PARA

LEGAL

WORK

BOOK

PARALEGAL WORKBOOK I

Charles P. Nemeth, *Esquire*
Director of Public Service Administration
Waynesburg College
Waynesburg, Pennsylvania
Member of the Pennsylvania and North Carolina Bar

Anderson Publishing Co. / Cincinnati

NEMETH, PARALEGAL WORKBOOK I

© 1989 by Anderson Publishing Co.

Printed in the United States of America.

ISBN: 0-87084-610-8

To Mary Claire, my sixth angel from heaven.

CONTENTS

ACKNOWLEDGMENT

It is always my distinct pleasure to acknowledge individuals and entities that have assisted me in the authorship of this work. So many aspects of textbook production are both taxing and mundane and require steadfast dedication and concern. The gratitude I extend is heartfelt and not merely obligatory.

First and foremost, to my beloved extended family including my dear wife, Jean Marie, and our most cherished children, Eleanor, Stephen, Anne Marie, John and Joe and the newest addition, Mary Claire, to whom this book is dedicated. Born August 30, 1989, Mary Claire triggers in me a continuing desire to produce and author such works, first, from an economic perspective—that is, the necessity of feeding this large brood—but also from my inherent desire to leave her, as well as all my children a legacy of words.

To Michelle Kretzler, a skilled typist and editor as well as a provocative critic, this author expresses the deepest of gratitude. Without question, and Michelle will confirm, I was not born with an eye towards detail—a function she so ably performs and has no rival in my experience.

To numerous personalities at Anderson Publishing goes my regular appreciation. From production to editing, Anderson Publishing Company is always a positive experience. Problems dissipate under a spirit of cooperation, and this is especially evident in the paste-up and production end of this first volume of a series. With Anderson, one need never convince that the appearance of a text, its layout and design, has a great deal to do with its functionality and efficacy in the learning process. In particular, I need to mention Dee Dunn, Dale Hartig and Bill Burden.

At Waynesburg College, I am indebted to Dr. Thomas Pavick for the time I am afforded by the selection of my own scheduling. His type of administrative oversight fosters an author's activity.

On the permissions end, this workbook needs to acknowledge the following companies who graciously granted us access to their materials: Associated Press, *The Cincinnati Enquirer*, John C. Clark Company, the Lawyer's Co-operative Publishing Company, Matthew Bender & Company and Yeo and Lukens Company.

Finally, I extend my sincere thanks to Thomas Williams, Esquire, a long-time business associate, friend and promoter of these types of educational expressions. He has truly been in the forefront of paralegal education.

Charles P. Nemeth, Esquire

In Midway, Western Pennsylvania Coal Country
October 3, 1989

PRACTICUM EXERCISES NO. 1
THE NATURE OF REAL PROPERTY

	Time Allotted (hours)	Point Value
Agreement of Sale:		
Assignment #1	0.6	7.0
Application for Financing:		
Assignment #2	0.5	5.0
Truth-in-Lending Disclosure Statement:		
Assignment #3	0.2	2.0
Power of Attorney:		
Assignment #4	0.2	2.0
Good Faith Estimate:		
Assignment #5	0.2	2.0
Endorsements:		
Assignment #6	0.2	2.0
Legal Descriptions of Land:		
Assignment #7 (3 parts)	1.0	5.0
Searching the Title:		
Tracing Your House's Heritage		
Assignment #8 — Part 1	0.3	5.0
Office of the Recorder of Deeds		
Assignment #8 — Part 2	0.5	5.0
Acquisition of Title Insurance:		
Assignment #9 (5 parts)	1.1	10.0
Cleaning Up Title:		
Assignment #10 (4 parts)	1.0	5.0
Preparation of Mortgage:		
Assignment #11 (2 parts)	0.7	10.0
Deeds:		
Assignment #12 (2 parts)	0.5	10.0
Closing and Settlement Process:		
Assignment #13 (3 parts)	3.0	30.0
	10.0	100.0

I.
INTRODUCTION

It is often said that real property is the single largest economic investment and expenditure in an individual's life. To be sure, the value of real property has been escalating dramatically over the last two decades in most geographic regions. Real property has historically been considered one of the safest investments, especially over the long term. However, practitioners in the field must be aware that it is subject to cyclical influences such as employment trends and projections, inflation, interest rates and the changing character of communities. Lawyers, paralegals and legal assistants, real estate agents, brokers, bankers, insurance agents, surveyors and title abstracters all have a stake in the nature of real property.

Consider the diversity of real property interest. Real property can simply be raw land as evidenced by *Photo 1.1,* a panoramic view of Cape Hatteras National Seashore.

Photo 1.1

On its face, it appears to be a pristine ocean front of sand and beaches. In reality, such land is extremely valuable given its aesthetic and investment quality. Some make a career of doing nothing but buying raw pieces of land for speculation, investment or charitable purposes.

Photo 1.2 presents the opposite angled view of the same territory. In contrast to the barren, yet pleasingly aesthetic, ocean front plot, this photo portrays the enhanced utility of raw land when improvements such as condominiums, residential and rental structures are added.

Photo 1.2

The size and expanse of a piece of property is determined by numerous influences as well. *Photo 1.3* shows a residential building on a lot 100 x 100.

Photo 1.3

This is the typical citizen's view of what real estate is, but interests in land are, at times, indescribable. Ponder *Photo 1.4*. What possible interests in land, real property or specific rights might exist in the body of water immediately in front of this house?

Photo 1.4

Notice the small stakes out in this particular bay. Believe it or not, this is a clam farm in which seabed clams are raised and then released into the estuarine water for the purposes of propagating a diminishing species. Is this an enforceable real property right?

Real property interests range from freehold to licenses and privileges. Review the chart below at *Figure 1.1*.

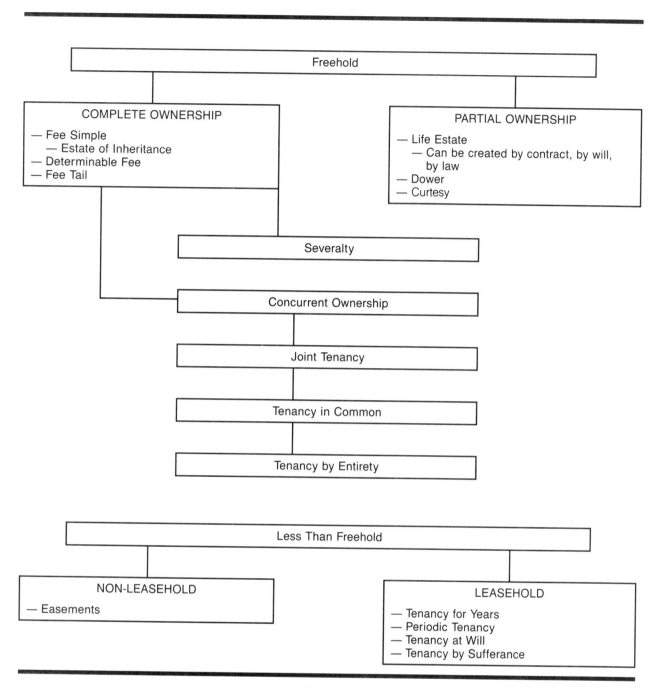

Figure 1.1

It is presumed that the student has a rudimentary understanding of interests in real property as he or she proceeds with the assignment. This introduction reviews the basics for a practical examination of a typical real estate transaction.

II.
THE REAL ESTATE TRANSACTION

What follows is a step-by-step examination of a typical, standardized and fairly nationalized real estate transaction. Please be aware that there are substantial jurisdictional differences in the transfer and alienation of real estate and that your instructor should be able to provide the insight, forms, exhibits, checklists and other needed information and input to highlight these distinct differences. However, for purposes of these assignments, we will approach these tasks in a generic way. Please be cognizant of the objectives listed below as well as the explicitly stated student and instructor obligations. The value of the assignment and the time allotted for each task is formally calculated, giving deference to both the level of expertise and experience the reader has to date and the average time frames these duties usually take to perform.

In the fact patterns to follow, information not cited or described is not considered critical for evaluation purposes. The student may complete these facts as he or she feels appropriate.

1. **The Agreement of Sale**

    A. Objectives

    To be able to:
    (1) Read and interpret a typical agreement of sale;
    (2) Spot and highlight specific issues such as conditions, contingencies and other legal issues that might emerge in the drafting of an agreement of sale;
    (3) Prepare a complete agreement of sale; and
    (4) Monitor terms and conditions to assure adherence to the contract.

    B. Student Obligations

    (1) To analyze a fact pattern and thereafter complete an entire agreement of sale.

    C. Instructor Obligations

    (1) To assist the student in the preparation of the agreement of sale; and
    (2) To point out any local distinctions, differences or traits that are necessary in the student's local area of practice. Instructors must correct, modify and make the facts fit or be compatible with the local practice of his or her area.

    D. Time Allotted: 0.6 hours

    E. Value of Assignment: 7.0 points

ASSIGNMENT #1

FACT PATTERN

Bob and Sally Quinn desire to purchase the home currently owned and occupied by Ron and Mary Bartkowski. The address of the property is 418 Queens Highway, Mercer, Georgia 45690. The residence of the buyers is 1100 Champlain Lane, Wilmington, Delaware 19801. The sellers in this case are willing to part with the entire estate except for their personal possessions and an antique laundry tub, a television antenna and certain carpeting recently installed on the upper floor. The buyers of the property are insisting that any appraisal fees and charges that must be paid in advance to the bank be borne by the sellers. An oral agreement has been reached on these topics. The buyers also insist on a mortgage contingency for a mortgage amount of $100,000 on a sale price of a home at $300,000. Buyers will be offering $200,000 as a down payment and earnest money payable as follows: $30,000 upon signing the agreement on June 1, 1989; balance at time of settlement. Again, purchase price is the sum of $300,000. Sellers are asking that settlement be made within sixty (60) days of this signed agreement of sale or before if at all possible. Transfer tax, fees, assessments, taxes, rents and other municipal services will be prorated and shared accordingly. Buyers desire a mortgage amount of $100,000 over a 30-year period at a mortgage rate that is fixed and conventional and not to exceed 12 percent. The property is located at the address listed above in the county of Dauphin, and it has been zoned for residential purposes only. Since a settlement and closing within 60 days is faster than normal, sellers are insisting that the buyers apply to a bank for the financing within a two-day period and request a written commitment from the bank within 30 days of the application. No other issues of contention, dispute or concern exist.

COMPLETE THE AGREEMENT OF SALE AT *FORM 1.1 (2 PAGES)*.

AGREEMENT FOR THE SALE OF REAL ESTATE

```
COPIES
1. White ............. Seller
2. Yellow ........... Agent
3. Pink ............. Buyer
4. Blue .......... Mortgagee
5. Gold ...................
6. Green ........... Buyer's
copy at time of signing.
```

This Agreement, this .... day of .... A.D. 19 ....

1. PRINCIPALS (1-78) Between ....
....

(residing at .... Zip ....) hereinafter called Seller,

and ....
....

(residing at .... Zip ....) hereinafter called Buyer.

2. PROPERTY (3-85) Seller hereby agrees to sell and convey to Buyer, who hereby agrees to purchase:
ALL THAT CERTAIN lot or piece of ground with buildings and improvements thereon erected, if any, known as:
....
....

in the .... of .... County of ....
State of .... , Zip ....
Zoned ....

3. TERMS (3-85) (a) Purchase Price .... **Dollars**
....
which shall be paid to the Seller by the Buyer as follows:

    (b) Cash or check at signing this agreement: .... $ ....
    (c) Cash or check to be paid on or before: .... 19 .... $ ....
    (d) .... $ ....
    (e) Cash or certified check at time of settlement: .... $ ....
                                          TOTAL $ ....

    (f) Written approval of Seller to be on or before: .... 19 ....
    (g) Settlement to be made on or before: .... 19 ....
    (h) Conveyance from Seller will be by fee simple deed of special warranty.
    (i) Payment of transfer taxes will be divided equally between Buyer and Seller.
    (j) The following shall be apportioned pro-rata as of and at time of settlement: Taxes as levied and assessed, rents, interest on mortgage
        assumptions, condominium fees and homeowner association fees if any, water and or sewer rents if any, together with any other
        lienable municipal services.

4. MORTGAGE CONTINGENCY (8-85) This sale is NOT contingent upon any mortgage financing except as hereinafter provided.
    (a) Mortgage terms required by Buyer. Amount of mortgage loan $ .... , Term .... years.
        Type of mortgage ....
        Interest rate...................... % HOWEVER, BUYER AGREES TO ACCEPT THE INTEREST RATE AS MAY BE
        COMMITTED BY THE MORTGAGE LENDER, not to exceed a maximum interest rate of .... %
    (b) Within ten(10) days of Seller's approval of this agreement, Buyer shall make a completed mortgage application to a responsible
        mortgage lending institution through the office of ....
        who for the purposes of negotiating for the said mortgage loan, shall be considered the Agent for the Buyer.
    (c) (1) Buyer will, upon receipt of a mortgage commitment, promptly provide a copy to Seller, Agent and/or Sub-agent, if any.
        (2) Mortgage commitment date .... 19 .... If a written commitment is not received
        by the above date, Buyer agrees to extend the commitment date until Seller terminates this agreement, in writing.
        (3) Should the mortgage commitment not be valid until the date of settlement, be conditioned upon the sale or settlement of any other
        property or contain any other condition not specified herein, Seller has the option to terminate this agreement, in writing.
        In the event Seller terminates this agreement as specified in paragraphs (c) (2) or (3), all deposit monies paid on account shall
        be returned to the Buyer, subject to the payments required, if any, provided for in paragraph #7(c), 1, 2, and 3.
    (d) Seller hereby agrees to permit inspections by authorized appraisers, reputable certifiers and/or Buyer as may be required by the
        lending institution or insuring agencies.

5. SPECIAL CLAUSES
    (a) This sale is NOT contingent in any manner upon the sale or settlement of any other real estate except as may be hereinafter provided.

Form 1.1

6. **NOTICES & ASSESSMENTS (3-85)**
   (a) Seller represents as of the approval date of this agreement, that no public improvement, condominium or homeowner association assessments have been made against the premises which remain unpaid and that no notice by any government or public authority has been served upon the Seller or anyone on the Seller's behalf, including notices relating to violations of zoning, housing, building, safety or fire ordinances which remain uncorrected unless otherwise specified herein.
   (b) If required by law, Seller shall deliver to Buyer on or before settlement, a certification from the appropriate municipal department or departments disclosing notice of any uncorrected violation of zoning, housing, building, safety or fire ordinances.
   (c) Seller will be responsible for any notice of improvements or assessments received on or before the date of Sellers approval of this agreement, unless improvements consist of sewer or water lines not in use.
   (d) Buyer will be responsible for any notice served upon Seller after the approval date of this agreement and for the payment thereafter of any public improvement, condominium or homeowner association assessments.
7. **TITLE AND COSTS (3-85)**
   (a) The premises are to be conveyed free and clear of all liens, encumbrances, and easements, EXCEPTING HOWEVER, the following: existing building restrictions, ordinances, easements of roads, easements visible upon the ground, privileges or rights of public service companies, if any; otherwise the title to the above described real estate shall be good and marketable or such as will be insured by a reputable Title Insurance Company at the regular rates.
   (b) In the event the Seller is unable to give a good and marketable title or such as will be insured by a reputable Title Company, subject to aforesaid, Buyer shall have the option of taking such title as the Seller can give without abatement of price or of being repaid all monies paid by Buyer to the Seller on account of the purchase price and the Seller will reimburse the Buyer for any costs incurred by the Buyer for those items specified in paragraph 7(c) items (1), (2), (3), and in paragraph 7(d); and in the latter event there shall be no further liability or obligation on either of the parties hereto and this agreement shall become NULL AND VOID and all copies will be returned to Seller's agent for cancellation.
   (c) The Buyer will pay for the following:
      (1) The premium for mechanics lien insurance and/or title search, or fee for cancellation of same, if any.
      (2) The premiums for flood insurance and/or fire insurance with extended coverage, insurance binder charges or cancellation fee, if any.
      (3) Appraisal fees and charges paid in advance to mortgagee if any.
      (4) Buyer's normal settlement costs and accruals.
   (d) Any survey or surveys which may be required by the Title Insurance Company or the abstracting attorney, for the preparation of an adequate legal description of the premises (or the correction thereof), shall be secured and paid for by the Seller. However, any survey or surveys desired by the Buyer or required by his/her mortgagee shall be secured and paid for by the Buyer.
8. **FIXTURES, TREES, SHRUBBERY, ETC. (1-81)** All existing plumbing, heating and lighting fixtures (including chandeliers) and systems appurtenant thereto and forming a part thereof, and other permanent fixtures, as well as all ranges, laundry tubs, T.V. antennas, masts and rotor systems, together with wall to wall carpeting, screens, storm sash and/or doors,shades, awnings, venetian blinds, couplings for automatic washers and dryers, etc., radiator covers, cornices, kitchen cabinets, drapery rods, drapery rod hardware, curtain rods, curtain rod hardware, all trees, shrubbery, plantings now in or on property, if any, unless specifically excepted in this agreement, are included in the sale and purchase price. None of the above mentioned items shall be removed by the Seller from the premises after the date of this agreement.; Any remaining heating and/or cooking fuels stored on the premises at time of settlement are also included under this agreement. Seller hereby warrants that he will deliver good title to all of the articles described in this paragraph, and any other fixtures or items of personalty specifically scheduled and to be included in this sale.
9. **DEPOSIT AND RECOVERY FUND (5-85)** Deposits or hand monies shall be paid to agent for Seller, who shall retain the same until consummation or termination of this agreement in conformity with all applicable laws and regulations. Agent for the Seller may, at his/her sole option, hold any uncashed check tendered as deposit or hand monies, pending the acceptance of this offer.
   A real estate recovery fund exists to reimburse persons who have suffered monetary loss and have obtained an uncollectable judgment due to fraud, misrepresentation or deceit in a real estate transaction by a Pennsylvania licensee. For complete details, call 717-783-3658.
10. **POSSESSION AND TENDER (3-85)**
   (a) Possession is to be delivered by deed, keys and physical possession to a vacant building (if any) broom clean, free of debris at day and time of settlement, or by deed and assignment of existing lease(s) at time of settlement if premises is tenant occupied at the signing of this agreement, unless otherwise specified herein. Buyer will acknowledge existing lease(s) by initialing said lease(s) at time of signing of this agreement of sale if tenant occupied.
   (b) Seller will not enter into any new leases, written extension of existing leases, if any, or additional leases for the premises without expressed written consent of the Buyer.
   (c) Formal tender of an executed deed and purchase money is hereby waived.
   (d) Buyer reserves the right to make a pre-settlement inspection of the subject premises.
11. **MAINTENANCE AND RISK OF LOSS (3-85)**
   (a) Seller shall maintain the property (including all items mentioned in paragraph #8 herein) and any personal property specifically scheduled herein in its present condition, normal wear and tear excepted.
   (b) Seller shall bear risk of loss from fire or other casualties until time of settlement. In the event of damage to any property included in this sale by fire or other casualties, not repaired or replaced prior to settlement, Buyer shall have the option of rescinding this agreement and receiving all monies paid on account or of accepting the property in its then condition together with the proceeds of any insurance recovery obtainable by Seller. Buyer is hereby notified that he may insure his equitable interest in this property as of the time of the acceptance of this agreement.
12. **RECORDING (3-85)** This agreement shall not be recorded in the Office for the Recording of Deeds or in any other office or place of public record and if Buyer causes or permits this agreement to be recorded, Seller may elect to treat such act as a breach of this agreement.
13. **ASSIGNMENT (3-85)** This agreement shall be binding upon the parties, their respective heirs, personal representatives, guardians and successors, and to the extent assignable, on the assigns of the parties hereto, it being expressly understood, however, that the Buyer shall not transfer or assign this agreement without the written consent of the Seller.
14. **DEFAULT (1-79)** The said time for settlement and all other times referred to for the performance of any of the obligations of this agreement are hereby agreed to be of the essence of this agreement. Should the Buyer:
   (a) Fail to make any additional payments as specified in paragraph #3, or
   (b) Furnish false or incomplete information to the Seller, the Seller's agent, or the mortgage lender, concerning the Buyer's legal or financial status, or fail to cooperate in the processing of the mortgage loan application, which acts would result in the failure to obtain the approval of a mortgage loan commitment, or
   (c) Violate or fail to fulfill and perform any other terms or conditions of this agreement,
   then in such case, all deposit money and other sums paid by the Buyer on account of the purchase price, whether required by this agreement or not, may be retained by the Seller:
      (1) On account of the purchase, or
      (2) As monies to be applied to the Seller's damages, or
      (3) As liquidated damages for such breach,
   as the Seller may elect, and in the event that the Seller elects to retain the monies as liquidated damages in accordance with paragraph #14(3), the Seller shall be released from all liability or obligations and this agreement shall be NULL AND VOID and all copies will be returned to the Seller's agent for cancellation.
15. **AGENT(S) (3-85)** It is expressly understood and agreed between the parties that the named Agent, Broker, and any Sub Agent, Broker and their salespeople, employees, officers and or partners, are Agent(s) for the Seller, not the Buyer, however, the Agent(s) may perform services for the Buyer in connection with financing, insurance and document preparation.
16. **REPRESENTATIONS (3-85)** It is understood that Buyer has inspected the property, or hereby waives the right to do so and has agreed to purchase it as a result of such inspection and not because of or in reliance upon any representation made by the Seller or any other officer, partner or employee of Seller, or by the Agent, Sub Agent, if any, of the Seller, their salespeople and employees, officers and or partners.
   The Buyer has agreed to purchase it in its present condition unless otherwise specified herein. It is further understood that this agreement contains the whole agreement between the Seller and the Buyer and there are no other terms, obligations, covenants, representations, statements or conditions, oral or otherwise of any kind whatsoever concerning this sale. Furthermore, this agreement shall not be altered, amended, changed or modified except in writing executed by the parties.

APPROVAL BY BUYER BUYER...(SEAL)
WITNESS AS
TO BUYER.. BUYER...(SEAL)
WITNESS AS
TO BUYER.. BUYER...(SEAL)

APPROVAL BY SELLER
Seller hereby approves the above contract this .... day of .... A.D. 19 ....
and in consideration of the services rendered in procuring the Buyer, Seller agrees to pay the named Agent a fee of.................................
of/from the herein specified sale price. In the event Buyer defaults hereunder, any monies paid on account shall be divided ...., Seller,
................., Agent, but in no event will the sum paid to the Agent be in excess of the above specified Agent's fee.
WITNESS AS
TO SELLER.. SELLER...(SEAL)
WITNESS AS
TO SELLER.. SELLER...(SEAL)
AGENT BY:.. SELLER...(SEAL)

TO:.. (Agent) Date.. 19 ....

In conjunction with the purchase of the premises described in this agreement of sale attached hereto, I/We hereby authorize your firm to perform the services as indicated below by my/our initials.
A. Order Title insurance in any reputable title insurance company ....(INITIALS)
B. Order insurance in the amount of $ .... ☐ Homeowners ☐ Fire & Extended Coverage ☐ Flood ....(INITIALS)
C. ....(INITIALS)

Form 1.1—*concluded*

2.   Application for Financing

As the agreement of sale dictates, an application for financing must be filed within a prescribed period of time. Unfortunately, the complexities of financing require a great deal of paperwork, and the average citizen has an extremely difficult time completing all of the necessary financial information. Practitioners in real estate can be called upon by buyers of real estate for assistance in the completion of a residential or commercial loan application, the subject matter of our next assignment.

A.   Objectives

    (1)   To be able to complete and calculate a residential loan application; and

    (2)   To assist the client in making a timely bank application.

B.   Student Obligations

    (1)   To complete a residential loan application.

C.   Instructor Obligations

    (1)   To check the mathematical integrity and completeness of the information on the student's residential loan application; and

    (2)   To point out any information that is unique to the locality in which they practice that might have to be cited on this application.

D.   Time Allotted: 0.5 hours

E.   Value of Assignment: 5.0 points

ASSIGNMENT #2

FACT PATTERN

Borrower: John Michaelson
Mortgage Type: Conventional
Mortgage Amount: $80,000
Interest Rate: 12 percent
Number of Months: 360
Monthly Payment and Principal: $1,050
All Other Amounts: In Escrow
Prepayment Option: Yes
Property Street Address: 44 Dixon St.
City: Charlotte
County: Mecklinburg
State & Zip Code: North Carolina 12666
Purpose of Loan: Purchase; not a construction loan
Borrower: Same
Address: 1110 Broad St., Columbia, SC 18888
Length of Residency: Five (5) years
Annual Income: $62,000
Dividends and Interest: $1,000 per year
Current Rent Payment: $495.00 per month

Purchase Price: $100,000
Closing Costs: $8,000
Prepaid Escrow: $1,000
Other Financing or Equity: No
Cash Deposit: $20,000
Marital Status: Unmarried
Dependents: No
Employer: Dupont Corporation, 1111 Stage St., Columbia, SC 68888
Years Employed: 15 years
Position Title: Engineer
Type of Business: Chemical
SS #: 444-88-9999
Phone: 868-8843
Business Phone: 263-8194
Reference: Sears, McArthur Blvd., Wilmington, DE Acct. 888-999; revolving credit line, highest balance $8,000.
Reference: GMAC Financing, P.O. Box 568, Charlotte, NC Acct. 11644; auto loan, $12,000
Checking and Savings Account: $10,000
Stocks and Bonds: $10,000
Life Insurance Value: $5,000
Retirement Fund: $5,000
Automobiles: 1987 Cadillac; $18,000
Personal Property: $100,000
Debt: GMAC; $342.00 per month; $6,000 unpaid balance
Debt: Sears; $120.00 per month; $8,000 unpaid balance
Year Property Built: 1904

COMPLETE THE RESIDENTIAL LOAN APPLICATION AT *FORM 1.2 (2 PAGES)*.

RESIDENTIAL LOAN APPLICATION

Appl. No. _____

| MORTGAGE APPLIED FOR | ☐ Conventional ☐ VA ☐ FHA | Amount $ | Interest Rate % | No. of Months | Monthly Payment Principal & Interest $ | Escrow/Impounds (to be collected monthly) ☐ Taxes ☐ Hazard Ins. ☐ Mtg. Ins. ☐ _____ |

Prepayment Option

SUBJECT PROPERTY

| Property Street Address | City | County | State | Zip | No. Units |

Legal Description (Attach description if necessary) — Year Built

Purpose of Loan: ☐ Purchase ☐ Construction-Permanent ☐ Construction ☐ Refinance ☐ Other (Explain)

| Complete this line if Construction-Permanent or Construction Loan | Lot Value Data Year Acquired $ | Original Cost $ | Present Value (a) $ | Cost of Imps. (b) $ | Total (a + b) $ | ENTER TOTAL AS PURCHASE PRICE IN DETAILS OF PURCHASE. |

Complete this line if a Refinance Loan — Year Acquired | Original Cost $ | Amt. Existing Liens $ — Purpose of Refinance — Describe Improvements [ ] made [ ] to be made Cost: $

Title Will Be Held In What Name(s) — Manner In Which Title Will Be Held

Source of Down Payment and Settlement Charges

This application is designed to be completed by the borrower(s) with the lender's assistance. The Co-Borrower Section and all other Co-Borrower questions must be completed and the appropriate box(es) checked if ☐ another person will be jointly obligated with the Borrower on the loan, or ☐ the Borrower is relying on income from alimony, child support or separate maintenance or on the income or assets of another person as a basis for repayment of the loan, or ☐ the Borrower is married and resides, or the property is located, in a community property state.

BORROWER				CO-BORROWER			
Name		Age	School Yrs	Name		Age	School Yrs
Present Address No. Years ___ ☐ Own ☐ Rent				Present Address No. Years ___ ☐ Own ☐ Rent			
Street				Street			
City/State/Zip				City/State/Zip			
Former address if less than 2 years at present address				Former address if less than 2 years at present address			
Street				Street			
City/State/Zip				City/State/Zip			
Years at former address ☐ Own ☐ Rent				Years at former address ☐ Own ☐ Rent			
Marital Status ☐ Married ☐ Separated ☐ Unmarried (incl. single, divorced, widowed)	DEPENDENTS OTHER THAN LISTED BY CO-BORROWER NO. AGES			Marital Status ☐ Married ☐ Separated ☐ Unmarried (incl. single, divorced, widowed)	DEPENDENTS OTHER THAN LISTED BY BORROWER NO. AGES		
Name and Address of Employer	Years employed in this line of work or profession? ___ years Years on this job ___ ☐ Self Employed*			Name and Address of Employer	Years employed in this line of work or profession? ___ years Years on this job ___ ☐ Self Employed*		
Position/Title	Type of Business			Position/Title	Type of Business		
Social Security Number***	Home Phone	Business Phone		Social Security Number***	Home Phone	Business Phone	

GROSS MONTHLY INCOME				MONTHLY HOUSING EXPENSE**			DETAILS OF PURCHASE	
Item	Borrower	Co-Borrower	Total		PRESENT	PROPOSED	Do Not Complete If Refinance	
Base Empl. Income	$	$	$	Rent	$		a. Purchase Price	$
Overtime				First Mortgage (P&I)		$	b. Total Closing Costs (Est.)	
Bonuses				Other Financing (P&I)			c. Prepaid Escrows (Est.)	
Commissions				Hazard Insurance			d. Total (a + b + c)	$
Dividends/Interest				Real Estate Taxes			e. Amount This Mortgage	( )
Net Rental Income				Mortgage Insurance			f. Other Financing	( )
Other† (Before completing, see notice under Describe Other Income below.)				Homeowner Assn. Dues			g. Other Equity	( )
				Other			h. Amount of Cash Deposit	( )
				Total Monthly Pmt.	$	$	i. Closing Costs Paid by Seller	( )
				Utilities			j. Cash Reqd. For Closing (Est.)	$
Total	$	$	$	Total	$	$		

DESCRIBE OTHER INCOME

◁ B-Borrower C-Co-Borrower	NOTICE: † Alimony, child support, or separate maintenance income need not be revealed if the Borrower or Co-Borrower does not choose to have it considered as a basis for repaying this loan.	Monthly Amount
		$

IF EMPLOYED IN CURRENT POSITION FOR LESS THAN TWO YEARS COMPLETE THE FOLLOWING

B/C	Previous Employer/School	City/State	Type of Business	Position/Title	Dates From/To	Monthly Income
						$

THESE QUESTIONS APPLY TO BOTH BORROWER AND CO-BORROWER

If a "yes" answer is given to a question in this column, explain on an attached sheet.	Borrower Yes or No	Co-Borrower Yes or No	If applicable, explain Other Financing or Other Equity (provide addendum if more space is needed).
Have you any outstanding judgments? In the last 7 years, have you been declared bankrupt?			
Have you had property foreclosed upon or given title or deed in lieu thereof?			
Are you a co-maker or endorser on a note?			
Are you a party in a law suit?			
Are you obligated to pay alimony, child support, or separate maintenance?			
Is any part of the down payment borrowed?			

*FHLMC/FNMA require business credit report, signed Federal Income Tax returns for last two years, and, if available, audited Profit and Loss Statements plus balance sheet for same period.
**All Present Monthly Housing Expenses of Borrower and Co-Borrower should be listed on a combined basis.
***Neither FHLMC nor FNMA requires this information.

Form No. 80 · FHLMC 65 Rev. 8/78 · FNMA 1003 Rev. 8/78

Form 1.2

This Statement and any applicable supporting schedules may be completed jointly by both married and unmarried co-borrowers if their assets and liabilities are sufficiently joined so that the Statement can be meaningfully and fairly presented on a combined basis; otherwise separate Statements and Schedules are required (FHLMC 65A/FNMA 1003A). If the co-borrower section was completed about a spouse, this statement and supporting schedules must be completed about that spouse also.   ☐ Completed Jointly   ☐ Not Completed Jointly

ASSETS		LIABILITIES AND PLEDGED ASSETS			
Indicate by (*) those liabilities or pledged assets which will be satisfied upon sale of real estate owned or upon refinancing of subject property					
Description	Cash or Market Value	Creditors' Name, Address and Account Number	Acct. Name If Not Borrower's	Mo. Pmt. and Mos. left to pay	Unpaid Balance
Cash Deposit Toward Purchase Held By	$	Installment Debts (include "revolving" charge accts)		$ Pmt./Mos. /	$
				/	
Checking and Savings Accounts (Show Names of Institutions/Acct. Nos.)				/	
				/	
Stocks and Bonds (No./Description)					
Life Insurance Net Cash Value Face Amount ($)		Other Debts Including Stock Pledges			
SUBTOTAL LIQUID ASSETS	$			/	
Real Estate Owned (Enter Market Value from Schedule of Real Estate Owned)		Real Estate Loans			
Vested Interest in Retirement Fund					
Net Worth of Business Owned (ATTACH FINANCIAL STATEMENT)					
Automobiles (Make and Year)		Automobile Loans			
				/	
Furniture and Personal Property		Alimony, Child Support and Separate Maintenance Payments Owed To			
Other Assets (Itemize)					
				/	
		TOTAL MONTHLY PAYMENTS		$	
TOTAL ASSETS	A $	NET WORTH (A minus B) $		TOTAL LIABILITIES	B $

SCHEDULE OF REAL ESTATE OWNED (If Additional Properties Owned Attach Separate Schedule)							
Address of Property (Indicate S if Sold, PS if Pending Sale or R if Rental being held for income)	Type of Property	Present Market Value	Amount of Mortgages & Liens	Gross Rental Income	Mortgage Payments	Taxes, Ins. Maintenance and Misc.	Net Rental Income
		$	$	$	$	$	$
TOTALS →		$	$	$	$	$	$

LIST PREVIOUS CREDIT REFERENCES					
B - Borrower C - Co Borrower	Creditor's Name and Address	Account Number	Purpose	Highest Balance	Date Paid
				$	

List any additional names under which credit has previously been received _____

AGREEMENT.   The undersigned applies for the loan indicated in this application to be secured by a first mortgage or deed of trust on the property described herein, and represents that the property will not be used for any illegal or restricted purpose, and that all statements made in this application are true and are made for the purpose of obtaining the loan. Verification may be obtained from any source named in this application. The original or a copy of this application will be retained by the lender, even if the loan is not granted.   The undersigned ☐ intend or ☐ do not intend to occupy the property as their primary residence.

I/we fully understand that it is a federal crime punishable by fine or imprisonment, or both, to knowingly make any false statements concerning any of the above facts as applicable under the provisions of Title 18, United States Code, Section 1014.

_____ Date _____   _____ Date _____
Borrower's Signature   Co-Borrower's Signature

INFORMATION FOR GOVERNMENT MONITORING PURPOSES

The following information is requested by the Federal Government if this loan is related to a dwelling, in order to monitor the lender's compliance with equal credit opportunity and fair housing laws. You are not required to furnish this information, but are encouraged to do so. The law provides that a lender may neither discriminate on the basis of this information, nor on whether you choose to furnish it. However, if you choose not to furnish it, under Federal regulations this lender is required to note race and sex on the basis of visual observation or surname. If you do not wish to furnish the above information, please initial below.

BORROWER: I do not wish to furnish this information (initials)_____ | **CO-BORROWER:** I do not wish to furnish this information (initials)_____

RACE/ ☐ American Indian, Alaskan Native ☐ Asian, Pacific Islander | RACE/ ☐ American Indian, Alaskan Native ☐ Asian, Pacific Islander
NATIONAL ☐ Black ☐ Hispanic ☐ White SEX: ☐ Female | NATIONAL ☐ Black ☐ Hispanic ☐ White SEX ☐ Female
ORIGIN ☐ Other (specify) _____ ☐ Male | ORIGIN ☐ Other (specify) _____ ☐ Male

FOR LENDER'S USE ONLY

(FNMA REQUIREMENT ONLY) This application was taken by ☐ face to face interview ☐ by mail ☐ by telephone

_____   _____
(Interviewer)   Name of Employer of Interviewer

FHLMC 65 Rev. 8/78   REVERSE   FNMA 1003 Rev. 8/78

Form 1.2—*concluded*

3. Regulation Z Disclosure Statement

Once an application for a bank has been filed, the bank is required to disclose what charges and costs the buyer will accrue during the life of the loan. Required under federal law is the completion of what is known as a Regulation Z Disclosure Statement.

A. Objectives

(1) To learn what federal financial disclosures are required in a finance application.

B. Student Obligations

(1) To complete a Regulation Z, Truth-in-Lending, Disclosure Statement.

C. Instructor Obligations

(1) To monitor and provide oversight in the completion of the Truth-in-Lending disclosure statement.

D. Time Allotted: 0.2 hours

E. Value of Assignment: 2.0 points

ASSIGNMENT #3

FACT PATTERN

Total of Payments: $146,724.16
Finance Charge: $78,490.08
Amount Financed: $68,234.08
Annual Percentage Rate: 10.904
Date, Address and Phone Numbers: (By student)
Life Insurance: Buyers do not desire.
Security: Property itself
Recording Fees: $35
Payment Schedule: 179 payments of $815.13; 1 payment of $815.89.
Late Charges: 5% of principal and interest
Prepayment: No penalty
Assumption: Possible

*Other terms and conditions to be completed by the student.

COMPLETE THE TRUTH-IN-LENDING DISCLOSURE STATEMENT AT *FORM 1.3.*

TRUTH-IN-LENDING DISCLOSURE STATEMENT

ANNUAL PERCENTAGE RATE	FINANCE CHARGE	Amount Financed	Total of Payments	Loan No.:
The cost of your credit as a yearly rate.	The dollar amount the credit will cost you.	The amount of credit provided to you or on your behalf.	The amount you will have paid after you have made all payments.	Borrower: Address:
_____ %	$ _____	$ _____	$ _____	

Your payment schedule will be:

Number of Payments	Amount of Payments*	When Payments Are Due
		The first day of the month, beginning _____ .

*Payments may vary due to increasing or decreasing mortgage insurance premiums.

Variable Rate: ☐ If this box is checked, the annual percentage rate may increase during the term of this transaction. For an explanation of the circumstances under which the rate may increase, the limitations and effects of such an increase and an example of the resultant payment terms, see the Lender's Adjustable Rate Mortgage Loan Disclosure Statement.

Refinance: ☐ If this box is checked, the loan is a refinance and you have the right to receive at this time an itemization of the amount financed. ☐ I do want an itemization. ☐ I do not want an itemization.

Security: You are giving a security interest in (only applicable box(es) checked):
☐ the property being purchased; and
☐ Other (describe): _____

Late Charge: If a payment is late, you will be charged _____% of the payment

Prepayment: If you pay off early, you (only applicable box checked):
(a) ☐ will   ☐ will not   have to pay a penalty; and
(b) ☐ may   ☐ will not   be entitled to a refund of part of the finance charge.

Assumption: Someone buying your house ☐ may, under certain circumstances, ☐ cannot assume the remainder of the mortgage on the original terms.

☐ IF CHECKED, THIS OBLIGATION HAS A DEMAND FEATURE.

Filing Fees: $ _____ recording fees $ _____e mortgage satisfaction fees

Insurance: You may obtain property/flood insurance from anyone you want that is acceptable to the Lender.

INSURANCE:	Credit life insurance and credit disability insurance are not required to obtain credit and will not be provided unless you sign and agree to pay the additional cost. I do not want credit life insurance _____.		
Cost Over The Loan Term	$		
Single Credit Life	$	/Mo.	I want Single Credit Life Insurance. _____ (Initial)
Joint Credit Life	$	/Mo.	I want Joint Credit Life Insurance. _____ _____ (Initial)
Single Credit Life and Disability	$	/Mo.	I want Single Credit Life and Disability. _____ (Initial)
Joint Credit Life and Single Disability	$	/Mo.	I want Joint Credit Life and Single Disability. _____ _____ (Initial)

Variable Rate Example: If this loan has a variable rate feature, you have received separately an example of how an increase in the rate affects the payment terms in a typical variable rate loan.

See your contract documents for any additional information about interest rate adjustments, graduated payment options, nonpayment, default, any required repayment in full before the scheduled date, and prepayment refunds and penalties.

☐ If this box is checked, all numerical disclosures except for late charges are estimates or, if used above, (e) means estimate.

I have received a copy of this statement.

_____
Signature of Borrower   Date

_____
Signature of Borrower

This form completed by Lender's employee _____ who certifies that a completed copy of this disclosure statement was given/mailed to Borrower(s) on _____ , 19___.

┌   ┐   Signature
                      LOAN AMT:
                      LOAN TYPE:
└   ┘   INTEREST RATE:

Form 1.3

4. Power of Attorney

Perplexed and sometimes perturbed buyers and sellers in modern real estate transactions are turning over the responsibilities of handling the transaction to other parties. Attorneys frequently represent buyers and sellers in an entire transaction. Depending on your local area and the restrictions imposed by banks and title companies, the use of a power of attorney to delegate this responsibility is a common practice.

    A. Objectives

        (1) To learn the legal requirements in the grant of a standard power of attorney.

    B. Student Obligations

        (1) To prepare, draft and complete a power of attorney.

    C. Instructor Obligations

        (1) To monitor and oversee the process and, if applicable, provide local forms.

    D. Time Allotted: 0.2 hours

    E. Value of Assignment: 2.0 points

ASSIGNMENT #4

FACT PATTERN

Person Granted Power of Attorney: Charles L. Lumford
Person Granting Power of Attorney: Pearl E. Stolak
Purpose of Power of Attorney: To handle all paperwork, documentation, attestation, execution and documents in a real estate transaction at 1314 Grant St., Polermo, Ohio 49688.
Date: June 15, 1989
Notary: Michael Ambrocelli
County: Polermo

COMPLETE THE POWER OF ATTORNEY FORM AT *FORM 1.4 (2 PAGES)*.

Know all Men by these Presents,

THAT ....

....

................do make, constitute and appoint...

....

................true and lawful ATTORNEY for...............and in............name..............

....

....

....

....

....

....

....

....

....

....

....

....

....

....

....

....

....

....

....

....

....

with power also as attorney or attorneys, under.........................for that purpose

to make and substitute, and to do all lawful acts requisite for effecting the premises;

hereby ratifying and confirming all that the said attorney or substitute or substitutes

shall do therein by virtue of these presents.

In Witness whereof,...............have hereunto set...............hand and seal

..............................day of.........................in the year of our Lord one

thousand nine hundred and

Signed, Sealed and Delivered
IN THE PRESENCE OF

.... (SEAL)

.... (SEAL)

Form 1.4

This⸺⸺day of⸺⸺A. D., 19⸺ *personally appeared*
before me,⸺

the above-named⸺
⸺*and acknowledged the foregoing*
Power of Attorney to be⸺*act and deed, and desired the same might*
be recorded as such, according to law.

Witness *my hand and*⸺*seal, the day and year aforesaid.*

Power of Attorney.

TO

FOR

Dated⸺19⸺

John C. Clark Co., Phila.

324

Form 1.4—*concluded*

5. Good Faith Estimate

Of regular confusion to buyers and other parties to a real estate transaction is the financial institution's *Good Faith Estimate of Closing Costs*. It is imperative that the buyer be made aware that good faith estimate means just what it says. At best, it is the bank's perception of what the closing costs will be — not the eventual arrangements that buyers will make with their own attorneys, title and insurance companies.

A. Objectives

 (1) To learn about *Good Faith Estimations* conducted by banking and financial institutions.

B. Student Obligations

 (1) To complete a *Good Faith Estimate* form.

C. Instructor Obligations

 (1) To monitor and oversee the completion of a *Good Faith Estimate* form.

D. Time Allotted: 0.2 hours

E. Value of Assignment: 2.0 points

ASSIGNMENT #5

FACT PATTERN

 Loan Amount: $70,000
 Loan Origination Fees: 1.25%
 Application Fee: $200
 Loan Set-Up Fee: $100
 29 Days of Interest: $590.92
 Notary Fees: $5
 Attorney's Fee: $150.00
 Title Insurance: $963
 Recording Fees: $35
 Transfer Tax: 1%
 Special Endorsements to Title Insurance: $50

COMPLETE THE GOOD FAITH ESTIMATE AT *FORM 1.5*.

GOOD FAITH ESTIMATE

	PAID OR WITHHELD FROM BORROWER'S SETTLEMENT
This form does not cover all items which will be withheld from your loan proceeds at closing or which you will be required to pay in cash at settlement, for example, deposit in escrow for real estate taxes and insurance. You may wish to inquire as to the amounts of such other items. You may be required to pay other additional amounts at settlement.	
800. ITEMS PAYABLE IN CONNECTION WITH LOAN	
801. Loan Origination Fee %	
802. Loan Discount %	
803. Appraisal Fee to	
804. Credit Report to	
805. Lender's Inspection Fee	
806. Mortgage Insurance Application Fee to	
807. Assumption Fee	
808. APPLICATION FEE (PAID)	
809. LOAN SET UP FEE	
810.	
811.	
900. ITEMS REQUIRED BY LENDER TO BE PAID IN ADVANCE	
901. Interest from to @	
902. Mortgage Insurance Premium for months to	
904. years to	
905.	
1100. TITLE CHARGES	
1101. Settlement or closing fee to	
1102. Abstract or title search to	
1103. Title examination to	
1104. Title insurance binder to	
1105. Document preparation to	
1106. Notary fees to	
1107. Attorney's fees to	
(includes above items numbers;)	////////
1108. Title insurance to TITLE COMPANY	////////
(includes above items numbers;)	////////
1109. Lender's coverage $	////////
1110. Owner's coverage $	
1111. ENDORSEMENT TO TITLE	
1112.	
1113.	
1200. GOVERNMENT RECORDING AND TRANSFER CHARGES	
1201. Recording fees: Deed $; Mortgage $; Releases $	
1202. City/county tax/stamps: Deed $; Mortgage $	
1203. State tax/stamps: Deed $; Mortgage $	
1204. TRANSFER TAX @ 1.0%	
1205.	
1300. ADDITIONAL SETTLEMENT CHARGES	
1301. Survey to	
1302. Pest inspection to	
1303.	
1304.	
1305.	
1400. TOTAL SETTLEMENT CHARGES	

The above range of Good Faith Estimates of Loan Closing Costs are made pursuant to the requirements of the Real Estate Settlement Procedures Act. Exact figures can only be known at the time of final settlement.

THE LENDER'S ESTIMATE IS BASED UPON THE CHARGES OF THE DESIGNATED PROVIDERS.

PROVIDERS (Designated By Lender)   NAME _____
                                      ADDRESS _____
                                      _____ PHONE _____

              SERVICES RENDERED _____
                                      DOES PROVIDER HAVE A BUSINESS RELATIONSHIP WITH THE LENDER? YES ☐ NO ☐

PROVIDERS (Designated By Lender)   NAME _____
                                      ADDRESS _____
                                      _____ PHONE _____

              SERVICES RENDERED _____
                                      DOES PROVIDER HAVE A BUSINESS RELATIONSHIP WITH THE LENDER? YES ☐ NO ☐

              LENDER'S NAME _____
                    ADDRESS _____
                    ADDRESS _____

801-212-01-0185

Form 1.5

6. Endorsements to the Agreement of Sale

When a change of circumstances warrants a change in the agreement of sale, an endorsement or an addendum to the basic contract is necessary. Predictably, financing commitment dates are not necessarily met. Zoning or other conditional or contingent matters may affect the timetable outlined in the underlying agreement. As a result, the real estate practitioner must be on his or her guard to keep the contract current and to extend or modify its underlying terms and conditions to keep it contractually viable.

A. Objectives

    (1) To learn about the nature of an endorsement or addendum to an underlying agreement of sale.

B. Student Obligations

    (1) To prepare and complete an endorsement or addendum to an agreement of sale.

C. Instructor Obligations

    (1) To monitor and oversee the completion of the endorsement or addendum; and

    (2) To provide whatever local forms are necessary to address specific local needs.

D. Time Allotted: 0.2 hours

E. Value of Assignment: 2.0 points

ASSIGNMENT #6

FACT PATTERN

Change settlement date from June 20, 1989, to July 20, 1989.
Change mortgage amount from $50,000 to $59,000.
Change interest rate from 10% to 11%.

COMPLETE THE ENDORSEMENT TO AGREEMENT OF SALE AT *FORM 1.6.*

ENDORSEMENT TO AGREEMENT OF SALE

RE PROPERTY _____

SELLERS _____

BUYERS _____

DATE OF AGREEMENT _____ SETTLEMENT DATE _____

SALE PRICE $_____

It is understood and agreed that the above agreement of sale shall be amended as follows:

BUYERS AND SELLERS agree to_____

_____

_____

_____

_____

_____

_____

All other terms and conditions of the said agreement shall remain unchanged and in full effect.

WITNESS_____BUYER_____

WITNESS_____BUYER_____

WITNESS_____SELLER _____

AGENT_____SELLER _____

Form 1.6

7. Legal Descriptions of Land

Various options exist in how a legal description of land can be written. Historically, oral descriptions of land were often passed down generation to generation using particularized reference markers, boundaries or objects that were easily visible to the eye. Over time, the description of any land often becomes formalized in a deed or by a graphic reproduction such as a survey or photograph. This series of exercises will try to hone the skills necessary to compose appropriate legal descriptions. These principles will be approached from three different scenarios: first, using a survey, a pictorial, graphic representation of a piece of real property, to translate into a written description; secondly, using a description in a deed, often complex and arcane language, to reproduce a picture; and lastly, visually inspecting a land area to draw up a legal description, albeit not scientifically accurate, to reflect that parcel in as close and accurate a description as possible.

  A. Objectives

   (1) To learn about the varied techniques of describing a real property interest, including the following: deed descriptions, surveys, pictorial representations and reference points.

  B. Student Obligations

   (1) To translate a survey into narrative language;

   (2) To translate a pictorial representation into a real property description; and

   (3) To translate a written deed description into a graphic representation.

  C. Instructor Obligations

   (1) To provide guidance in the preparation of the legal description assignments; and

   (2) To provide forms or other information highlighting local custom and practice.

  D. Time Allotted: 1.0 hours

  E. Value of Assignment: 5.0 points

ASSIGNMENT #7 — PART 1

View the survey at *Figure 1.2*. Write out a narrative, literary exposition of what this pictorial survey represents. Employ the numbers and data provided and assume that the two individual parcels are being joined as one.

USE YOU OWN STATIONERY TO COMPLETE THIS ASSIGNMENT.

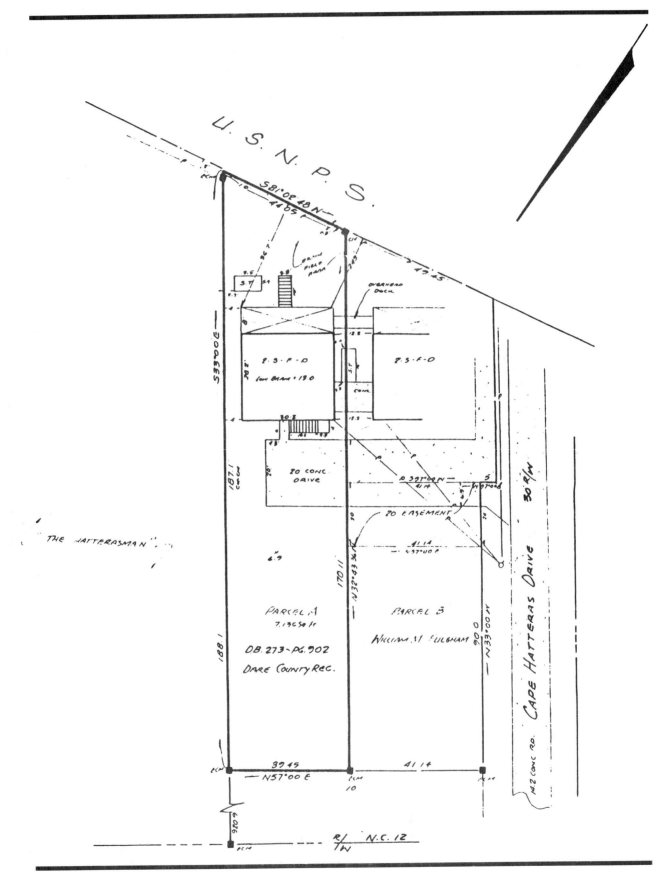

Figure 1.2

ASSIGNMENT #7 — PART 2

Review the legal description *(Figure 1.3)* provided in a deed which outlines a piece of rural, agricultural farmland. Draw as close a visual reproduction of this language as possible — a mirror image of sorts.

USE THE SPACE BELOW TO COMPLETE THIS ASSIGNMENT.

PRINTED BY: MATTHEWS BROS.
WILMINGTON, DEL.

016622

This Deed, Made this

day of   in the year of

our LORD one thousand nine hundred and   eighty-eight (1988)
    BETWEEN,

Witnesseth, *That the said part y   of the first part, for and in consideration of the sum of*

FORTY-SEVEN THOUSAND ($47,000.00) DOLLARS *lawful money of the United States of America,*

the receipt whereof is hereby acknowledged, hereby grant   and convey   unto the said

part ies *of the second part,* and by these presents does grant, bargain, sell,
release, convey and confirm, unto the said parties of the second part, their
heirs and assigns forever: **ALL**   that certain lot or parcel of
land located in Smith Township, Washington County, Pennsylvania, beginning
a portion of a larger tract of land known as the Virgil McDowell tract,
bounded and described as follows, to wit:

BEGINNING at a stake, a corner common to the within described tract
and lands of Warner C. Massey and on line of lands now or formerly of Thomas
Taylor and T. Burr Robbins; thence by said lands formerly of Taylor and
Robbins North one degree nine minutes East (N. 1° 9' E.) four hundred
thirty-six and two tenth (436.2) feet to a post; thence by same South
eighty degrees eight minutes East (S. 80° 8' E.) one hundred fifty-two and
six tenth (152.6) feet to a fence corner; thence North two degrees forty-two
minutes East (N. 2° 42' E.) two hundred forty-two and two tenth (242.2)
feet to a stake; thence South eighty-four degrees thirty-seven minutes
East (S. 84° 37' E.) forty-six and seven tenth (46.7) feet to a stone
corner; thence North one degree no minutes East (N. 1° 0' E.) fifty-six
and seven tenth (56.7) feet to a stake on the southerly side of a roadway;
thence along Southerly side of said roadway South eighty degrees twenty-
eight minutes East (S. 80° 28' E.) two hundred seventy-nine and four tenth
(279.4) feet to an iron pin on westerly side of a fifty foot roadway;
thence along said westerly side of said roadway South twelve degrees six
minutes West (S. 12° 6' W.) seven hundred thirty and one tenth (730.1)
feet to an iron pin on line of lands of Warner C. Massey; thence by said lands
North eighty degrees thirty-eight minutes West (N. 80° 38' W.) three hundred
forty-five (345.) feet to the place of beginning. CONTAINING 5.82 acres
more or less and having erected thereon one two-story frame dwelling house.

This conveyance is subject to the reservation of the coal and other
minerals with the mining rights and privileges appurtenant thereto as
reserved in conveyance from G. W. Crawford, et. ux., to Nancy W. Moses
dated January 9, 1880, and of record in the Recorder's Office of Washington
County aforesaid in Deed Book Volume 5, Page 507. This conveyance is also
subject to an oil and gas lease covering the said premises.

Figure 1.3

ASSIGNMENT #7 — PART 3

Finally, evaluate the photograph below at Photo 1.5. Assume that the water tower is in a southerly direction and that the parcel you will describe in writing is raw land with no structures of any kind on it. It is one parcel. To the east is the Atlantic Ocean. To the west is a bay or sound. To the north is a military installation.

Photo 1.5

*Both students and instructors must be reminded that there is no absolute response to this series of exercises. The thrust of the evaluation should rest in whether or not the student is grasping the nature of legal description and is able to translate, compare, contrast and differentiate words with pictorial representations, surveys and other well-accepted reference points.

USE YOU OWN STATIONERY TO COMPLETE THIS ASSIGNMENT.

8.   Searching the Title

As the agreement of sale demands, and unless waived, good and marketable title is a necessary component of an eventual settlement. Paralegals, legal assistants, attorneys, title officers and banking and finance specialists all have an interest in the quality of title and a chronological exposition of its chain. So important is this matter that the number of title companies providing insurance to the buyer, assuaging fears of competing claims, unpaid judgments, liens, encumbrances, zoning violations and other matters is steadily growing. The search of title — or as it is called in some jurisdictions, the abstraction — calls for specialized research which is far from uniform or national in design. Local practice and dictates, on a county-by-county basis, often influence the procedure to be employed. Your instructor should advise you in great depth as to what is to be expected at your Register or Recorder of Deeds office. Conveyancing and cataloging practices and how they are maintained for posterity are far from standardized, though all systems have some foundational similarities. In any event, the abstractor has to assist sellers and buyers in the clarification of title, the cleansing of outstanding obligations and the removal of judgments, liens and encumbrances. In addition, in order to understand the dynamics of these activities, the search for title should produce a chain of ownership that is without doubt or exception — airtight. The following assignments will give the student an understanding of what will be expected in this type of research.

ASSIGNMENT #8 — PART 1

TRACING YOUR HOUSE'S HERITAGE

A.   Objectives

   (1)   To learn about the process of title abstraction and the construction of chain of title.

B.   Student Obligations

   (1)   To complete a tracking of ownership of a selected residence.

C.   Instructor Obligations

   (1)   To give guidance and understanding as to what sources could assist a student in tracking the historical ownership of a house.

D.   Time Allotted: 0.3 hours

E.   Value of Assignment: 5.0 points

COMPLETE *FORM 1.7* BEGINNING WITH THE CURRENT OWNER AND ENDING WITH, AS FAR BACK AS YOU CAN TRACE, THE FIRST KNOWN OWNER AND OCCUPIER OF THE RESIDENCE.

HISTORICAL OWNERSHIP IN HOUSE

(Beginning with most recent owner)

NAME OF RESIDENCE_____

NAME OF OWNERS_____

DATES OF OWNERSHIP_____

NAME OF RESIDENCE_____

NAME OF OWNERS_____

DATES OF OWNERSHIP_____

NAME OF RESIDENCE_____

NAME OF OWNERS_____

DATES OF OWNERSHIP_____

NAME OF RESIDENCE_____

NAME OF OWNERS_____

DATES OF OWNERSHIP_____

NAME OF RESIDENCE_____

NAME OF OWNERS_____

DATES OF OWNERSHIP_____

NAME OF RESIDENCE_____

NAME OF OWNERS_____

DATES OF OWNERSHIP_____

NAME OF RESIDENCE_____

NAME OF OWNERS_____

DATES OF OWNERSHIP_____

(Copy this page if additional pages will be needed.)

Form 1.7

ASSIGNMENT #8 — PART 2
THE OFFICE OF THE RECORDER OF DEEDS

Most jurisdictions have a centralized location for the recordation of deeds and other instruments evidencing an interest in real property. In most jurisdictions, the term Recorder of Deeds is applicable. You are required to become familiar with your Recorder of Deeds Office by either direct visitation or a phone consultation. If you need a letter of introduction in order to get answers to the following questions, one will be provided by your instructor.

A. Objectives

    (1) To learn about the office of the Recorder of Deeds; and

    (2) To become familiar with the recordation techniques, storage mechanisms and tracking indexes utilized in real property documentation.

B. Student Obligations

    (1) To visit or call the local Recorder of Deeds to collect information on operation, recordation methods and indexing systems.

C. Instructor Obligations

    (1) To provide students with the address, phone number and any responsible party at the local Recorder of Deeds or other relevant office; and

    (2) To give students a brief introduction into the systems of recording real property documentation; and

    (3) To provide permission slips and other letters of introduction.

D. Time Allotted: 0.5 hours

E. Value of Assignment: 5.0 points

COMPLETE THE QUESTIONNAIRE AT *FORM 1.8*.

RECORDER OF DEEDS QUESTIONNAIRE

1. Who currently holds the position of Recorder of Deeds?_____

_____

_____

_____

_____

2. Name, address and phone number of the Recorder of Deeds office._____

_____

_____

3. Is there any other agency of government which holds, tracks and records instruments relating to real property ownership?_____

_____

_____

_____

_____

_____

4. What techniques of tracking and indexing are employed by your **Recorder of Deeds? Please list.**_____

_____

_____

_____

a. Is there a grantor/grantee index?   ☐ Yes   ☐ No

b. Is there a grantee/grantee index?   ☐ Yes   ☐ No

c. Is there an address index?   ☐ Yes   ☐ No

d. Is there a system which employs a code or other cryptic system of abbreviation which will assist the title
    abstracter?   ☐ Yes   ☐ No
    (1) If so, reproduce a picture of the code employed and attach.

e. Is there a cross-referencing or other indexing system which officially records liens, encumbrances, tax liabilities
    or other matters against the real property?   ☐ Yes   ☐ No

f. If the answer is YES to any of the above questions, make a photocopy of sample pages from those indexing
    systems. (For those who cannot visit the local office, this requirement is waived.)

5. What are the legal requisites such as fees, attestations, executory and notary requirements for the filing of real
    property documentation in your local office? Be specific and list._____

    _____

    _____

    _____

    _____

6. Is it advisable or proper for a deed to be submitted to this office by mail?   ☐ Yes   ☐ No

7. Note any peculiar practices or issues of great importance in your local office where real property documents are
    recorded._____

    _____

    _____

    _____

    _____

    _____

Form 1.8

9.   The Acquisition of Title Insurance

Title insurance plays a key role in the transferability and alienability of modern real estate. Assuring that defects in title and other legal impediments do not haunt a purchaser of real property, title insurance is a critical component in the settlement process. A title insurer will not provide a policy unless assured that the property is good and marketable or the insurer excepts itself from specific conditions, covenants or other legal requirements.

A.   Objectives

 (1)   To become familiar with the purposes of title insurance;

 (2)   To be able to read, comprehend and file appropriate documentation for the acquisition of title insurance;

 (3)   To become familiar with the types of objections that attorneys raise in their reports of title; and

 (4)   To be able to comprehend and prepare a final certificate of title.

B.   Student Obligations

 (1)   To prepare an application for title insurance;

 (2)   To prepare owner's and purchaser's affidavits for title insurance;

 (3)   To prepare an attorney's report of title; and

 (4)   To prepare a final certificate of title.

C.   Instructor Obligations

 (1)   To provide students with whatever forms are necessary to adhere to local practice and procedure in the acquisition of title insurance. (Forms provided in the sample assignment are merely illustrative.)

D.   Time Allotted: 1.1 hours

E.   Value of Assignment: 10.0 points

ASSIGNMENT #9 — PART 1
APPLICATION FOR TITLE INSURANCE

FACT PATTERN

Name of Insured (Buyers):   Mary and Bill Davidson
Address: 1800 Left Blvd., Amarillo, TX 81119
Consideration: $48,000
File No.:   168849
Address of Property: 1350 Benton Blvd., Hollywood, CA 99964
Description of Property: All that certain lot or piece of ground with buildings and improvements thereon erected, situated in the township of Hollywood, County of Washington, State of California, and described as follows:

Beginning at a point at the intersection of the southerly side of Shadeland Avenue and the northwesterly side of Benton Blvd. Containing in front or breadth on the said side of Shadeland Avenue 100 feet and extending of that width in length or depth, 100 feet; the southeasterly line thereof being the long, the northwesterly side of Benton Blvd.

Name of Owners/Occupiers: Sally and Philip Testa (husband and wife)
Amount of mortgage or deed of trust to be insured: $40,000
Type of Mortgage: Conventional
Mortgagors: City Bank of New York
Title by: Tenancy by the entireties
Deed Book: 64 at Page 100
Will Book: 846 at Page 44
Intestacy: Not Applicable
Use of property: Residential
Interim Binder: Desired
Deliver Binder To: Stephen Wilcox, Attorney at Law, 1418 Maidenchoice Lane, Baltimore, MD 21120
Settlement To Be Held At: Attorney's Office
Assessments Paid Until: July 31, 1989; none unpaid
Taxes Paid Until: July 31, 1989; none unpaid
Notary Public: Fred Williams of Baltimore County, Maryland
Notary Commission Expires: June 10, 1990
All Rents Accrue: July 31; on an annual basis
Title Commitment No.:   6218
Tax Parcel No.:   412
Conflicts with Adjoining Properties, Public or Discoverable Easements or Variations: No
Liens: None
Mineral Region: Yes
Date of Deed Book: Deed from Anna Schwartz to sellers dated July 9, 1957; recorded in Deed Book
     64 at Page 100.

COMPLETE THE APPLICATION FOR TITLE INSURANCE AT *FORM 1.9* BASED ON THE FACT PATTERN ABOVE.

No._____

APPLICATION FOR TITLE INSURANCE

Application is hereby made to Berks Title Insurance Company by the undersigned for Title Insurance, in its usual form, on the title to real estate identified below. The undersigned, in order to secure such insurance from Berks Title Insurance Company, represents the data and information given below to be true and correct and avers that no knowledge of any unrecorded deeds, adverse claims, agreements or objections have come to applicant's attention and that no material fact is being suppressed relating to said title. Applicant(s) agrees that should there occur or come to knowledge before the Title Policy is issued, only matter which would affect (a) the answers herein (b) the title to said real estate or (c) the instrument to be insured, such knowledge will be immediately communicated to said Berks Title Insurance Company. Applicant(s) agrees that the entire charge for the service of Berks Title Insurance Company, including the policy fee, shall be due and payable immediately upon the presentation and delivery of the Interim Binder (Settlement Certificate) and/or Title Policy.

FOR OWNER INSURANCE

Name of Owner(s) to be Insured:

Address of Insured:

Consideration paid or to be paid for Property: $

(NOTE: Owner's Policy must be for full value of property.)

FOR MORTGAGE OR DEED OF TRUST INSURANCE

Name of Insured:

Address of Insured:

Name of Proposed Mortgagors:

Amount of Mortgage or Deed of Trust to be Insured: $

Property is (a) now owned ( ) (b) being purchased ( ) or (c) leased ( ) by Proposed Mortgagors.

GENERAL INFORMATION

Name of present Owner(s) of Property and Marital status

Address of present Owner(s):

Title is vested in present Owner(s) by:
{ Deed Book No._____ Page _____ from
Will Book No. _____ Page _____ of
Intestacy of _____

Property is now occupied by:

If tenant, give particulars of lease: Does tenant have renewal and/or purchase option?

When were buildings or last alterations fully completed? Month_____ Year _____

How is property used?

Is Interim Binder (Settlement Certificate) desired?

NOTE: Owner's Policy cannot be issued until consideration for property has been fully paid and deed recorded. Mortgagee Policy cannot be issued until loan proceeds have been disbursed to satisfaction of Company.

Deliver Interim Binder (Settlement Certificate) to   by

Settlement to be held at   on

Description of Property: (Complete description to be attached.)

Date:

_____

FORM TC 1 (REV. 6-72)   (Applicant(s)

Form 1.9

ASSIGNMENT #9 — PART 2
OWNER'S AFFIDAVIT

PREPARE THE OWNER'S AFFIDAVIT AT *FORM 1.10* BASED ON THE FACT PATTERN ABOVE.

American Title Insurance Company
A ⊗ Meridian Company
10 BRYN MAWR AVE., BRYN MAWR, PA 19010
OWNER'S AFFIDAVIT (INDIVIDUAL)

STATE OF   :
                ss:

COUNTY OF   :   No. ....

ON THE ....day of .... , A.D. 19 ..... ,

before me, the Subscriber, a Notary Public for the State of .... , duly commissioned,

personally appeared .... ,
who being duly sworn according to law, depose/s and say/s:

That .... is/are

the owner/s of premises situate ....

....

and the same person/s as the grantee/s in Book .... , Page No. ....;

....

That there are no liens or encumbrances (Mortgages, Deeds of Trust, Judgments, Tax Liens, Mechanics' Liens, etc.) known to the undersigned which are not being properly provided for in this transaction;

That there have been no repairs, additions or improvements made, ordered or contracted to be made on or to the premises, nor are there any appliances or fixtures attached to said premises which have not been paid for in full; and that there are no outstanding or disputed claims for any such work or item;

That there has been no work done, or notice received that work is to be done, by the Municipality (City, Borough or Township), or at its direction, in connection with the installation of sewer or water or for improvements such as paving or repaving of streets or alleys, or the installation of curbs or sidewalks;

That no notice has been served by any government authority for the removal or abatement of any nuisance, for the violation of any Zoning Regulation or concerning the condemnation of any portion of said premises;

That there has been no violation of any restrictions affecting the premises;

That there are no disputes with any adjoining property owners as to the location of property lines or the encroachment of any improvements;

That there are no purchase money obligations being created in this transfer;

That there are no unrecorded leases or agreements affecting premises in question;

That the present transaction is not made for the purpose of hindering, delaying or defrauding any creditors of said owner/s and does not come within the provisions of the Bankruptcy or Insolvency Acts (or any amendments thereof);

That the said owner/s has/have not been divorced, or that the said owner/s is/are not involved in any pending divorce action in any jurisdiction;

That all Real Estate Taxes assessed upon said premises have been paid in full to and including 19 .... and water rent to .... and sewer rent to .... ;

That the grantor/s and/or mortgagor/s in this transaction is/are of full legal age and in every respect competent to convey or encumber the title to the premises in question;

That none of the improvements nor any part thereof on the insured premises was ever a mobile home or trailer and was never registered in the Department of Motor Vehicles of any State or Subdivision of the United States;

That the land to be insured hereunder is not under any contract covenant for preferential assessment as farm or forest land;

That this affidavit is made for the purpose of enabling American Title Insurance Company to remove certain objections from the commitment issued under the above cited number, and affiant/s aver/s the foregoing statements are true and correct to the best of his/her knowledge and belief.

SUBSCRIBED and SWORN to before me,
the day and year aforesaid.

....

                                                   (Affiant)

....

                                                   (Affiant)

FL-21A (10-86)

Form 1.10

ASSIGNMENT #9 — PART 3
PURCHASER'S AFFIDAVIT

PREPARE THE PURCHASER'S AFFIDAVIT AT *FORM 1.11* BASED ON THE FACT PATTERN ABOVE.

PURCHASER'S AFFIDAVIT

STATE OF   :   ss: No. . . . .
COUNTY OF   :

ON THE . . . . day of . . . . , A. D. 19 . . . . ,

before me, the Subscriber, a Notary Public for the State of . . . . ,

duly commissioned, personally appeared the undersigned who, being duly sworn according to law, depose/s and say/s:

That . . . . is/are

the purchaser/s of premises situate . . . .

. . . .

. . . . ,

That it is the intention of said purchaser/s to take title as (state the estate or interest) . . . .

. . . . ,

That the said premises are to be owned in the following fractional interests, if any: . . . .

. . . . ,

That the newly-erected building/s, if any, on said premises is/were completed on or about (if none, so state),

. . . .

That said purchaser/s (if individual/s) is/are of full legal age and sui juris,

That said purchaser/s has/have not entered into any unrecorded leases or agreements affecting said premises,

That there are no judgments against said purchaser/s,

That no part of the funds used for the purchase of said premises has been borrowed except . . . .

. . . . ,

That this affidavit is made for the purpose of enabling Berks Title Insurance Company to remove certain

objections from Interim Binder No. . . . . , and affiant/s aver/s the foregoing statements are true

and correct to the best of his/her/their knowledge and belief.

SUBSCRIBED and SWORN to before me,
the day and year aforesaid.

. . . .
                                                           (Affiant)
. . . .
                                                            (Affiant)

TF-6 5/81

Form 1.11

ASSIGNMENT #9 — PART 4
ATTORNEY'S REPORT OF TITLE

PREPARE THE ATTORNEY'S REPORT OF TITLE AT *FORM 1.12* BASED ON THE FACT PATTERN ABOVE.

ATTORNEY'S REPORT of TITLE

No. _____

I have examined the record title to the real estate described in Schedule "A" to the date hereof for the protection of:

OWNER or LEASEHOLDER to be insured: _____ $_____

LENDER to be insured: _____ $_____

Type of Mortgage/Deed of Trust: Conv._____ VA_____ FHA_____ VRM_____ Const._____ Other_____ (Specify)

Title vested in: _____

Estate or Interest:_____Type of Tenancy:_____

Being (the same) (part of the same) premises acquired by Deed from _____

_____ dated____ /____ /____ and recorded____ /____ /____ in Deed Book _____ page _____

Note: if acquired by more than one deed or through an estate set forth the additional information and attach hereto.

Schedule A

Attach complete description of Real Estate (including heading) to be insured.

Schedule B

ATTORNEY'S OBJECTIONS
NOTE: Please fill all spaces; "None" where applicable.

1. Property is occupied by: _____
    If tenant, give particulars of lease: Does tenant have renewal and/or purchase option? _____
2. Taxes are paid to and including the year 19_____. Tax Parcel No._____
3. Water Rent accruing from_____
4. Sewer Rent accruing from_____
        Note: if 3 and 4 are private sources, so state.
5. Any unpaid water and sewer connections, paving charges or other assessments_____
                                                                                                              (define)
6. Easements, servitudes, variation in dimensions or area content, improper location of buildings and improvements, conflict with lines of adjoining property, encroachments, projections or other matters which might be disclosed by an accurate survey of the premises.
7. Liability for claims for work done or materials furnished for which a lien might be filed.
    Construction (if applicable) is. (   ) contemplated   (   ) in progress   (   ) completed_____and statutory lien period has
    (   ) expired – (   ) has not expired.   (date)
8. Is property located in a coal area? Yes_____No_____. If so, Bituminous_____; Anthracite_____.

List all liens and other exceptions and conditions disclosed by the examination. (Furnish verbatim copies of easements, rights of way and restrictions INCLUDING REVERTER CLAUSE, IF ANY).

Certified at_____this_____day of_____, 19_____.
                              (AM/PM)

            (Signature) _____ Attorney at Law

                                                        (Note – Please type name under signature.)

No liability is assumed by   Title Insurance Company under this Attorney's Report of Title until a commitment, title binder or title policy is issued pursuant to this report.

TF5 (Rev. 11/84)

Form 1.12

ASSIGNMENT #9 — PART 5
FINAL CERTIFICATE OF TITLE

PREPARE THE FINAL CERTIFICATE OF TITLE AT *FORM 1.13* BASED ON THE FACT PATTERN ABOVE TAKING INTO ACCOUNT THE FOLLOWING ADDITIONS TO AND/OR CHANGES OF FACT.

Mechanic's Lien: $4,000; Arthur Construction Co.; unsatisfied

Tax Lien: County of Washington; $4,212; unsatisfied

Mortgage Recorded: Volume 35 at Page 464

Deed Recorded: Deed Book 65, Volume 28 at Page 1000

Date Recorded: August 1, 1989

FINAL CERTIFICATE OF TITLE

IN RE: Report of Title or Interim Binder No. ....

I hereby certify that I have searched all the records which affect the title to the premises described in the above numbered Report of Title or Interim Binder from the date of said Report or Binder to the date of this Final Certificate and I find that the following instrument(s) affecting title thereto have been placed of record subsequent to the date of said Report or Binder:

DEED: *Grantor:*

       Grantee:

       Dated:
       Recorded: 19   ; *Instrument #*
          Deed Book   , *Vol.*   , *Page*
       Consideration:
       Transfer Taxes:

DEED/TR. or   *Grantor/Mortgagor:*
MORTGAGE

       Trustees/Mortgagee:

       Note Holder:

Check Type:
VA.....................*Dated:*
FHA.................*Recorded:*   19   ;   *Instrument #*
CONV.............. ....*Book*   Vol.   , *Page*
         Amount

OTHER   *(All other instruments affecting title, including Assignment(s) of above Deed of Trust or Mortgage, placed of record subsequent to the date of the above numbered Report of Title or Interim Binder):*

I HAVE COMPARED THE DESCRIPTIONS, AND COVENANTS AND RESTRICTIONS, IF ANY, CONTAINED IN SAID DEED AND/OR DEED OF TRUST/MORTGAGE WITH THOSE CONTAINED IN THE REPORT OR BINDER AND HEREBY CERTIFY THAT THEY ARE THE SAME IN ALL RESPECTS UNLESS AN EXCEPTION IS NOTED IMMEDIATELY HEREUNDER:

Water rent (if any) is paid to and including: ....★
Sewer rent (if any) is paid to and including: ....★
★   DATE OF METER READING OR DATE PERIOD ENDS; if not applicable, or lienable, so state.

Real Estate Taxes were paid to Taxing Authorities to and including: ....

I further certify that the liens or encumbrances on Schedule "B" of said Report or Schedule "C" of said Binder have been fully satisfied of record or the premises in question properly released therefrom in the following manner on the dates shown: IF NOT SATISFIED OR RELEASED, SHOW PROVISIONS MADE FOR SAME:

Exception No. ...., ...
Exception No. ...., ...
Exception No. ...., ...
Exception No. ...., ...

and I further certify that there are no liens or encumbrances of record against the said premises other than the Deed of Trust/Mortgage noted above, if any, which Deed of Trust/Mortgage, in my opinion, is a good, valid, first lien on the said premises.

I further certify that, so far as I know, no question as to the validity of the title to the premises concerned has at any time been raised by any persons, nor has there been any dispute, to my knowledge, among attorneys of the local Bar as to its validity.

Searches were extended to cover recordation of the instrument(s) listed above.

Date of search: ....   ------------------------------------
                                                     Attorney

TF 2 - (Form TC-28 Rev. 2/80)

Form 1.13

10. Cleaning Up Title

In order for any title policy to be issued, the title company must be satisfied that all matters relating to defects in the chain of title, outstanding obligations, encumbrances, liens, judgments and unsatisfied mortgages have been taken care of. Paralegals and legal assistants and other real estate practitioners will be given the responsibility of collecting and compiling information relative to these types of matters.

A. Objectives

   (1) To become familiar with the technique for proving that a mortgage has been satisfied;

   (2) To learn about those issues that must be resolved before a title insurance policy can be issued;

   (3) To understand the dynamics involved in acquiring a release;

   (4) To learn and comprehend the influence judgments have upon the transferability and alienability of an interest in real property; and

   (5) To see how liens can be extinguished through the techniques of waiver or satisfaction;

B. Student Obligations

   (1) To prepare a mortgage satisfaction piece;

   (2) To draft and compile a general release document;

   (3) To draft and compile a release from judgment document; and

   (4) To draft and compile a waiver of lien document.

C. Instructor Obligations

   (1) To point out the major or subtle differences between the suggested uniform practice and that of your locality;

   (2) To provide examples of local forms and documents which serve the same purpose; and

   (3) To monitor and to give advice to students as they complete these assignments.

D. Time Allotted: 1.0 hours

E. Value of Assignment: 5.0 points

ASSIGNMENT #10 — PART 1
PREPARATION OF A MORTGAGE SATISFACTION PIECE

The mortgage satisfaction indicates that the mortgage has been fully and totally satisfied, thereby insuring free and marketable title of an underlying property, assuming no other issues are outstanding.

FACT PATTERN

Notary: George Lynch
Place of Mortgage Satisfaction: Dare Township, Washington County, Virginia
Date of Satisfaction: June 1, 1985
Mortgagor: Harry and Rebecca Brown
Name of Last Assignment: None
Mortgagee: Bank of Hyde Park
Mortgagee Representative: Grace Williams, Secretary

Date of Mortgage: January 1, 1983

Original Mortgage amount: $18,600

Recorded on: January 1, 1983

Location of Mortgage Recording: Dare Township, Washington County, Virginia

Mortgage Book: Volume 1681 at Page 900

Description of Premises: All that certain lot or piece of ground with buildings and improvements thereon erected, situated in the township of Dare, County of Washington, Commonwealth of Virginia, and described as follows:

Beginning at a point at the intersection of the southerly side of Shadeland Avenue and the northwesterly side of Marveen Avenue. Containing in front or breadth on the said side of Shadeland Avenue 100 feet and extending of that width in length or depth, 100 feet, the southeasterly line thereof being the long, the northwesterly side of Marveen Avenue.

COMPLETE THE MORTGAGE SATISFACTION PIECE FORM AT *FORM 1.14*.

Mortgage Satisfaction Piece — Corporation No. 845 C   Copyright 1977 Printed and Sold by John C. Clark Co., 1326 Walnut St., Phila., Pa.
Act of Assembly No. 382 of 1961.

....   Prems: ....

....

TO

....**Township**

.... County

Mortgage Satisfaction Piece

Made this   day of   19
Name of Mortgagor(s)

Name of Mortgagee(s)

Name of Last Assignee(s)

Date of Mortgage
Original Mortgage Debt $
Mortgage recorded on   19   , in the Office of the Recorder of Deeds of
                        County,   , in Mortgage Book   page
*Last assignment recorded on   19   , in the Office of the Recorder of Deeds of
                        County,   in Mortgage Book*   Assignment of Mortgage Book*
No.   page

**Mortgage Premises:

The undersigned hereby certifies that the debt secured by the above mentioned Mortgage has been fully
paid or otherwise discharged and that upon the recording hereof said Mortgage shall be and is hereby fully
and forever satisfied and discharged.

In Witness Whereof, the said Corporation has caused its common or corporate seal to be hereunto
affixed the   day of   A. D., 19

Signed, Sealed and Delivered
   in the presence of:

                                            ....
                                                                        President
                        ATTEST: ....
                                                                        Secretary

STATE of   ⎫
COUNTY of   ⎬ SS:
                                            ⎭
   On the   day of   , A. D. 19   . before me, the undersigned officer,
personally appeared   , who acknowledged
himself—herself— to be the   of
a corporation, and that   he as such   , being authorized to do so, executed the foregoing instrument for the purposes therein contained by signing the name of the Corporation by himself
herself—as

   In Witness Whereof.   I have hereunto set my hand and   Seal.

* Delete if not applicable.
** Brief Description or Statement of location of mortgaged premises. ....

Form 1.14

ASSIGNMENT #10 — PART 2
GENERAL RELEASE

In order to insure that property is fully alienable, some financial institutions and title companies will insist on a general release as relates to an entire property interest. General release forms are employed in many contexts of legal practice.

FACT PATTERN

Person Releasing: John and Mary Green

Person Released: Eleanor Regina

Subject Matter Released From: Money judgments acquired by Irvin Construction Company against the real property and interest at 1416 Johnson Street, Boise, Idaho

Date of Release: September 4, 1984

PREPARE THE RELEASE AT *FORM 1.15 (2 PAGES).*

Printed   No. 135—GENERAL RELEASE
by Yeo & Lukens Co.,   Philadelphia

Know all Men by these Presents

That _____

_____

_____

_____

do hereby remise, release and forever discharge _____

_____

_____

heirs, executors and administrators, of and from all _____

_____

_____

and all manner of actions and causes of action, suits, debts, dues, accounts, bonds, covenants, contracts, agreements, judgments, claims and demands whatsoever in law or equity; which against the said

_____

_____

ever had, now have, or which   heirs, executors, administrators or assigns, or any of them hereafter can, shall or may have, for or by reason of any cause, matter or thing whatsoever, from the beginning of the world to the date of these presents

In Witness Whereof,

have hereunto set   hand and seal   the

_____ day of _____ in the year of our Lord one thousand

nine hundred and _____

SIGNED, SEALED AND DELIVERED

IN THE PRESENCE OF US

_____

_____

_____ (SEAL)

_____ (SEAL)

Form 1.15

General Release

FROM

Date _____

No. 135—Yeo and Lukens Co., Philadelphia

P 51898

Form 1.15—*concluded*

ASSIGNMENT #10 — PART 3
RELEASE OF JUDGMENT

For a more specific example of a release of a judgment against an identifiable piece of real property, adopt the following facts to complete a "Release of Judgment."

FACT PATTERN

Entity Possessing Judgment: Joseph Manufacturing Company, Inc.

Judgment Against: Real property situated at 1812 Merdland Blvd., Nashville, TN 86611

Consideration Paid for Release of Judgment: $35,000

Date of Release: June 4, 1988

Purchaser of Real Property Subject to Judgment: Robert Anglen

COMPLETE *FORM 1.16*

RELEASE OF JUDGMENT

WHEREAS, _____ holds
and possesses a judgment against real property situated at ____
_____.

WHEREAS, _____ wishes and desires to
purchase said _____ free and clear of any outstanding
judgments, liens, or other encumbrances, said _____
____ agrees to pay _____ the
sum of _____ (_____)
____ for a release extending to _____, _____
heirs and assigns.

On this date, the party granting the release, namely, ____
_____ to bone fide purchaser
_____ hereby agree to these terms and conditions.

_____   _____
Witness

_____   _____
Witness

Form 1.16

ASSIGNMENT #10 — PART 4
WAIVER OF LIENS

Before issuing a title policy, the title company will want to be assured that all liens, especially in a construction project, will have been taken care of.

FACT PATTERN

Property at: Balcor Avenue, Portland, Maine 00049

Owned by: Gregory Williams of 1359 Beckett Lane, Canterbury, Oklahoma

Types of Claims: Excavation (Kretzler Excavation Co., $3,000); Electric (Speer Electric Co., $8,000); Stonework (Sanders Stone, $8,000); Plumbing (Fehl Plumbing, $11,000)

State: Maine

County: Bath

General Contractor: Nembar Construction

Notary: Fred Williams

COMPLETE THE WAIVER OF LIENS FORM AT *FORM 1.17 (2 PAGES).*

WAIVER OF LIENS

INSTRUCTIONS

1. This instrument will not be satisfactory or acceptable unless ALL of the signature blanks in Part I are filled in by signatures of proper parties or if no such material or labor has been furnished, such fact is shown by the word "none" inserted in the blank. When materials furnished by the general contractor pursuant to his contract with the owner were obtained from sources other than his own stock or manufacture of such materials, the persons, firms or corporations from which the materials were obtained, rather than the general contractor, must sign for such materials.

2. In the middle of the third line in Part I the name of the owner of the property should be inserted.

3. In the space after the third line in Part I a description of the property should be inserted, care being taken to identify the property with the record description. Please be certain that this part of the waiver is completed before same is executed by any party.

4. The signatures to the waiver should be in accordance with the following: Unless the party signing be an individual, it should be stated whether a partnership or corporation. If a partnership, one of the partners must sign the name of the firm by him and show after his signature on behalf of the firm the fact that he is a partner. If a corporation, then the name of the corporation must be written and signed by an executive officer, the official title of such officer being placed after his signature and the corporate seal affixed. A signature by one individual on behalf of another individual will not be accepted unless the waiver is accompanied by power of attorney showing the authority of such individual to sign on behalf of the other individual. If an individual is doing business under a trade name and executes the waiver in such trade name, he should affix his signature after such trade name and show that he is the owner. Unless the signatures are taken in the presence of special counsel, he should be sure to verify their genuineness. Where a subcontractor or materialman has been fully paid and no waiver is to be taken, his name should be type-written in Part I, showing contract price, and receipt showing payment in full should accompany the waiver.

5. The affidavit, Part II, should be executed by the general contractor, if any. The affidavit, Part III, should be executed by the owner. If the owner is also the general contractor, both affidavits should be executed by him.

Part I—Waiver of Liens

We, the undersigned, are general or subcontractors, materialmen, or other persons furnishing services or labor or materials, as indicated under our respective signatures below, in the construction or repair of improvements upon real estate owned

by .... and described as follows:

Complete Waiver to Show Description of Property Before Same is Executed by Any Party

In consideration of the sum of $1.00 to each of us in hand paid, receipt whereof is hereby acknowledged, and other benefits accruing to us, and in order to induce the making of one or more loans on said real estate, as improved, and the insuring of the title to the premises we do hereby waive, release and quit-claim in favor of each and every party making a loan on said real estate, as improved, and his or its successors and assigns, and the title company insuring the title all right that we, or any of us, may now or hereafter have to a lien upon the land and improvements above described, by virtue of the laws of the state wherein said land is situate, or any amendments of said laws; and we do further warrant that we have not and will not assign our claims for payment, nor our right to perfect a lien against said property, and that we have the right to execute this waiver and release thereof.

ALL of the subscribers to this instrument respectively warrant that all laborers employed by them upon the aforesaid premises have been fully paid and that none of such laborers have any claim, demand or lien against said premises; and further, that no chattel mortgage, conditional bill of sale or retention of title agreement, has been given or executed by the said owner or any general contractor or other party or any of us, for or in connection with any material, appliances, machinery, fixtures, or furnishings placed upon or installed in the aforesaid premises by any of us, other than:

It is understood and agreed that any and all signatures hereto are for all services rendered, work done and material furnished heretofore and hereafter by the signers in any and all capacities, and are not understood to be only for the particular item against which the signature is affixed.

Witness the following signatures and seals this .... day of ...., 19 ......

AMOUNT OF CLAIM PAID OR UNPAID		AMOUNT OF CLAIM PAID OR UNPAID	
($ ....) Architect	(SEAL)	($ ....) Elevators	(SEAL)
($ ....) General Contractor	(SEAL)	($ ....) Excavation	(SEAL)
($ ....) Brick	(SEAL)	($ ....) Flooring	(SEAL)
($ ....) Bricklaying	(SEAL)	($ ....) Floor Scraping	(SEAL)
($ ....) Carpentry	(SEAL)	($ ....) Glass	(SEAL)
($ ....) Concrete	(SEAL)	($ ....) Glass Work	(SEAL)
($ ....) Electric Fixtures	(SEAL)	($ ....) Gutters and Downspouts	(SEAL)
($ ....) Electric Wiring	(SEAL)	($ ....) Hardware	(SEAL)

SEE AFFIDAVITS ON THE REVERSE SIDE HEREOF. THIS WAIVER WILL NOT BE ACCEPTED UNLESS THESE AFFIDAVITS ARE EXECUTED.

FORM T. 46   REPRINTED (11/84)

Form 1.17

($............)..(SEAL)   ($............)..(SEAL)
Heating/Air Conditioning   Roofing Work

($............)..(SEAL)   ($............)..(SEAL)
Iron and Steel   Sand and Gravel

($............)..(SEAL)   ($............)..(SEAL)
Iron and Steel Work   Screens

($............)..(SEAL)   ($............)..(SEAL)
Lime and Cement   Shades

($............)..(SEAL)   ($............)..(SEAL)
Linoleum   Sheet Metal Work

($............)..(SEAL)   ($............)..(SEAL)
Lumber   Sprinkler System

($............)..(SEAL)   ($............)..(SEAL)
Materials for insulation Against Weather Conditions   Stone

($............)..(SEAL)   ($............)..(SEAL)
Millwork   Stone Work

($............)..(SEAL)   ($............)..(SEAL)
Paint   Stucco

($............)..(SEAL)   ($............)..(SEAL)
Painting   Tile and Marble

($............)..(SEAL)   ($............)..(SEAL)
Plaster Materials   Tile and Marble Setting

($............)..(SEAL)   ($............)..(SEAL)
Plastering   Wall Paper

($............)..(SEAL)   ($............)..(SEAL)
Plumbing Fixtures   Wall Papering

($............)..(SEAL)   ($............)..(SEAL)
Plumbing   Weather Strips

($............)..(SEAL)   ($............)..(SEAL)
Refrigeration

($............)..(SEAL)   ($............)..(SEAL)
Roofing Materials

Part II—Affidavit

STATE OF .... TO-WIT:
.... of ....

I, ..., having been first duly sworn, doth now depose and say: That the persons, firms and corporations who have executed the waiver of liens on the reverse side hereof are all of the persons, firms and corporations who have furnished services, labor, or materials in the construction or repair of improvements on the real estate described in said waiver and that, as of the date of this affidavit, such work has been fully completed and accepted by the owner of said real estate.

....
General Contractor, if any.

Subscribed and sworn to before the undersigned, a Notary Public for the .... of ....,

State of .... in said ...., this .... day of ...., 19 ....

....
Notary Public.

Part III—Affidavit

STATE OF .... TO-WIT:
.... of ....

I, ..., having been first duly sworn, doth now depose and say: That the persons, firms and corporations who have executed the waiver of liens on the reverse side hereof include all of the persons, firms and corporations with whom or with which I have contracted for services, labor, or materials in the construction or repair of improvements on the real estate described in said waiver; that, as of the date of this affidavit, such work has been fully completed and accepted by me; that the general contractor, if any, and all other parties with whom I have contracted have been paid in full; that, at the time of paying said parties in full, I had no notice of any claim of any subcontractor, laborer or materialman, and that I do not now have notice of any claim of any subcontractor, laborer or materialman.

....
Owner.

Subscribed and sworn to before the undersigned, a Notary Public for the .... of ....,

State of .... in said ...., this .... day of ...., 19 ....

....
Notary Public.

Form 1.17—*concluded*

11. Preparation of Mortgage

If title has been made clear and marketable, lending institutions will proceed with the issuance of a positive commitment, assuming a positive credit analysis and all other conditions and contingencies have been satisfied. Understanding the nature of a mortgage and an accompanying note is important for the specialist in real estate.

A. Objectives

   (1) To evaluate and assess those terms, conditions, clauses and provisions necessary in a mortgage document; and

   (2) To evaluate and analyze those terms and conditions necessary for an enforceable mortgage note.

B. Student Obligations

   (1) To prepare a mortgage document; and

   (2) To prepare a mortgage note.

C. Instructor Obligations

   (1) To monitor and oversee the preparation of a mortgage and accompanying note; and

   (2) To point out all major differences and distinctions given local practice and custom.

D. Time Allotted: 0.7 hours

E. Value of Assignment: 10.0 points

ASSIGNMENT #11 — PART 1
MORTGAGE

FACT PATTERN

Legal Description of Property: All that certain lot of land situated in the Township of Hope, County of Appaloosa, Minnesota, being lot No. 29 in the Hope Township Re-Subdivision Plan, recorded in the Recorder's Office of Appaloosa County, Minnesota, in the Plan Book Volume 32, page 78, bounded and described as follows:

Beginning at a point on the Easterly side of 1400 Washington Blvd. in said Plan at the dividing line between Lots No. 29 and 30 in said Plan; thence along Easterly side of Washington Boulevard North 12 14' West, 127.89 feet to a point of tangent; thence along the said side of said Washington Boulevard curving to the right by a curve having a radius of 57.84 feet, a distance of 147.84 feet to a point on the Southwesterly side of Jefferson Street in said Plan; thence along the Southwesterly side of Kings Highway, South 45 47' East, a distance of 170.00 feet to a point; thence along the Westerly boundary line of the Park designated in said Plan, South between Lots No. 29 and 30 in said Plan; then along said dividing line South 77 46' West, a distance of 200.00 feet to the Easterly side of Rosslyn Road at the Place of Beginning.

Having erected thereon a two-story brick building.

Address: 1400 Washington Blvd., Minneapolis, MN 31865

Township: Hope

County: Appaloosa

Attachments: Adjustable rate rider

Notary: Fred Williams
Date of Mortgage: July 1, 1989
Mortgagor: Charles P. and Jean Marie Conway
Mortgagee: Mellon Bank, 100 West Mall Plaza, Pittsburgh, PA 15106
Sum of Mortgage: $70,000

COMPLETE THE MORTGAGE NOTE AT *FORM 1.18 (4 PAGES)*.

[Space Above This Line For Recording Data]

MORTGAGE

THIS MORTGAGE ("Security Instrument") is given on
19   The mortgagor is

("Borrower").

This Security Instrument is given to
which is organized and existing under the laws of   , and whose address is

("Lender").

Borrower owes Lender the principal sum of

Dollars (U.S.$). This debt is evidenced by Borrower's note dated the same date as this Security Instrument ("Note"), which provides for monthly payments, with the full debt, if not paid earlier, due and payable on   . This Security Instrument secures to Lender: (a) the repayment of the debt evidenced by the Note, with interest, and all renewals, extensions and modifications; (b) the payment of all other sums, with interest, advanced under paragraph 7 to protect the security of this Security Instrument; and (c) the performance of Borrower's covenants and agreements under this Security Instrument and the Note. For this purpose, Borrower does hereby mortgage, grant and convey to Lender the following described property located in

County, Pennsylvania:

BEING MORE PARTICULARLY DESCRIBED ACCORDING TO A LEGAL DESCRIPTION ATTACHED HERETO AND MADE A PART HEREOF.

which has the address of

[Street]   [City]

Pennsylvania   ("Property Address");
            [Zip Code]

TOGETHER WITH all the improvements now or hereafter erected on the property, and all easements, rights, appurtenances, rents, royalties, mineral, oil and gas rights and profits, water rights and stock and all fixtures now or hereafter a part of the property. All replacements and additions shall also be covered by this Security Instrument. All of the foregoing is referred to in this Security Instrument as the "Property."

BORROWER COVENANTS that Borrower is lawfully seised of the estate hereby conveyed and has the right to mortgage, grant and convey the Property and that the Property is unencumbered, except for encumbrances of record. Borrower warrants and will defend generally the title to the Property against all claims and demands, subject to any encumbrances of record.

THIS SECURITY INSTRUMENT combines uniform covenants for national use and non-uniform covenants with limited variations by jurisdiction to constitute a uniform security instrument covering real property.

CONV PA MORTGAGE—Single Family—FNMA/FHLMC UNIFORM INSTRUMENT
MM CL-400-C Rev. 5/87 jtr   Form 3039 12/83

Form 1.18

UNIFORM COVENANTS. Borrower and Lender covenant and agree as follows:

1. **Payment of Principal and Interest; Prepayment and Late Charges.** Borrower shall promptly pay when due the principal of and interest on the debt evidenced by the Note and any prepayment and late charges due under the Note.

2. **Funds for Taxes and Insurance.** Subject to applicable law or to a written waiver by Lender, Borrower shall pay to Lender on the day monthly payments are due under the Note, until the Note is paid in full, a sum ("Funds") equal to one-twelfth of: (a) yearly taxes and assessments which may attain priority over this Security Instrument; (b) yearly leasehold payments or ground rents on the Property, if any; (c) yearly hazard insurance premiums; and (d) yearly mortgage insurance premiums, if any. These items are called "escrow items." Lender may estimate the Funds due on the basis of current data and reasonable estimates of future escrow items.

The Funds shall be held in an institution the deposits or accounts of which are insured or guaranteed by a federal or state agency (including Lender if Lender is such an institution). Lender shall apply the Funds to pay the escrow items. Lender may not charge for holding and applying the Funds, analyzing the account or verifying the escrow items, unless Lender pays Borrower interest on the Funds and applicable law permits Lender to make such a charge. Borrower and Lender may agree in writing that interest shall be paid on the Funds. Unless an agreement is made or applicable law requires interest to be paid, Lender shall not be required to pay Borrower any interest or earnings on the Funds. Lender shall give to Borrower, without charge, an annual accounting of the Funds showing credits and debits to the Funds and the purpose for which each debit to the Funds was made. The Funds are pledged as additional security for the sums secured by this Security Instrument.

If the amount of the Funds held by Lender, together with the future monthly payments of Funds payable prior to the due dates of the escrow items, shall exceed the amount required to pay the escrow items when due, the excess shall be, at Borrower's option, either promptly repaid to Borrower or credited to Borrower on monthly payments of Funds. If the amount of the Funds held by Lender is not sufficient to pay the escrow items when due, Borrower shall pay to Lender any amount necessary to make up the deficiency in one or more payments as required by Lender.

Upon payment in full of all sums secured by this Security Instrument, Lender shall promptly refund to Borrower any Funds held by Lender. If under paragraph 19 the Property is sold or acquired by Lender, Lender shall apply, no later than immediately prior to the sale of the Property or its acquisition by Lender, any Funds held by Lender at the time of application as a credit against the sums secured by this Security Instrument.

3. **Application of Payments.** Unless applicable law provides otherwise, all payments received by Lender under paragraphs 1 and 2 shall be applied: first, to late charges due under the Note; second, to prepayment charges due under the Note; third, to amounts payable under paragraph 2; fourth, to interest due; and last, to principal due.

4. **Charges; Liens.** Borrower shall pay all taxes, assessments, charges, fines and impositions attributable to the Property which may attain priority over this Security Instrument, and leasehold payments or ground rents, if any. Borrower shall pay these obligations in the manner provided in paragraph 2, or if not paid in that manner, Borrower shall pay them on time directly to the person owed payment. Borrower shall promptly furnish to Lender all notices of amounts to be paid under this paragraph. If Borrower makes these payments directly, Borrower shall promptly furnish to Lender receipts evidencing the payments.

Borrower shall promptly discharge any lien which has priority over this Security Instrument unless Borrower: (a) agrees in writing to the payment of the obligation secured by the lien in a manner acceptable to Lender; (b) contests in good faith the lien by, or defends against enforcement of the lien in, legal proceedings which in the Lender's opinion operate to prevent the enforcement of the lien or forfeiture of any part of the Property; or (c) secures from the holder of the lien an agreement satisfactory to Lender subordinating the lien to this Security Instrument. If Lender determines that any part of the Property is subject to a lien which may attain priority over this Security Instrument, Lender may give Borrower a notice identifying the lien. Borrower shall satisfy the lien or take one or more of the actions set forth above within 10 days of the giving of notice.

5. **Hazard Insurance.** Borrower shall keep the improvements now existing or hereafter erected on the Property insured against loss by fire, hazards included within the term "extended coverage" and any other hazards for which Lender requires insurance. This insurance shall be maintained in the amounts and for the periods that Lender requires. The insurance carrier providing the insurance shall be chosen by Borrower subject to Lender's approval which shall not be unreasonably withheld.

All insurance policies and renewals shall be acceptable to Lender and shall include a standard mortgagee clause. Lender shall have the right to hold the policies and renewals. If Lender requires, Borrower shall promptly give to Lender all receipts of paid premiums and renewal notices. In the event of loss, Borrower shall give prompt notice to the insurance carrier and Lender. Lender may make proof of loss if not made promptly by Borrower.

Unless Lender and Borrower otherwise agree in writing, insurance proceeds shall be applied to restoration or repair of the Property damaged, if the restoration or repair is economically feasible and Lender's security is not lessened. If the restoration or repair is not economically feasible or Lender's security would be lessened, the insurance proceeds shall be applied to the sums secured by this Security Instrument, whether or not then due, with any excess paid to Borrower. If Borrower abandons the Property, or does not answer within 30 days a notice from Lender that the insurance carrier has offered to settle a claim, then Lender may collect the insurance proceeds. Lender may use the proceeds to repair or restore the Property or to pay sums secured by this Security Instrument, whether or not then due. The 30-day period will begin when the notice is given.

Unless Lender and Borrower otherwise agree in writing, any application of proceeds to principal shall not extend or postpone the due date of the monthly payments referred to in paragraphs 1 and 2 or change the amount of the payments. If under paragraph 19 the Property is acquired by Lender, Borrower's right to any insurance policies and proceeds resulting from damage to the Property prior to the acquisition shall pass to Lender to the extent of the sums secured by this Security Instrument immediately prior to the acquisition.

6. **Preservation and Maintenance of Property; Leaseholds.** Borrower shall not destroy, damage or substantially change the Property, allow the Property to deteriorate or commit waste. If this Security Instrument is on a leasehold, Borrower shall comply with the provisions of the lease, and if Borrower acquires fee title to the Property, the leasehold and fee title shall not merge unless Lender agrees to the merger in writing.

7. **Protection of Lender's Rights in the Property; Mortgage Insurance.** If Borrower fails to perform the covenants and agreements contained in this Security Instrument, or there is a legal proceeding that may significantly affect Lender's rights in the Property (such as a proceeding in bankruptcy, probate, for condemnation or to enforce laws or regulations), then Lender may do and pay for whatever is necessary to protect the value of the Property and Lender's rights in the Property. Lender's actions may include paying any sums secured by a lien which has priority over this Security Instrument, appearing in court, paying reasonable attorneys' fees and entering on the Property to make repairs. Although Lender may take action under this paragraph 7, Lender does not have to do so.

Any amounts disbursed by Lender under this paragraph 7 shall become additional debt of Borrower secured by this Security Instrument. Unless Borrower and Lender agree to other terms of payment, these amounts shall bear interest from the date of disbursement at the Note rate and shall be payable, with interest, upon notice from Lender to Borrower requesting payment.

Form 1.18—*continued*

If Lender required mortgage insurance as a condition of making the loan secured by this Security Instrument, Borrower shall pay the premiums required to maintain the insurance in effect until such time as the requirement for the insurance terminates in accordance with Borrower's and Lender's written agreement or applicable law.

8. **Inspection.**   Lender or its agent may make reasonable entries upon and inspections of the Property. Lender shall give Borrower notice at the time of or prior to an inspection specifying reasonable cause for the inspection.

9. **Condemnation.**   The proceeds of any award or claim for damages, direct or consequential, in connection with any condemnation or other taking of any part of the Property, or for conveyance in lieu of condemnation, are hereby assigned and shall be paid to Lender.

In the event of a total taking of the Property, the proceeds shall be applied to the sums secured by this Security Instrument, whether or not then due, with any excess paid to Borrower. In the event of a partial taking of the Property, unless Borrower and Lender otherwise agree in writing, the sums secured by this Security Instrument shall be reduced by the amount of the proceeds multiplied by the following fraction: (a) the total amount of the sums secured immediately before the taking, divided by (b) the fair market value of the Property immediately before the taking. Any balance shall be paid to Borrower.

If the Property is abandoned by Borrower, or if, after notice by Lender to Borrower that the condemnor offers to make an award or settle a claim for damages, Borrower fails to respond to Lender within 30 days after the date the notice is given, Lender is authorized to collect and apply the proceeds, at its option, either to restoration or repair of the Property or to the sums secured by this Security Instrument, whether or not then due.

Unless Lender and Borrower otherwise agree in writing, any application of proceeds to principal shall not extend or postpone the due date of the monthly payments referred to in paragraphs 1 and 2 or change the amount of such payments.

10. **Borrower Not Released; Forbearance By Lender Not a Waiver.**   Extension of the time for payment or modification of amortization of the sums secured by this Security Instrument granted by Lender to any successor in interest of Borrower shall not operate to release the liability of the original Borrower or Borrower's successors in interest. Lender shall not be required to commence proceedings against any successor in interest or refuse to extend time for payment or otherwise modify amortization of the sums secured by this Security Instrument by reason of any demand made by the original Borrower or Borrower's successors in interest. Any forbearance by Lender in exercising any right or remedy shall not be a waiver of or preclude the exercise of any right or remedy.

11. **Successors and Assigns Bound; Joint and Several Liability; Co-signers.**   The covenants and agreements of this Security Instrument shall bind and benefit the successors and assigns of Lender and Borrower, subject to the provisions of paragraph 17. Borrower's covenants and agreements shall be joint and several. Any Borrower who co-signs this Security Instrument but does not execute the Note: (a) is co-signing this Security Instrument only to mortgage, grant and convey that Borrower's interest in the Property under the terms of this Security Instrument; (b) is not personally obligated to pay the sums secured by this Security Instrument; and (c) agrees that Lender and any other Borrower may agree to extend, modify, forbear or make any accommodations with regard to the terms of this Security Instrument or the Note without that Borrower's consent.

12. **Loan Charges.**   If the loan secured by this Security Instrument is subject to a law which sets maximum loan charges, and that law is finally interpreted so that the interest or other loan charges collected or to be collected in connection with the loan exceed the permitted limits, then: (a) any such loan charge shall be reduced by the amount necessary to reduce the charge to the permitted limit; and (b) any sums already collected from Borrower which exceeded permitted limits will be refunded to Borrower. Lender may choose to make this refund by reducing the principal owed under the Note or by making a direct payment to Borrower. If a refund reduces principal, the reduction will be treated as a partial prepayment without any prepayment charge under the Note.

13. **Legislation Affecting Lender's Rights.**   If enactment or expiration of applicable laws has the effect of rendering any provision of the Note or this Security Instrument unenforceable according to its terms, Lender, at its option, may require immediate payment in full of all sums secured by this Security Instrument and may invoke any remedies permitted by paragraph 19. If Lender exercises this option, Lender shall take the steps specified in the second paragraph of paragraph 17.

14. **Notices.**   Any notice to Borrower provided for in this Security Instrument shall be given by delivering it or by mailing it by first class mail unless applicable law requires use of another method. The notice shall be directed to the Property Address or any other address Borrower designates by notice to Lender. Any notice to Lender shall be given by first class mail to Lender's address stated herein or any other address Lender designates by notice to Borrower. Any notice provided for in this Security Instrument shall be deemed to have been given to Borrower or Lender when given as provided in this paragraph.

15. **Governing Law; Severability.**   This Security Instrument shall be governed by federal law and the law of the jurisdiction in which the Property is located. In the event that any provision or clause of this Security Instrument or the Note conflicts with applicable law, such conflict shall not affect other provisions of this Security Instrument or the Note which can be given effect without the conflicting provision. To this end the provisions of this Security Instrument and the Note are declared to be severable.

16. **Borrower's Copy.**   Borrower shall be given one conformed copy of the Note and of this Security Instrument.

17. **Transfer of the Property or a Beneficial Interest in Borrower.**   If all or any part of the Property or any interest in it is sold or transferred (or if a beneficial interest in Borrower is sold or transferred and Borrower is not a natural person) without Lender's prior written consent, Lender may, at its option, require immediate payment in full of all sums secured by this Security Instrument. However, this option shall not be exercised by Lender if exercise is prohibited by federal law as of the date of this Security Instrument.

If Lender exercises this option, Lender shall give Borrower notice of acceleration. The notice shall provide a period of not less than 30 days from the date the notice is delivered or mailed within which Borrower must pay all sums secured by this Security Instrument. If Borrower fails to pay these sums prior to the expiration of this period, Lender may invoke any remedies permitted by this Security Instrument without further notice or demand on Borrower.

18. **Borrower's Right to Reinstate.**   If Borrower meets certain conditions, Borrower shall have the right to have enforcement of this Security Instrument discontinued at any time prior to the earlier of: (a) 5 days (or such other period as applicable law may specify for reinstatement) before sale of the Property pursuant to any power of sale contained in this Security Instrument; or (b) entry of a judgment enforcing this Security Instrument. Those conditions are that Borrower: (a) pays Lender all sums which then would be due under this Security Instrument and the Note had no acceleration occurred; (b) cures any default of any other covenants or agreements; (c) pays all expenses incurred in enforcing this Security Instrument, including, but not limited to, reasonable attorneys' fees; and (d) takes such action as Lender may reasonably require to assure that the lien of this Security Instrument, Lender's rights in the Property and Borrower's obligation to pay the sums secured by this Security Instrument shall continue unchanged. Upon reinstatement by Borrower, this Security Instrument and the obligations secured hereby shall remain fully effective as if no acceleration had occurred. However, this right to reinstate shall not apply in the case of acceleration under paragraphs 13 or 17

MM CL-400A-C Rev. 5/87 jtr

Form 1.18—*continued*

NON-UNIFORM COVENANTS. Borrower and Lender further covenant and agree as follows:

19. Acceleration; Remedies. Lender shall give notice to Borrower prior to acceleration following Borrower's breach of any covenant or agreement in this Security Instrument (but not prior to acceleration under paragraphs 13 and 17 unless applicable law provides otherwise). Lender shall notify Borrower of, among other things: (a) the default; (b) the action required to cure the default; (c) when the default must be cured; and (d) that failure to cure the default as specified may result in acceleration of the sums secured by this Security Instrument, foreclosure by judicial proceeding and sale of the Property. Lender shall further inform Borrower of the right to reinstate after acceleration and the right to assert in the foreclosure proceeding the non-existence of a default or any other defense of Borrower to acceleration and foreclosure. If the default is not cured as specified, Lender at its option may require immediate payment in full of all sums secured by this Security Instrument without further demand and may foreclose this Security Instrument by judicial proceeding. Lender shall be entitled to collect all expenses incurred in pursuing the remedies provided in this paragraph 19, including, but not limited to, attorneys' fees and costs of title evidence to the extent permitted by applicable law.

20. Lender in Possession. Upon acceleration under paragraph 19 or abandonment of the Property, Lender (in person, by agent or by judicially appointed receiver) shall be entitled to enter upon, take possession of and manage the Property and to collect the rents of the Property including those past due. Any rents collected by Lender or the receiver shall be applied first to payment of the costs of management of the Property and collection of rents, including, but not limited to, receiver's fees, premiums on receiver's bonds and reasonable attorneys' fees, and then to the sums secured by this Security Instrument.

21. Release. Upon payment of all sums secured by this Security Instrument, Lender shall discharge this Security Instrument without charge to Borrower. Borrower shall pay any recordation costs.

22. Reinstatement Period. Borrower's time to reinstate provided in paragraph 18 shall extend to one hour prior to the commencement of bidding at a sheriff's sale or other sale pursuant to this Security Instrument.

23. Purchase Money Mortgage. If any of the debt secured by this Security Instrument is lent to Borrower to acquire title to the Property, this Security Instrument shall be a purchase money mortgage.

24. Interest Rate After Judgment. Borrower agrees that the interest rate payable after a judgment is entered on the Note or in an action of mortgage foreclosure shall be the rate payable from time to time under the Note.

25. Riders to this Security Instrument. If one or more riders are executed by Borrower and recorded together with this Security Instrument, the covenants and agreements of each such rider shall be incorporated into and shall amend and supplement the covenants and agreements of this Security Instrument as if the rider(s) were a part of this Security Instrument. [Check applicable box(es)]

☐ Adjustable Rate Rider   ☐ Condominium Rider   ☐ 2–4 Family Rider

☐ Graduated Payment Rider   ☐ Planned Unit Development Rider

☐ Other(s) [specify]

BY SIGNING BELOW, Borrower accepts and agrees to the terms and covenants contained in this Security Instrument and in any rider(s) executed by Borrower and recorded with it.

_____ (Seal)
                                —Borrower

_____   _____ (Seal)
                   WITNESS   —Borrower

_____   _____ (Seal)
                   WITNESS   —Borrower

                                         _____ (Seal)
                                                         —Borrower

_____ [Space Below This Line For Acknowledgment] _____

)
) ss:
COUNTY OF   )

On this   day of   , A.D. 19   , before me,
the Subscriber, a Notary Public

                          came the above-named

                                                                              and
                                              act and deed, and desired the
acknowledged the within indenture of Mortgage to be
same to be recorded as such.

WITNESS my hand and seal, the day and year aforesaid.

                                         _____
                                                    NOTARY PUBLIC

ASSIGNMENT #11 — PART 2
MORTGAGE NOTE

USE THE FACT PATTERN ABOVE AND THESE ADDITIONAL FACTS TO COMPLETE THE ADJUSTABLE RATE NOTE AT *FORM 1.19.*

FACT PATTERN

Interest rate: 8.875%

Change date of interest rate: Annual

Basis Percentage Points Added to Current Index: 2.75%

Grace Period: 15 days

Highest First Change Date Interest: 2%

Lowest First Change Date Interest: 2%

Highest Possible Interest Rate: 13.875%

Late Charge: 5% of principal and interest

Payments Commence: April 1, 1989

Payments End: March 1, 2016

Initial Monthly Payments: $556.95

ADJUSTABLE RATE NOTE
(1 Year Treasury Index—Rate Caps)

THIS NOTE CONTAINS PROVISIONS ALLOWING FOR CHANGES IN MY INTEREST RATE AND MY MONTHLY PAYMENT. THIS NOTE LIMITS THE AMOUNT MY INTEREST RATE CAN CHANGE AT ANY ONE TIME AND THE MAXIMUM RATE I MUST PAY.

.............................., 19..86   ...., ...
                                                 [City]   [State]

....
                                               [Property Address]

1. BORROWER'S PROMISE TO PAY

In return for a loan that I have received, I promise to pay U.S. $ .... (this amount is called "principal"), plus interest. to the order of the Lender. The Lender is ....
....
I understand that the Lender may transfer this Note. The Lender or anyone who takes this Note by transfer and who is entitled to receive payments under this Note is called the "Note Holder."

2. INTEREST

Interest will be charged on unpaid principal until the full amount of principal has been paid. I will pay interest at a yearly rate of ....%. The interest rate I will pay will change in accordance with Section 4 of this Note.

The interest rate required by this Section 2 and Section 4 of this Note is the rate I will pay both before and after any default described in Section 7(B) of this Note.

3. PAYMENTS

(A) Time and Place of Payments

I will pay principal and interest by making payments every month.

I will make my monthly payments on the first day of each month beginning on .... , 19 .... I will make these payments every month until I have paid all of the principal and interest and any other charges described below that I may owe under this Note. My monthly payments will be applied to interest before principal. If, on ...., 20 ...., I still owe amounts under this Note, I will pay those amounts in full on that date, which is called the "maturity date."

I will make my monthly payments at ....
.... or at a different place if required by the Note Holder.

(B) Amount of My Initial Monthly Payments

Each of my initial monthly payments will be in the amount of U.S. $................ .... This amount may change.

(C) Monthly Payment Changes

Changes in my monthly payment will reflect changes in the unpaid principal of my loan and in the interest rate that I must pay. The Note Holder will determine my new interest rate and the changed amount of my monthly payment in accordance with Section 4 of this Note.

4. INTEREST RATE AND MONTHLY PAYMENT CHANGES

(A) Change Dates

The interest rate I will pay may change on the first day of ...., 19 .. .., and on that day every 12th month thereafter. Each date on which my interest rate could change is called a "Change Date."

(B) The Index

Beginning with the first Change Date, my interest rate will be based on an Index. The "Index" is the weekly average yield on United States Treasury securities adjusted to a constant maturity of 1 year, as made available by the Federal Reserve Board. The most recent Index figure available as of the date 45 days before each Change Date is called the "Current Index."

MULTISTATE ADJUSTABLE RATE NOTE—ARM 5-2—Single Family—Fannie Mae/Freddie Mac Uniform Instrument   Form 3502 3/85

515-500-00-0785 (1 of 4)   274780
S

If the Index is no longer available, the Note Holder will choose a new index which is based upon comparable information. The Note Holder will give me notice of this choice.

(C) Calculation of Changes

Before each Change Date, the Note Holder will calculate my new interest rate by adding........... .... percentage points (..............%) to the Current Index. The Note Holder will then round the result of this addition to the nearest one-eighth of one percentage point (0.125%). Subject to the limits stated in Section 4(D) below, this rounded amount will be my new interest rate until the next Change Date.

The Note Holder will then determine the amount of the monthly payment that would be sufficient to repay the unpaid principal that I am expected to owe at the Change Date in full on the maturity date at my new interest rate in substantially equal payments. The result of this calculation will be the new amount of my monthly payment.

(D) Limits on Interest Rate Changes

The interest rate I am required to pay at the first Change Date will not be greater than ....% or less than ....%. Thereafter, my interest rate will never be increased or decreased on any single Change Date by more than two percentage points (2.0%) from the rate of interest I have been paying for the preceding twelve months. My interest rate will never be greater than ....%.

(E) Effective Date of Changes

My new interest rate will become effective on each Change Date. I will pay the amount of my new monthly payment beginning on the first monthly payment date after the Change Date until the amount of my monthly payment changes again.

(F) Notice of Changes

The Note Holder will deliver or mail to me a notice of any changes in my interest rate and the amount of my monthly payment before the effective date of any change. The notice will include information required by law to be given me and also the title and telephone number of a person who will answer any question I may have regarding the notice.

5. BORROWER'S RIGHT TO PREPAY

I have the right to make payments of principal at any time before they are due. A payment of principal only is known as a "prepayment." When I make a prepayment, I will tell the Note Holder in writing that I am doing so.

I may make a full prepayment or partial prepayments without paying any prepayment charge. The Note Holder will use all of my prepayments to reduce the amount of principal that I owe under this Note. If I make a partial prepayment, there will be no changes in the due dates of my monthly payments unless the Note Holder agrees in writing to those changes. My partial prepayment may reduce the amount of my monthly payments after the first Change Date following my partial prepayment. However, any reduction due to my partial prepayment may be offset by an interest rate increase.

6. LOAN CHARGES

If a law, which applies to this loan and which sets maximum loan charges, is finally interpreted so that the interest or other loan charges collected or to be collected in connection with this loan exceed the permitted limits, then: (i) any such loan charge shall be reduced by the amount necessary to reduce the charge to the permitted limit; and (ii) any sums already collected from me which exceeded permitted limits will be refunded to me. The Note Holder may choose to make this refund by reducing the principal I owe under this Note or by making a direct payment to me. If a refund reduces principal, the reduction will be treated as a partial prepayment.

7. BORROWER'S FAILURE TO PAY AS REQUIRED

(A) Late Charges for Overdue Payments

If the Note Holder has not received the full amount of any monthly payment by the end of .... calendar days after the date it is due, I will pay a late charge to the Note Holder. The amount of the charge will be .... · of my overdue payment of principal and interest. I will pay this late charge promptly but only once on each late payment.

(B) Default

If I do not pay the full amount of each monthly payment on the date it is due, I will be in default.

Form 1.19—*continued*

(C) Notice of Default

If I am in default, the Note Holder may send me a written notice telling me that if I do not pay the overdue amount by a certain date, the Note Holder may require me to pay immediately the full amount of principal which has not been paid and all the interest that I owe on that amount. That date must be at least 30 days after the date on which the notice is delivered or mailed to me.

(D) No Waiver By Note Holder

Even if, at a time when I am in default, the Note Holder does not require me to pay immediately in full as described above, the Note Holder will still have the right to do so if I am in default at a later time.

(E) Payment of Note Holder's Costs and Expenses

If the Note Holder has required me to pay immediately in full as described above, the Note Holder will have the right to be paid back by me for all of its costs and expenses in enforcing this Note to the extent not prohibited by applicable law. Those expenses include, for example, reasonable attorneys' fees.

8. GIVING OF NOTICES

Unless applicable law requires a different method, any notice that must be given to me under this Note will be given by delivering it or by mailing it by first class mail to me at the Property Address above or at a different address if I give the Note Holder a notice of my different address.

Any notice that must be given to the Note Holder under this Note will be given by mailing it by first class mail to the Note Holder at the address stated in Section 3(A) above or at a different address if I am given a notice of that different address.

9. OBLIGATIONS OF PERSONS UNDER THIS NOTE

If more than one person signs this Note, each person is fully and personally obligated to keep all of the promises made in this Note, including the promise to pay the full amount owed. Any person who is a guarantor, surety or endorser of this Note is also obligated to do these things. Any person who takes over these obligations, including the obligations of a guarantor, surety or endorser of this Note, is also obligated to keep all of the promises made in this Note. The Note Holder may enforce its rights under this Note against each person individually or against all of us together. This means that any one of us may be required to pay all of the amounts owed under this Note.

10. WAIVERS

I and any other person who has obligations under this Note waive the rights of presentment and notice of dishonor. "Presentment" means the right to require the Note Holder to demand payment of amounts due. "Notice of dishonor" means the right to require the Note Holder to give notice to other persons that amounts due have not been paid.

11. UNIFORM SECURED NOTE

This Note is a uniform instrument with limited variations in some jurisdictions. In addition to the protections given to the Note Holder under this Note, a Mortgage, Deed of Trust or Security Deed (the "Security Instrument"), dated the same date as this Note, protects the Note Holder from possible losses which might result if I do not keep the promises which I make in this Note. That Security Instrument describes how and under what conditions I may be required to make immediate payment in full of all amounts I owe under this Note. Some of those conditions are described as follows:

Transfer of the Property or a Beneficial Interest in Borrower. If all or any part of the Property or any interest in it is sold or transferred (or if a beneficial interest in Borrower is sold or transferred and Borrower is not a natural person) without Lender's prior written consent, Lender may, at its option, require immediate payment in full of all sums secured by this Security Instrument. However, this option shall not be exercised by Lender if exercise is prohibited by federal law as of the date of this Security Instrument. Lender also shall not exercise this option if: (a) Borrower causes to be submitted to Lender information required by Lender to evaluate the intended transferee as if a new loan were being made to the transferee; and (b) Lender reasonably determines that Lender's security will not be impaired by the loan assumption and that the risk of a breach of any covenant or agreement in this Security Instrument is acceptable to Lender.

To the extent permitted by applicable law, Lender may charge a reasonable fee as a condition to Lender's consent to the loan assumption. Lender may also require the transferee to sign an assumption agreement that is acceptable to Lender and that obligates the transferee to keep all the promises and agreements made in the Note and in this Security Instrument. Borrower will continue to be obligated under the Note and this Security Instrument unless Lender releases Borrower in writing.

Form 1.19—*continued*

If Lender exercises the option to require immediate payment in full, Lender shall give Borrower notice of acceleration. The notice shall provide a period of not less than 30 days from the date the notice is delivered or mailed within which Borrower must pay all sums secured by this Security Instrument. If Borrower fails to pay these sums prior to the expiration of this period, Lender may invoke any remedies permitted by this Security Instrument without further notice or demand on Borrower.

WITNESS THE HAND(S) AND SEAL(S) OF THE UNDERSIGNED.

.... (Seal)
-Borrower

.... (Seal)
-Borrower

.... (Seal)
-Borrower

[Sign Original Only]

Form 1.19—*concluded*

12. Deeds

A deed is evidence of ownership. It can be recorded or unrecorded; however, recording gives a certain priority over other interests under a race or notice formula. In order for a transfer to be effective, a deed must be tendered or delivered.

A. Objectives

(1) To understand the clauses and provisions necessary in the construction of an effective deed; and

(2) To have some familiarity with the language and requirement of a limited warranty and quit-claim deed.

B. Student Obligations

(1) To draft and compose a general warranty deed; and

(2) To be aware of the procedures and processes for recording the deed upon closing.

C. Instructor's Obligations

(1) To monitor and advise students regarding the proper authorship of a deed;

(2) To provide names, addresses and phone numbers and accompanying forms necessary for the filing and recordation of a completed deed; and

(3) To give advice regarding local rules, custom and practice.

D. Time Allotted: 0.5 hours

E. Value of Assignment: 10.0 points

ASSIGNMENT #12 — PART 1
STANDARDIZED DEED

The standardized deed that is employed at *Form 1.20* contains all the requisites necessary for an effective legal transfer.

FACT PATTERN

Date of Deed: May 21, 1988

Parties to the Deed: Don and Janet Loeffler, grantors; Bart and Tona Brizee, grantees

Consideration: $200,000

Legal Description of Property: All that certain lot of land situated in the Township of Hope, County of Appaloosa, Minnesota, being lot No. 29 in the Hope Township Re-Subdivision Plan, recorded in the Recorder's Office of Appaloosa County, Minnesota, in the Plan Book Volume 32, page 78, bounded and described as follows:

Beginning at a point on the Easterly side of 1400 Washington Blvd. in said Plan at the dividing line between Lots No. 29 and 30 in said Plan; thence along Easterly side of Washington Boulevard North 12 14' West, 127.89 feet to a point of tangent; thence along the said side of said Washington Boulevard curving to the right by a curve having a radius of 57.84 feet, a distance of 147.84 feet to a point on the Southwesterly side of Jefferson Street in said Plan; thence along the Southwesterly side of Kings Highway, South 45 47' East, a distance of 170.00 feet to a point; thence along the Westerly boundary line of the Park designated in said Plan, South between Lots No. 29 and 30 in said Plan; then along said dividing line South 77 46′ West, a distance of 200.00 feet to the Easterly side of Rosslyn Road at the Place of Beginning.

Having erected thereon a two-story brick building.

Notary Public: Fred Williams

Location: County of Washington; State of Florida

COMPLETE THE DEED AT FORM 1.20 (4 PAGES). *Be certain on the cover page of the deed to put Grantor to Grantee names and addresses. Please note: student or instructor will need to make two additional copies of Form 1.20 in order to complete Part 2 of this assignment.

Form 1.20

DEED. No. 760.   Printed for and Sold by John C. Clark Co., 1326 Walnut St., Phila.

This Deed, MADE this   day of
in the year nineteen hundred and

Between

(hereinafter called the Grantor),

and

(hereinafter called the Grantee),

Witnesseth, *That in consideration of*

Dollars,
in hand paid, the receipt whereof is hereby acknowledged, the said Grantor   do hereby grant and convey to the said Grantee   heirs and assigns,

And *the said Grantor   do   hereby covenant and agree to and with the said Grantee   that the Grantor   heirs, executors and administrators, SHALL and WILL*
WARRANT and forever DEFEND the herein above

described premises, with the hereditaments and appurtenances, unto the said Grantee
heirs and assigns, against the said Grantor   and against every other person lawfully
claiming or who shall hereafter claim the same or any part thereof.

In Witness Whereof, *said Grantor   ha   hereunto set   hand and seal*
the day and year first above written.

Sealed and Delivered
IN THE PRESENCE OF

.... (SEAL)

.... (SEAL)

.... (SEAL)

.... (SEAL)

State of

County of } *ss.*

On the   *day of*   *, 19   , before me*

the undersigned officer, personally appeared

known to me (or satisfactorily proven) to be the person   whose name   subscribed to the
within instrument, and acknowledged that   he   executed the same for the
purposes therein contained, and desired the same might be recorded as such.

In Witness Whereof, I hereunto set my hand and official seal.

The address of the within-named Grantee   ....

is ....

....   *Title of Officer*
On behalf of the Grantee

Form 1.20—*continued*

.... Recorder

Given under my hand and the seal of the said office, the date above written.

Recorded on this .... day of .... A. D. 19 ...., in the Recorder's Office of the said County, in Deed Book .... Vol. .... Page ....

STATE OF ....

County of .... } ss.

Deed.

1985 John C. Clark Company, Phila. 760

ASSIGNMENT #12 — PART 2
DEED MODIFICATION

MODIFY AND ADJUST THE DEED JUST COMPLETED BY USING LIMITED WARRANTY AND QUIT-CLAIM LANGUAGE. CITE SPECIFICALLY WHERE THE LANGUAGE OF *FIGURES 1.4 AND 1.5* SHOULD BE PLACED.

Certificate of Title No:

LIMITED WARRANTY DEED

<NAMES/GRANTOR> , husband and wife, of <NAME/COUNTY> County, <NAME/STATE>, for valuable consideration paid, grants, with limited warranty covenants, to <NAME/GRANTEE> , whose tax-mailing address is <STATE-COMPLETE-ADDRESS-INCLUDING-COUNTY> County, the following real property:
<FULL-LEGAL-DESCRIPTION-OF-PROPERTY-AND-ANY-ENCUMBRANCES-RESERVATIONS-OR-EXCEPTIONS>.
Prior Instrument Reference: Volume <NUMBER>, Page <NUMBER>.

Figure 1.4

Certificate of Title No:

QUIT-CLAIM DEED

<NAMES/GRANTOR>, husband and wife, of <NAME/COUNTY> County, <NAME/STATE>, for valuable consideration paid, grants to <NAME/GRANTEE>, whose tax-mailing address is <STATE-COMPLETE-ADDRESS-INCLUDING-COUNTY> County, the following real property:
<FULL-LEGAL-DESCRIPTION-OF-PROPERTY-AND-ANY-ENCUMBRANCES-RESERVATIONS-OR-EXCEPTIONS>.
Prior Instrument Reference: Volume <NUMBER>, Page <NUMBER>.

Figure 1.5

13. Closing and Settlement Process

No other part of real estate practice will absorb as much time and energy as the closing and settlemen process, which is the culmination of the above steps. A checklist outlining the necessary information for closing and settlement is the initial phase of these exercises. The culmination of all of these endeavors is the calculated settlement sheet. Note that more than the average time is being allotted to this activity since student will need time to work through this complex process.

A. Objectives

  (1) To become aware of the varied information that must be collected to effect a closing an settlement;

  (2) To learn how to make a checklist or master information form which will assist in the collec tion of closing and settlement information; and

  (3) To become aware of the mathematical formulas and calculation techniques necessary for the accurate and complete compilation of a settlement sheet.

B. Student Obligations

  (1) To prepare a master checklist for a closing and settlement process; and

  (2) To prepare and compute a settlement sheet using a specific fact pattern.

C. Instructor Obligations

  (1) To provide local forms to students in order that closing and settlement assignments can be completed;

  (2) To point out jurisdictional differences in closing and settlement processes; and

  (3) To assist students in the mathematical reconciliation of the settlement sheets.

D. Time Allotted: 3.0 hours

E. Value of Assignment: 30.0 points

ASSIGNMENT #13 — PART 1
MASTER CHECKLIST FOR CLOSING AND SETTLEMENT

Complete the checklist at *Form 1.21* as you prepare for any actual or hypothetical closing. Assume that you are performing a closing within your local jurisdiction. Look to the instructor for specific advice regarding the unique issues of local practice and custom.

All of these questions are important considerations in the closing and settlement process. What is imperative is that the real estate specialist have access to a wide array of information. At times, the process can be mind-boggling.

CLOSING CHECKLIST

1. What is the current real estate commission rate in your jurisdiction?

_____ %

2. Are the current agreement of sale and all attached extensions, addenda and endorsements legally enforceable and timely?

☐ Yes ☐ No

3. State specifically (name, address and phone) to whom you make tax payments in your jurisdiction.

Real Estate Tax Payments: _____

_____

_____

4. State specifically (name, address and phone) to whom you pay sewer assessments.

_____

_____

_____

5. State specifically (name, address and phone) to whom you pay water rent, water bills and other assessments relating to water.

_____

_____

_____

6. What are the recording fees on a page-by-page basis in your jurisdiction?

_____

7. How much of a transfer tax is required to be paid on a real estate transaction?

_____ %

8. Is the transfer tax divisible between the buyer and the seller? ☐ Yes ☐ No   If yes, by what formula? _____

9. What are the names, addresses and phone numbers of your local gas, electric and telephone companies?

Gas _____

Electric _____

Telephone _____

10. What are the names, addresses and phone numbers of three infestation carriers that might be required to perform an inspection on the property?

_____

_____

_____

11. What is the name, address and phone number of a notary who will assist you in the preparation and completion c closing documentation?

_____

_____

_____

12. What is the name, address and phone number of the bank official or officer who serves as a liaison between the closing and settlement parties for financing parties?

_____

_____

13. What are the names, addresses and phone numbers of the agents involved for seller and buyer, if applicable?

Seller's Agent_____

_____

_____

Buyer's Agent_____

_____

_____

14. What are the names, addresses and phone numbers of two or three hazard insurance agencies most likely to issue a policy in your jurisdiction?

1._____

_____

2._____

_____

3._____

_____

15. What are the names, addresses and phone numbers of the most prominent and commonly employed title insurance companies in your region?

1._____

_____

2._____

_____

3._____

_____

6. Do title agents perform the functions of closing in your region? ☐ Yes ☐ No

7. Have all the terms and conditions of the agreement of sale been met?

   Financing conditions? ☐ Yes ☐ No
   Zoning conditions? ☐ Yes ☐ No
   Appraisal? ☐ Yes ☐ No
   Engineering Report? ☐ Yes ☐ No
   Percolation Test? ☐ Yes ☐ No
   Repairs? ☐ Yes ☐ No

18. Have all mortgages been satisfied? ☐ Yes ☐ No

19. Will the mortgage subject to this property be assumed? ☐ Yes ☐ No

20. Have all assumption documents been prepared? ☐ Yes ☐ No

21. What are the names, addresses and phone numbers of the attorneys for buyers and sellers?

   Buyer's Attorney_____

   _____

   _____

   Seller's Attorney_____

   _____

   _____

22. What documents need to be prepared?

   _____ Indenture or deed

   _____ Deed of trust

   _____ Note

   _____ Bill of sale

   _____ Leases

   _____ Truth in Lending Disclosures

   _____ Release of trust

   _____ Right of rescission

——————— Settlement abstract

——————— Title Abstraction

——————— Escrow documentation

——————— Insurance assignments

——————— Commission agreements

——————— Title insurance documentation

——————— Mortgage assumption statements

——————— Loan payoff statements

——————— Attorney's opinion of title

——————— Judgment certificate

——————— Personal property tax statements

——————— Releases

——————— Lien documentation

——————— Affidavits

23. Does your jurisdiction require that a survey be performed? ☐ Yes ☐ No

24. What are the names, addresses and phone numbers of three reliable surveyors in your area?

1. _____

_____

2. _____

_____

3. _____

_____

OTHER CONSIDERATIONS

CHECKLIST OF QUESTIONS IN THE CLOSING AND SETTLEMENT PROCESS

1. Are all documents properly notarized? ☐ Yes ☐ No

2. Are all lender's financing documents properly completed and filled out? ☐ Yes ☐ No

3. Are all monies deposited in escrow accounts properly accounted for and ready to be distributed? ☐ Yes ☐ No

4. Have all bills been accounted for as to be noted on the settlement sheet?   ☐ Yes   ☐ No

5. Do you have the seller's new address?   ☐ Yes   ☐ No

6. What provisions have you taken for the surrender of keys?

7. Are all checks properly signed and endorsed?   ☐ Yes   ☐ No

8. Have buyer and seller adjusted their obligations and liabilities regarding gas, electric, water and telephone services?   ☐ Yes   ☐ No

9. Are all insurance documents available?   ☐ Yes   ☐ No

10. Have insurance policies been acquired or cancelled as needed?   ☐ Yes   ☐ No

11. Have all settlement sheets been signed and executed?   ☐ Yes   ☐ No

12. Have buyer and seller exchanged phone numbers?   ☐ Yes   ☐ No

Form 1.21

ASSIGNMENT #13 — PART 2
SETTLEMENT PREPARATION AND COMPUTATION OF THE SETTLEMENT STATEMENT

The final culmination of a real estate transaction is in the preparation and calculation of the settlement statement. Two specific problems are outlined in this section of practical exercises.

FACT PATTERN 1

Type of loan: Conventional
Name and address of borrower: John and Fredericka Rumbaugh, 18 Genner St., Hickory Station, MD 22214
Name and address of seller: Estate of Anna M. Rupnik, 402 E. Dickson St., Washington, D.C. 20756
Name and address of lender: First National Bank of New York, 1819 South Wayside St., Washington, D.C. 20786
Property Location: 402 E. Dickson St., Washington, D.C. 20756
Settlement Agent: American Title Insurance Co., 1418 E. 29th St., N.W., Washington, D.C. 20666
Contract Sales Price: $89,900
Earnest Money Deposit or Hand Money: $1,000
Commission: 5% = $4,495
Realtor: Hatteras Realty
Loan Origination Fee: 1% = $750
Loan Discount: 2% = $1,500
Credit Report: $75
Lender's Inspection Fee: $100
Tax Service Fee: $35
Document Preparation Fee: $10
Date of Settlement: January 19, 1989
Interest from 1-19-89 to 2-1-89:   20.83/day = 270.79

Mortgage insurance premium: 12 months = $375

Reserve taxes: 8 months at $125/month = $1,000

Reserve mortgage insurance: 2 months at $27.50/month = $55

Title insurance binder: $10

Notary fees: $10

Attorney's fees: $600

Title insurance: $305

Recording fees: $48

Releases: $3 (seller)

State tax stamps: $414

State transfer tax: $324.50 (paid from borrower's funds only)

Survey: $195

Federal express charges: $50

CALCULATE THE STANDARD RESPA SETTLEMENT STATEMENT AT *FORM 1.22 (2 PAGES)* WITH NET AMOUNTS OF CASH TO AND FROM BORROWERS AND SELLERS NOTED.

HUD-1 (03-86) OMB NO. 2502-0265

A. **U.S. DEPARTMENT OF HOUSING & URBAN DEVELOPMENT** ## SETTLEMENT STATEMENT	B. TYPE OF LOAN: 1. ☐ FHA 2. ☐ FmHA 3. ☐ CONV. UNINS. 4. ☐ VA 5. ☐ CONV. INS. 6. FILE NUMBER: 7. LOAN NUMBER: 8. MORTGAGE INSURANCE CASE NUMBER:

C. NOTE: This form is furnished to give you a statement of actual settlement costs. Amounts paid to and by the settlement agent are shown. Items marked "(p.o.c.)" were paid outside the closing; they are shown here for informational purposes and are not included in the totals.

D. NAME OF BORROWER:	E. NAME OF SELLER:	F. NAME OF LENDER:

G. PROPERTY LOCATION:	H. SETTLEMENT AGENT PLACE OF SETTLEMENT	I. SETTLEMENT DATE:

J. SUMMARY OF BORROWER'S TRANSACTION		K. SUMMARY OF SELLER'S TRANSACTION	
100. GROSS AMOUNT DUE FROM BORROWER:		**400. GROSS AMOUNT DUE TO SELLER:**	
101. Contract sales price		401. Contract sales price	
102. Personal property		402. Personal property	
103. Settlement charges to borrower (line 1400)		403.	
104.		404.	
105.		405.	
Adjustments for items paid by seller in advance		*Adjustments for items paid by seller in advance*	
106. City/town taxes to		406. City/town taxes to	
107. County taxes to		407. County taxes to	
108. Assessments to		408. Assessments to	
109.		409.	
110.		410.	
111.		411.	
112.		412.	
120. **GROSS AMOUNT DUE FROM BORROWER**		420. **GROSS AMOUNT DUE TO SELLER**	
200. AMOUNTS PAID BY OR IN BEHALF OF BORROWER:		**500. REDUCTIONS IN AMOUNT DUE TO SELLER:**	
201. Deposit or earnest money		501. Excess deposit (see instructions)	
202. Principal amount of new loan(s)		502. Settlement charges to seller (line 1400)	
203. Existing loan(s) taken subject to		503. Existing loan(s) taken subject to	
204.		504. Payoff of first mortgage loan	
205.		505. Payoff of second mortgage loan	
206.		506.	
207.		507.	
208.		508.	
209.		509.	
Adjustments for items unpaid by seller		*Adjustments for items unpaid by seller*	
210. City/town taxes to		510. City/town taxes to	
211. County taxes to		511. County taxes to	
212. Assessments to		512. Assessments to	
213.		513.	
214.		514.	
215.		515.	
216.		516.	
217.		517.	
218.		518.	
219.		519.	
220. **TOTAL PAID BY/FOR BORROWER**		520. **TOTAL REDUCTION AMOUNT DUE SELLER**	
300. CASH AT SETTLEMENT FROM/TO BORROWER		**600. CASH AT SETTLEMENT TO/FROM SELLER**	
301. Gross amount due from borrower (line 120)		601. Gross amount due to seller (line 420)	
302. Less amounts paid by/for borrower (line 220)		602. Less reductions in amount due seller (line 520)	
303. CASH (☐ FROM) (☐ TO) BORROWER		603. CASH (☐ TO) (☐ FROM) SELLER	

The undersigned hereby acknowledge receipt of a completed copy of pages 1 and 2 of this statement and any attachments referred to herein.

Borrower _____   Seller _____

Borrower _____   Seller _____

Form 1.22

L. SETTLEMENT CHARGES

	PAID FROM BORROWER'S FUNDS AT SETTLEMENT	PAID FROM SELLER'S FUNDS AT SETTLEMENT
700. TOTAL COMMISSION based on price		
Division of Commission (line 700) as follows:		
701. $ to		
702. $ to		
703. Commission paid at Settlement		
704.		
800. ITEMS PAYABLE IN CONNECTION WITH LOAN.		
801. Loan Origination fee %		
802. Loan Discount %		
803. Appraisal Fee to		
804. Credit Report to		
805. Lender's Inspection Fee		
806. Mortgage Insurance Application Fee to		
807. Assumption Fee		
808.		
809.		
810.		
811.		
900. ITEMS REQUIRED BY LENDER TO BE PAID IN ADVANCE		
901. Interest from to @ $ /day		
902. Mortgage Insurance Premium for months to		
903. Hazard Insurance Premium for years to		
904. years to		
905.		
1000. RESERVES DEPOSITED WITH LENDER		
1001. Hazard Insurance months @ $ per month		
1002. Mortgage Insurance months @ $ per month		
1003. City Property Taxes months @ $ per month		
1004. County Property Taxes months @ $ per month		
1005. Annual Assessments months @ $ per month		
1006. months @ $ per month		
1007. months @ $ per month		
1008. months @ $ per month		
1100. TITLE CHARGES		
1101. Settlement or closing fee to		
1102. Abst.act or title search to		
1103. Title examination to		
1104. Title insurance binder to		
1105. Document preparation to		
1106. Notary fees to		
1107. Attorney's fees to		
(includes above items numbers:)		
1108. Title insurance to		
(includes above items numbers:)		
1109. Lender's coverage $		
1110. Owner's coverage $		
1111.		
1112.		
1113.		
1200. GOVERNMENT RECORDING AND TRANSFER CHARGES		
1201. Recording fees: Deed $; Mortgage $; Releases $		
1202. City/county tax/stamps: Deed $; Mortgage $		
1203. State tax/stamps: Deed $; Mortgage $		
1204.		
1205.		
1300. ADDITIONAL SETTLEMENT CHARGES		
1301. Survey to		
1302. Pest inspection to		
1303.		
1304.		
1305.		
1400. TOTAL SETTLEMENT CHARGES (enter on lines 103, Section J and 502, Section K)		

By signing Page 1 of this statement, the signatories of Page 1 also acknowledge receipt of a completed copy of Page 2 of this two page statement.

Form 1.22—Concluded

FACT PATTERN 2

Settlement agent: Marie F. Johnson, Attorney at Law, 1814 King St., Salisbury, KY 44431

Type of Loan: Conventional

Name of Borrower: Michael Kretzler, 945 Palm St., Dorman, LA 56432

Property Location: 3752 State St., Cannon, KY 44823

Name of Seller: Johnny LaRue

Settlement Agent: same

Name of Lender: Great Savings Bank of America, 457 W. Main St., McDonald, PA 15046

Place of Settlement: Settlement Agent

Date of Settlement: January 31, 1986

Contract Sales Price: $59,000/$54,000 new loan amount

Earnest Money Deposit: $2,000

Real Estate Commission: 7%; split equally; totalling $4,130

Loan origination fee: 2 1/4 points = $1,215 (pd. by seller)

Credit report: $27

Interest from 1/31 to 2/1: $14.62/day = $14.62

Mortgage insurance premium: 12 months = $540

Hazard insurance: 1 year = $217

Reserve hazard insurance: 2 months at 18.08/month = 36.16

Mortgage insurance: 2 months at 15.30/month = $30.60

County property taxes: 6 months at $31.22 = $187.32

Title Insurance Binder: $10

Attorney's fees: $350

Title insurance: $133

Recording fees: $67.50

Releases: $8.50 (by borrower)

State transfer tax: $1180 (split equally)

Survey: $120

Pest Inspection: $15

Sewer Assessment: $37 (by buyer)

Buyer's home equity line payoff: $9,884.60

Second equity line: $9,754.80

Sewer assessment: $3.14 from 1/31 to 2/1/86

Pre-payment Fee for Early Mortgage Satisfaction: $528.54 (imposed on seller)

CALCULATE THE SETTLEMENT SHEET AT *FORM 1.23 (2 PAGES).*

HUD-1 (03-86) OMB NO. 2502-0265

A.	B. TYPE OF LOAN:
U.S. DEPARTMENT OF HOUSING & URBAN DEVELOPMENT **SETTLEMENT STATEMENT**	1. ☐ FHA 2. ☐ FmHA 3. ☐ CONV. UNINS. 4. ☐ VA 5. ☐ CONV. INS. 6. FILE NUMBER: 7. LOAN NUMBER: 8. MORTGAGE INSURANCE CASE NUMBER:

C. NOTE: *This form is furnished to give you a statement of actual settlement costs. Amounts paid to and by the settlement agent are shown. Items marked "(p.o.c.)" were paid outside the closing; they are shown here for informational purposes and are not included in the totals.*

D. NAME OF BORROWER:	E. NAME OF SELLER:	F. NAME OF LENDER:
G. PROPERTY LOCATION:	H. SETTLEMENT AGENT PLACE OF SETTLEMENT	I. SETTLEMENT DATE:

J. SUMMARY OF BORROWER'S TRANSACTION		K. SUMMARY OF SELLER'S TRANSACTION	
100. GROSS AMOUNT DUE FROM BORROWER:		**400. GROSS AMOUNT DUE TO SELLER:**	
101. Contract sales price		401. Contract sales price	
102. Personal property		402. Personal property	
103. Settlement charges to borrower (line 1400)		403.	
104.		404.	
105.		405.	
Adjustments for items paid by seller in advance		*Adjustments for items paid by seller in advance*	
106. City/town taxes to		406. City/town taxes to	
107. County taxes to		407. County taxes to	
108. Assessments to		408. Assessments to	
109.		409.	
110.		410.	
111.		411.	
112.		412.	
120. GROSS AMOUNT DUE FROM BORROWER		**420. GROSS AMOUNT DUE TO SELLER**	
200. AMOUNTS PAID BY OR IN BEHALF OF BORROWER:		**500. REDUCTIONS IN AMOUNT DUE TO SELLER:**	
201. Deposit or earnest money		501. Excess deposit (see instructions)	
202. Principal amount of new loan(s)		502. Settlement charges to seller (line 1400)	
203. Existing loan(s) taken subject to		503. Existing loan(s) taken subject to	
204.		504. Payoff of first mortgage loan	
205.		505. Payoff of second mortgage loan	
206.		506.	
207.		507.	
208.		508.	
209.		509.	
Adjustments for items unpaid by seller		*Adjustments for items unpaid by seller*	
210. City/town taxes to		510 City/town taxes to	
211. County taxes to		511. County taxes to	
212. Assessments to		512. Assessments to	
213.		513.	
214.		514.	
215.		515.	
216.		516.	
217.		517.	
218.		518.	
219.		519.	
220. TOTAL PAID BY/FOR BORROWER		**520. TOTAL REDUCTION AMOUNT DUE SELLER**	
300. CASH AT SETTLEMENT FROM/TO BORROWER		**600. CASH AT SETTLEMENT TO/FROM SELLER**	
301. Gross amount due from borrower (line 120)		601. Gross amount due to seller (line 420)	
302. Less amounts paid by/for borrower (line 220)		602. Less reductions in amount due seller (line 520)	
303. CASH (☐ FROM) (☐ TO) BORROWER		**603. CASH (☐ TO) (☐ FROM) SELLER**	

The undersigned hereby acknowledge receipt of a completed copy of pages 1 and 2 of this statement and any attachments referred to herein.

Borrower _____   Seller _____

Borrower _____   Seller _____

Form 1.23

L. SETTLEMENT CHARGES		
700. TOTAL COMMISSION based on price	**PAID FROM BORROWER'S FUNDS AT SETTLEMENT**	**PAID FROM SELLER'S FUNDS AT SETTLEMENT**
Division of Commission (line 700) as follows:		
701. $ to		
702. $ to		
703. Commission paid at Settlement		
704.		
800. ITEMS PAYABLE IN CONNECTION WITH LOAN.		
801. Loan Origination fee %		
802. Loan Discount %		
803. Appraisal Fee to		
804. Credit Report to		
805. Lender's Inspection Fee		
806. Mortgage Insurance Application Fee to		
807. Assumption Fee		
808.		
809.		
810.		
811.		
900. ITEMS REQUIRED BY LENDER TO BE PAID IN ADVANCE		
901. Interest from to @ $ /day		
902. Mortgage Insurance Premium for months to		
903. Hazard Insurance Premium for years to		
904. years to		
905.		
1000. RESERVES DEPOSITED WITH LENDER		
1001. Hazard Insurance months @ $ per month		
1002. Mortgage Insurance months @ $ per month		
1003. City Property Taxes months @ $ per month		
1004. County Property Taxes months @ $ per month		
1005. Annual Assessments months @ $ per month		
1006. months @ $ per month		
1007. months @ $ per month		
1008. months @ $ per month		
1100. TITLE CHARGES		
1101. Settlement or closing fee to		
1102. Abstract or title search to		
1103. Title examination to		
1104. Title insurance binder to		
1105. Document preparation to		
1106. Notary fees to		
1107. Attorney's fees to		
(includes above items numbers:)		
1108. Title insurance to		
(includes above items numbers:)		
1109. Lender's coverage $		
1110. Owner's coverage $		
1111.		
1112.		
1113.		
1200. GOVERNMENT RECORDING AND TRANSFER CHARGES		
1201. Recording fees: Deed $; Mortgage $; Releases $		
1202. City/county tax/stamps: Deed $; Mortgage $		
1203. State tax/stamps: Deed $; Mortgage $		
1204.		
1205.		
1300. ADDITIONAL SETTLEMENT CHARGES		
1301. Survey to		
1302. Pest inspection to		
1303.		
1304.		
1305.		
1400. TOTAL SETTLEMENT CHARGES *(enter on lines 103, Section J and 502, Section K)*		

By signing Page 1 of this statement, the signatories of Page 1 also acknowledge receipt of a completed copy of Page 2 of this two page statement.

Form 1.23—*concluded*

PRACTICUM EXERCISES NO. 2
THE INCORPORATION OF A BUSINESS

	Time Allotted (hours)	Point Value
Background Information on a Business: Assignment #1	1.5	20.0
Reservation of Corporate Name: Assignment #2	0.5	5.0
Fictitious Name Registration: Assignment #3	0.5	5.0
Certificate of Incorporation: Assignment #4 (3 parts)	0.5	5.0
Registered Agent: Assignment #5	0.5	5.0
By-Laws of the Corporation: Assignment #6	1.5	15.0
Minutes of the Corporation: Assignment #7 (4 parts)	1.5	15.0
Waivers and Resolutions: Assignment #8 (7 parts)	1.5	10.0
Stock Record Keeping: Assignment #9 (3 parts)	1.0	10.0
Dissolution and Liquidation: Assignment #10 (3 parts)	1.0	10.0
	10.0	100.0

I.
INTRODUCTION

Practitioners in law will find most engaging the application of law in the business world. The complexities of operating a modern-day business require an examination of many legal issues involving the formation, operation and any eventual dissolution and liquidation. Those delegated these responsibilities must be excellent fact finders, analyzers of business and economic data and persons keenly aware of the regulatory requirements for business operation in their particular jurisdiction. While there are many uniform traits and characteristics in business operation, never lose sight of local influence. Your instructor, throughout the completion of all of these assignments, is responsible for providing you with local forms. The series of assignments outlined below are generically designed but, in order to receive proper credit, will have to be localized. Again, look to the instructor for that input and the distribution of forms and documentation.

In general, this series of exercises will afford the practitioner an opportunity, on a step-by-step basis, to incorporate a business enterprise. Some of these same steps and requirements exist for partnerships, both general and limited in form, as well as the sole proprietorship. However, chief attention will be given to the business form entitled — The Corporation.

Students are advised to collect packets of information from state authorities regarding the incorporation process. In most jurisdictions, the Secretary of State is responsible for regulating the process of business incorporation. As a result, many jurisdictions have form packets, informational brochures and specific guidelines which serve to demystify an often convoluted scheme. An example is a booklet published by the State of Delaware and its Division of Corporations entitled, "Incorporating in Delaware." For those of you who wish a copy of this booklet, you may write to the State of Delaware, Division of Corporations, John G. Townsend Building, Dover, Delaware 19901. If you are not aware, Delaware is the business incorporation capital of the world due to preferential tax and corporate formation and operational policies. Since Delaware's climate is so favorable, numerous businesses have cropped up which serve as incorporation agents for business and industry. Examples of these include some of the advertisements below (*Figures 2.1, 2.2 and 2.3*). Check in your own state's yellow pages and consult your instructor regarding other agencies which serve the same function in your local jurisdiction.

Figure 2.1

Figure 2.2

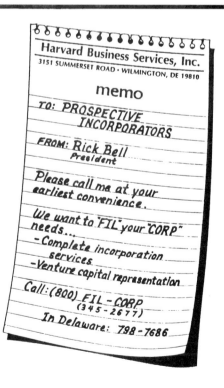

Figure 2.3

The student should list below the complete address and phone number of the governmental authority responsible for the regulation of corporations.

_____

_____

_____

_____

II.
THE INCORPORATION PROCESS

1. Background Information on a Business

A number of steps exists for the incorporation of a business, none more pressing or important than the collection of information during the initial client interview. This assignment requires that the student interview a local business owner or examine his or her own business holdings or enterprises. As in other practicums, the team approach is acceptable as long as the work is evenly divided and the instructor has been notified as to the team's membership. Of course, this requires some human relations skills, but the student is not constricted or constrained by time of day or normal business operating hours. The assignment may call for a visitation to a local gas station, bakery or to a large manufacturing or industrial concern. By and large, businesses are most cooperative with students who are engaged in the study of American enterprises, particularly their own. If you have difficulty locating a specific site, consult your instructor.

A. Objectives

   (1) To review and evaluate issues, both factual and legal in the formation of a business enterprise; and

   (2) To make an on-site visitation of a business soliciting information necessary for a business file.

B. Student Obligations

   (1) To complete a *Business Information Worksheet*.

C. Instructor Obligations

   (1) To provide general and local background information as students solicit the *Business Information Worksheet* information;

   (2) To refer students to possible business sites in order to conduct the interview process; and

   (3) To form teams or groups to work with a specific business enterprise.

D. Time Allotted: 1.5 hours

E. Value of Assignment: 20.0 points

ASSIGNMENT #1

COMPLETE THE BUSINESS INFORMATION WORKSHEET AT *FORM 2.1.*

BUSINESS INFORMATION WORKSHEET

1. Name of the business. _____

   _____

   _____

2. Describe the business. _____

   _____

   _____

3. List capital equipment (cars, machinery, etc.). _____

   _____

   _____

   _____

   _____

   _____

4. Where is the business conducted (in state, out of state)?

   _____

   _____

   _____

5. What are the rationales or reasons for this business desiring incorporation? _____

   _____

   _____

6. Who are the owners of this business? _____

   _____

   _____

   _____

7. Who will be appointed officers of the business?_____

    _____

    _____

    _____

8. What will be the full legal name of the business?_____

    _____

    _____

9. Where will the business be located?_____

    _____

    _____

10. What will be the initial expenditures to formulate the business, specifically?

    Lease costs:_____

    _____

    Out of state business locations:_____

    _____

    Telephone expense:_____

    _____

    Number of employees:_____

    _____

    Fringe benefits for employees:_____

    _____

    _____

    Wages for employees:_____

    _____

11. Are there requirements for business financing? If so, what are they?_____

_____

_____

12. What types of taxes will be assessed against the business?_____

_____

_____

_____

a. What is the name, address and phone number of the state tax office?_____

_____

_____

b. What is the name, address and phone number of the local tax office?_____

_____

_____

13. Does the corporation currently have a written business plan?   ☐ Yes   ☐ No

14. Are resources such as equity and labor available to the business?_____

_____

_____

15. What types of insurance coverages will be required?_____

_____

_____

a. Name and address of insurance company for business operation._____

_____

_____

b. Name and address of insurance company for workmen's compensation._____

_____

_____

16. Is unemployment compensation required?   ☐ Yes   ☐ No

17. What types of licenses are necessary?_____

_____

_____

    a. Names and addresses of licensing authorities.

        _____

        _____

        _____

        _____

        _____

        _____

18. What is the name and address of the person who will be the responsible keeper of records?_____

_____

_____

19. What kinds of tax returns will have to be filed?_____

_____

_____

_____

_____

20. Where are tax registration forms filed at the state and federal levels?

    State:_____

    _____

    _____

    Federal:_____

    _____

    _____

21. Does the business need an employer identification number?   ☐ Yes ☐ No

a.   Addresses to acquire state and federal identification numbers.

State:_____

_____

_____

Federal:_____

_____

_____

22.   Are there any promoters involved?   □ Yes   □ No

Names and addresses of promoters:

_____

_____

_____

_____

_____

_____

23.   Are there any SEC considerations regarding the issuance of stock?   □ Yes   □ No

Briefly discuss._____

_____

_____

_____

24.   Is there a specific corporate name which the parties wish and desire?_____

_____

25.   Attach a picture of the business or some other evidence that an actual visitation took place.

*For information that is not available, inapplicable or not relevant, simply state so in the response portion of the questionnaire.

Form 2.1

2.   Reservation of Corporate Name

As in all corporate record keeping activities, standardized forms from your jurisdiction are essential to successful practice. Ask your instructor for forms required to complete the reservation process in your area.

Once the decision is made to formulate a business corporation, a name is chosen. In order to insure the integrity of a name selection process, states promote a reservation system. Usually for a slight fee ranging from $10 to $50, the party seeking to incorporate with a selected name can accomplish two purposes: first, that the name they have selected is protected; and secondly, that they are not infringing or impinging upon the rights of another business enterprise with a similar name. Conflicting and competitive nomenclature cause legal problems relative to infringement, and a name with a similar description will not be permitted by the governmental agency regulating corporate organization.

A.   Objectives

   (1)   To discover that process necessary to reserve a corporate name in the business incorporation process.

B.   Student Obligations

   (1)   To complete an application to reserve a corporate name.

C.   Instructor Obligations

   (1)   To provide the necessary forms to complete the application to reserve a corporate name.

D.   Time Allotted: 0.5 hours

E.   Value of Assignment: 5.0 points

ASSIGNMENT #2

FACT PATTERN

Reservation Period: 6 months
Results of Reservation Research: No similar names
To Be Communicated To: Steelkin Enterprises, Inc., 1815 Buto Lane, Springfield, MA 09999
Reservation Name Requested: Steelkin Enterprises, Inc.
Consents: Not necessary

COMPLETE THE APPLICATION TO RESERVE A CORPORATE NAME AT *FORM 2.2.*

Applicant's Account No. _____
DSCB:
Filing Fee: $_____

Application to Reserve
Corporate Name

DEPARTMENT OF STATE
CORPORATION BUREAU

The Department of State is hereby requested to reserve a corporate name as follows:

1. The name for which reservation is requested is:

_____

2. The following forms are attached hereto and made a part hereof (strike out any inapplicable statements).

Form DSCB: 17-2 (Consent to Appropriation of Name) executed by the following corporation(s):

_____
_____

Form DSCB: 17-3 (Consent to Use of Similar Name) executed by the following corporation(s):

_____
_____

3. The period for which reservation is requested is:

_____ 60 days

_____ Six months (Applies to banking and savings institutions only — see Instruction B)

4. The response of the Department to this application should be mailed to:

_____
(NAME)

_____
(NUMBER)   (STREET)

_____
(CITY)   (STATE)   (ZIP CODE)

+---+
| For Department use only: The foregoing name: |
| |
| _____ is reserved until the close of business on _____; |
| |
| _____ unavailable because of conflict with _____ |
+---+

INSTRUCTIONS FOR COMPLETING FORM:

A. Only one name may be reserved on this form. If additional names are to be reserved additional copies of this form should be submitted.

B. If this form is submitted with a complete Form DSCB: 17.31A (Request for Corporate Name Search) Paragraph 1 of this form may be in blank, in which case the Department will insert in such blank and reserve the first in order of priority of the available names, if any, listed on the accompanying Form DSCB: 17.3A.

C. Banking and Savings Association names may be reserved for six months; all other names are reserved for 60 days.

D. The Department will assume that all requisite governmental approvals will be obtained in connection with the use of names to be reserved, and the reservation of a name will not eliminate the requirement for any such approvals.

Form 2.2

3. Fictitious Name Registration

All business entities from individuals to corporations can operate under a name that is "fictitious," that is, the name selected for operation does not correspond with the formal record. Often, a business chooses another name for purposes of marketing or other legal justification. In states which have a fictitious name registration, proper forms must be filed for a fee which ranges from $10 to $100.

A. Objectives

    (1) To become familiar with the fictitious name registration system and regulatory requirements.

B. Student Obligations

    (1) To complete a fictitious name registration form.

C. Instructor Obligations

    (1) To provide forms as necessary in the student's local jurisdiction.

D. Time Allotted: 0.5 hours

E. Value of Assignment: 5.0 points

ASSIGNMENT #3

FACT PATTERN

Individuals in the Business:
    John Michaelson, 1812 King Street, Wilmington, Delaware 19885
    Sally Strand, 11 Fenwick Way, Lewes, Delaware 19006
    Erica Longski, 18 VanBuren Street, Wilmington, Delaware 19448

Fictitious Name: Lady Luck Limited, Inc.

Address: 1317 Gateway, Wilmington, Delaware 19444

Brief Character of the Business: Cruise service on the Delaware River

Agencies Granted: None

Entity Other Than Individual Interested in the Business: Lukens Steel Corporation

Form of Entity: Corporation

Jurisdiction: Pennsylvania

Address: 165 Blain Lane, Coastal, Pennsylvania 19001

Registered Office: 41 King Street, Wilmington, Delaware 19802

President of the Corporation: Stanley Dove

Secretary: Roberta Ronson

*Many jurisdictions call for the publication of a fictitious name registration. What newspaper is considered a proper forum for legal notices and advertisements in your jurisdiction?

Name:_____

Address:_____

Phone:_____

COMPLETE THE FICTITIOUS NAME REGISTRATION FORM AT *FORM 2.3*.

FICTITIOUS NAME REGISTRATION

FILING FEE: _____ Corporate/Individual - $ _____
_____ Corporation $ _____
_____ Individual $ _____
_____ Check Enclosed
_____ Charge Account # _____

CORPORATION BUREAU
DEPARTMENT OF STATE

This undersigned entity(ies) desiring to carry on or conduct a business in this state under an assumed or fictitious name, style or designation, does (do) hereby certify that:

1. Fictitious Name:

_____

2. Address of the principal place of business (including street and number)

_____
(County)

3. Brief statement of the character or nature of the business:

_____

4. Individual or individuals interested in the business: (name and address)

(NAME)	(NUMBER)	(STREET)	(CITY)	(STATE)	(ZIP CODE)

5. Entity other than an individual interested in the business:

(NAME)	(FORM OF ENTITY)	ORGANIZING JURISDICTION	ADDRESS IN JURIS	REGISTERED OFFICE (if any)

6. I am familiar with the provisions of the Fictitious Names Act and understand that filing under the Act does not create any exclusive or other right to the fictitious name.

_____

7. Agent, if any, authorized to execute amendments, withdrawals, or cancellations.

_____

IN TESTIMONY WHEREOF, the undersigned have caused this registration to be executed this _____ day of _____, 19_____.

_____   _____
Individual   Individual

Individual		Individual	

Corporate Seal

_____
Name of Corporation

_____
Secretary or Assistant Secretary

_____
President or Vice President

Corporate Seal

_____
Name of Corporation

_____
Secretary or Assistant Secretary

_____
President or Vice President

INSTRUCTIONS FOR APPLYING FOR A FICTITIOUS NAME

1. Prepare an application for Conducting Business Under an Assumed or Fictitious Name in the proper format.

2. Send the following documents to the Secretary of State either by mail or in person:

   a. The application for Conducting Business Under an Assumed or Fictitious Name.

   b. A draft or money order payable to the Secretary of State in payment of the filing fee.

3. The Secretary of State will review, file, copy and microfilm and return the Fictitious Name Registration properly endorsed. NO CERTIFICATE WILL BE ISSUED.

4. Publish in a newspaper of general circulation and the legal newspaper if any, in English, in the county where the principal office or place of business is located, the intention to file or the filing of application only for individuals.

Form 2.3

4.   Certificate of Incorporation

In most American jurisdictions, a certificate of incorporation must be filed with state authorities, published in a newspaper or disseminated in some other fashion. The certificate of incorporation merely indicates that a certain business entity will and does operate in a corporate form.

A.   Objectives

    (1)   To become familiar with the legal requirement of filing a certificate of incorporation; and

    (2)   To know what steps and processes are necessary for an amendment to such.

B.   Student Obligations

    (1)   To complete a certificate of incorporation; and

    (2)   To complete an amendment to that certificate.

C.   Instructor Obligations

    (1)   To provide students with local forms.

D.   Time Allotted: 0.5 hours

E.   Value of Assignment: 5.0 points

ASSIGNMENT #4

FACT PATTERN

Corporation: Bulah Enterprises, Inc.
Incorporator: CSI Incorporators, 1311 James Way Avenue, Sacramento, CA 99684
Date of Statement of Intent: July 30, 1989
Purpose of the Corporation: To act and engage in construction activities and any lawfully related activities within the state of California
Registered Office: 884 Queen St., Wilmington, Delaware 19116
Registered Agent: Same as incorporator
Value of Capital Stock: $100,000; 10,000 shares at $10 each

Amended Information—

Board of Directors of Bulah Enterprises: President, Larry Gaines; Secretary, Mary Fornash
Matter of Amendment and Revision: That the amount of authorized shares and corresponding value be increased to a total value of $200,000 divided into 20,000 shares at $10 each.

ASSIGNMENT #4 — PART 1
CERTIFICATE OF INCORPORATION

COMPLETE *FORM 2.4* BASED ON THE FACT PATTERN ABOVE.

CERTIFICATE OF INCORPORATION
OF

....

A STOCK CORPORATION

FIRST: The name of this Corporation is ....

....

SECOND: Its Registered Office in the state of Delaware is to be located at

.... Street, in the City of .... ,

County of .... Zip Code .... The Registered Agent in charge

thereof is ....

....

....

THIRD: The purpose of the corporation is to engage in any lawful act or activity for which corporations may be organized under the General Corporation Law of Delaware.

FOURTH: The amount of the total authorized capital stock of this corporation is

.... Dollars ($.....................) divided

into .... shares, of .... Dollars ($.....................) each.

FIFTH: The name and mailing address of the incorporator are as follows:

Name ....

Mailing Address ....

.... Zip Code.................................

I, THE UNDERSIGNED, for the purpose of forming a corporation under the laws of the State of Delaware, do make, file and record this Certificate, and do certify that the facts herein stated are true, and I have accor-

dingly hereunto set my hand this .... day of .... , A.D. 19...........

.

....

STOCK
Doc. 20-05/81/08/09

Form 2.4

A response from the governmental authority usually results in a formal certification, an example of which is reproduced at *Figure 2.4* below.

Office of Secretary of State

I, MICHAEL HARKINS, SECRETARY OF STATE OF THE STATE OF DELAWARE DO HEREBY CERTIFY THE ATTACHED IS A TRUE AND CORRECT COPY OF THE CERTIFICATE OF INCORPORATION OF NEMBAR ENTERPRISES, INC. FILED IN THIS OFFICE ON THE FIFTEENTH DAY OF APRIL, A.D. 1987, AT 9 O'CLOCK A.M.

: : : : : : : : : : :

717105001

Michael Harkins, Secretary of State

AUTHENTICATION: !1205675

DATE: 04/16/1987

Figure 2.4

Paralegals and other practitioners must be certain that some form of acknowledgment is forthcoming to verify the integrity of the incorporation process.

ASSIGNMENT #4 — PART 2
AMENDMENT TO CERTIFICATE

COMPLETE THE AMENDMENT AT *FORM 2.5* BASED ON THE PREVIOUS FACT PATTERN.

CERTIFICATE OF AMENDMENT
OF
CERTIFICATE OF INCORPORATION

.... ,
a corporation organized and existing under and by virtue of the General Corporation Law of the State of Delaware,

DOES HEREBY CERTIFY:

FIRST: That at a meeting of the Board of Directors of ....

....
resolutions were duly adopted setting forth a proposed amendment of the Certificate of Incorporation of said corporation, declaring said amendment to be advisable and calling a meeting of the stockholders of said corporation for consideration thereof. The resolution setting forth the proposed amendment is as follows:

RESOLVED, that the Certificate of Incorporation of this corporation be amended by changing the

Article thereof numbered " ...." so that, as amended said Article shall be and read as follows:

"
....

....

.... "

SECOND: That thereafter, pursuant to resolution of its Board of Directors, a special meeting of the stockholders of said corporation was duly called and held, upon notice in accordance with Section 222 of the General Corporation law of the state of Delaware at which meeting the necessary number of shares as required by statute were voted in favor of the amendment.

THIRD: That said amendment was duly adopted in accordance with the provisions of Section 242 of the General Corporation Law of the State of Delaware.

FOURTH: That the capital of said corporation shall not be reduced under or by reason of said amendment.

IN WITNESS WHEREOF, said ....

has caused this certificate to be signed by

.... its President,

and .... , its Secretary,

this .... day of... , 19.............

BY:...
President

ATTEST: ....
Secretary

AMENDMENT
Doc. 20-05/78/03/03

Form 2.5

ASSIGNMENT #4 — PART 3
ARTICLES OF INCORPORATION

Another way of describing these preliminary stages is to refer to this initial corporate filing as the "Articles of Incorporation."

ADDITIONAL FACTS:
Number and Class of Shares: 1,000 par
Total Authorized Capital: $20,000.00
Par Value: $1.00
Term of Existence: Perpetual
Incorporator Address: 472 Marx Street, Wilmington, DE 19116
Number and Class of Shares Owned by Incorporator: 1,000
Incorporator: John Stephens

USING *FORM 2.6*, EMPLOY THE FACT PATTERN ABOVE AND THESE ADDITIONAL FACTS TO COMPLETE THE DOCUMENTATION.

ARTICLES OF INCORPORATION

DEPARTMENT OF STATE — CORPORATION BUREAU

PLEASE INDICATE (CHECK ONE) TYPE CORPORATION:

☐ DOMESTIC BUSINESS CORPORATION

☐ DOMESTIC BUSINESS CORPORATION
A CLOSE CORPORATION — COMPLETE BACK

☐ DOMESTIC PROFESSIONAL CORPORATION
ENTER BOARD LICENSE NO.

FEE

$

010 NAME OF CORPORATION (MUST CONTAIN A CORPORATE INDICATOR UNLESS EXEMPT

011 ADDRESS OF REGISTERED OFFICE

012 CITY	033 COUNTY	013 STATE	064 ZIP CODE

050 EXPLAIN THE PURPOSE OR PURPOSES OF THE CORPORATION

(ATTACH 8½ x 11 SHEET IF NECESSARY)

The Aggregate Number of Shares, Classes of Shares and Per Value of Shares Which the Corporation Shall have Authority to Issue:

040 Number and Class of Shares	041 Stated Par Value Per Share If Any	042 Total Authorized Capital	031 Term of Existence

The Name and Address of Each Incorporator, and the Number and Class of Shares Subscribed to by each Incorporator

060 Name	061, 062 063, 064 Address (Street, City, State, Zip Code)	Number & Class of Shares
	(ATTACH 8½ x 11 SHEET IF NECESSARY)	

IN TESTIMONY WHEREOF, THE INCORPORATOR (S) HAS (HAVE) SIGNED AND SEALED THE ARTICLES OF INCORPORATION

THIS_____ DAY OF _____ 19_____.

— FOR OFFICE USE ONLY —

030 FILED	002 CODE	003 REV BOX	SEQUENTIAL NO.	100 MICROFILM NUMBER	
	REVIEWED BY				
	DATE APPROVED	004 SICC	AMOUNT $	001 CORPORATION NUMBER	
	DATE REJECTED	CERTIFY TO ☐ REV.	INPUT BY	LOG IN	LOG IN (REFILE)
	MAILED BY DATE	☐ L & I ☐ OTHER	VERIFIED BY	LOG OUT	LOG OUT (REFILE)

1. The following provisions shall regulate the status of the corporation as a close corporation:

   (a)   (Strike out(i) or (ii) below, whichever is not applicable.)

       (i)   All of the issued shares of the corporation of all classes, exclusive of treasury shares, shall be held of record by not more than_____persons.
                         (NUMBER NOT TO EXCEED 30)

       (ii)   All of the issued shares of the corporation of all classes, exclusive of treasury shares, shall be held of record by not more than the smaller of twenty-five "shareholders" within the meaning of Subchapter S of the Internal Revenue Code of 1954, as amended, or 30 persons.

   (b)   All of the issued shares of all classes of the corporation shall be subject to one or more of the restrictions on transfer permitted by section 613.1 of the Business Corporation Law

   (c)   The corporation shall make no offering of any of its shares of any class which would constitute a "public offering" within the meaning of the Securities Act of 1933, as amended.

2. (Optional: BCL § 372B) A person (other than an estate) who is not an "individual" or who is a "non-resident alien," in either case within the meaning of the Internal Revenue Code of 1954, as amended ("Code"), shall not be entitled to be a holder of record of shares of the corporation. Only a person whose consent is currently in effect to the election of the corporation to be treated as an electing small business corporation under Subchapter S of the Code and a shareholder who has not affirmatively refused to consent to the election within sixty days after he acquires his stock, shall be entitled to be a holder of record of shares of the corporation.

3. (Optional: BCL § 382) The business and affairs of the corporation shall be managed by the shareholders of the corporation rather than by a board of directors.

4. (Optional: § 376B) The status of the corporation as a "close corporation" within the meaning of the Business Corporation Law shall not be terminated without the affirmative vote or written consent of (all holders of) (shareholders holding _____ of the) shares of all classes of the corporation.
     (FRACTION AT LEAST TWO-THIRDS)

5. (Optional: BCL § 384B) (Any shareholder) (shareholders holding_____of the shares) of the corporation may
                                           (FRACTION)
   apply for the appointment of a provisional director of the corporation in the manner and upon the circumstances provided by statute.

6. (Optional: BCL § 386) (Any shareholder) (shareholders holding_____of the shares) of the corporation shall
                                          (FRACTION)
   have the right at will to cause the corporation to be dissolved by proceeding in the manner provided by statute.

Form 2.6

5. Registered Agent

Corporations need a designated registered agent who will accept service of process, tax filings and other documentation. Since a corporation is a business entity rather than an individual person, complications in service of process are natural. This dilemma has caused legislatures to call for the designation of a specific entity, person or other legal being who will accept service on behalf of the corporation. In states such as New York and Delaware, companies are founded upon the premise that corporations need registered agent services, an example of which is shown in the advertisement below.

ANNUAL FEE: $35

For Registered Agent on enclosed forms, use:

Agents and Corporations, Inc.

Suite 600 • One Commerce Center
Wilmington, New Castle County, Delaware 19801

For Consultation Call: (302) 575-0873

$35 Annual Fee includes forwarding mail and annual report to corporation and filing report with Secretary of State.

Complete Start-Up Package: $199

Includes Minutes, By-Laws and Stock Issuance, Filing and Recording services, Minute Book, Seal, Stock Certificates, Filing and Recording fees and First Year Annual Fee.

Figure 2.5

Another step, in the filing of a certificate or article of incorporation, is the naming and designation of a registered agent. Frequently, that designation is altered or changed. Forms are generally provided at the state and local levels with a filing fee ranging from $10 to $100 required.

A. Objectives

(1) To become familiar with the dynamics of registered agents and the legal requirements for change.

B. Student Obligations

(1) To complete a change of registered office for corporate enterprise.

C. Instructor Obligations

(1) To provide local forms as needed.

D. Time Allotted: 0.5 hours

E. Value of Assignment: 5.0 points

ASSIGNMENT #5

FACT PATTERN

Name of Corporation: Nembar Enterprises, Inc.
Type of Corporation: Domestic
Address: 415 Kings Highway, Rosslyn Farms, PA 15106
County: Allegheny
Address of Change: P.O. Box 578, 402 E. Dickson St., Washington County, Midway, PA 15060
Authorization: By Board
President: Bart Brizee

COMPLETE *FORM 2.7* USING THE FACT PATTERN ABOVE.

PROCEDURE FOR CHANGING REGISTERED OFFICE

The Department of State is the granting authority for all corporations and is the storehouse for those papers and other related corporations papers. In order to change the registered office of a business:

1. Prepare the change of registered office form, as prescribed in the appropriate law and exemplified.
2. Send the following documents to the Secretary of State, either by mail or in person:
    a. Change of Registered Office form
    b. Check, draft or money order payable to the Secretary of State in payment of the filing fee.
3. The Secretary of State will review, microfilm and return the original Change of Registered Office formed.
4. Please note: in reference to line 3, a Post Office Box is not acceptable.

CHANGE OF REGISTERED OFFICE

Department of State-Corporation Bureau

Please indicate (check one) type corporation

☐ Domestic Business Corporation
☐ Foreign Business Corporation
☐ Domestic Non-Profit Corporation
☐ Foreign Non-Profit Corporation

FEE
$

1. Name of Corporation

2. Address of its present registered office   (the Department of State is hereby authorized to correct the following statement to conform to the records of the Dept).

(number)   (street)   (city)   (state)   (zip code)   (county)

3. Address to which the registered office   is to be changed:

(number)   (street)   (city)   (state)   (zip code)   (county)

4. (Check, and if appropriate, complete one of the following):
   ☐ Such change was authorized by resolution duly adopted by the Board of Directors of the corporation.
   ☐ The procedure whereby such change was authorized was:

IN TESTIMONY WHEREOF, the undersigned corporation has caused this statement to be signed by a duly authorized officer, and its corporate seal, duly attested by another such officer, to be hereunto affixed, this _____ day of _____ , 19_____ .

(Corporate Seal)

BY:

_____
(Name of Corporation)

_____
(Signature)

ATTEST:

_____
(Title: President, Vice-President, etc.)

_____
(Signature)

_____
(Title: Secretary, Assistant Secretary, etc.)

—FOR OFFICE USE ONLY—

030 FILED	002 CODE	003 REV BOX	SEQUENTIAL NO.	100 MICROFILM NUMBER	
	REVIEWED BY	004 ICC	AMOUNT	001 CORPORATION NUMBER	
	DATE APPROVED		$		
	DATE REJECTED	CERTIFY TO	INPUT BY	LOG IN	LOG IN (REFILE)
	MAILED BY DATE	☐ REV ☐ L & I ☐ OTHER	VERIFIED BY	LOG OUT	LOG OUT (REFILE)

Form 2.7

6.   By-Laws of the Corporation

By-laws are the rules and regulations of corporate operation and governance as adopted by the board of directors. Board members', officers' and shareholders' conduct is governed by the by-laws of the corporation. Many forms of by-laws are possible, though in an age of standardized corporate kits, by-law formats are available. Two companies which make available corporate kits, which are of great use to practitioners in this area, are All-State Legal Supply and Black Beauty. Review the advertisement below.

"In every business, there's always one name that stands out as the best. In corporate outfits, it's Corpex."

Like her colleagues across the country, attorney Elaine Zapfel won't settle for anything but the best. So when she wants a top quality corporate outfit that contains all the forms she needs, that makes the best impression, and is there when she needs it, there's only one name in her book. Corpex. For overnight delivery of our corporate outfits anywhere in the U.S.,* call us today before 2 p.m. EST.

We'll send you our best. Fast.

Every Corpex Kit comes in matching slipcase complete with:
- corporate seal in foldaway pocket
- 20 custom-printed stock certificates
- stock transfer ledger
- 50 blank sheets for minutes or time-saving printed minutes and by-laws
- special forms section with complete IRS requirements for Sub-Chapter S election, medical and dental reimbursement plans, Section 1244 forms, IRS SS4 form, annual meeting forms.
- **Standard outfit, $49.75; with printed minutes and by-laws, $52.25; 35 page "S" Election Section with kit, $6.75** (ordered separately, $13.25). Prices include delivery in Continental U.S., Alaska and Hawaii.

To order, or to receive our brochure or more information, call:

Corpex®

1-800-221-8181

In NY: 1-800-522-7299; 212-925-2400

NEW! FAX: 1-800-8CORPEX

Corpex Banknote Co., Inc. 480 Canal St., NY, NY 10013
*Some remote locations might require an additional day.

Figure 2.6

For the assignment below, we will employ standardized by-laws made available through Corporate Service Corporation of Wilmington, Delaware.

A.   Objectives

(1)   To become familiar with those provisions, clauses, articles and various forms of construction within a set of corporate by-laws;

(2) To appreciate the legal implications of by-laws as relates to the holding of meetings, voting rights, officers and their compensation and the distribution of dividends.

B. Student Obligations

(1) To complete a set of corporate by-laws.

C. Instructor Obligations

(1) To assist students in the completion of by-laws; and

(2) To provide whatever local input is necessary to reflect the student's jurisdiction.

D. Time Allotted: 1.5 hours

E. Value of Assignment: 15.0 points

ASSIGNMENT #6

FACT PATTERN

Election of Directors: Must be by written ballot
Registered Agent: CTI Services, 18 Johnson St., Boulder, Colorado 85387
Registered Office: Johnson and Wales, Attorneys at Law, 1013 Center St., Boulder, Colorado 85386
Annual Meeting: April 15 at 10:00 a.m.
Number of Directors: 6
Time of Board Meetings: Last day of each month; 10 a.m.
Registration of Stock Certificates: As customary, but signed by secretary and president
Fiscal Year: August 1 to July 31
Seal: Corporate seal, Colorado
Requirements for Notice of Special Meetings: 10 days

COMPLETE THE DRAFTING OF STANDARDIZED BY-LAWS AT *FORM 2.8.*

BY-LAWS

ARTICLE I - OFFICES

Section 1. The registered office of the corporation in the State of   shall be at

The registered agent in charge thereof shall be

Section 2. The corporation may also have offices at such other places as the Board of Directors may from time to time appoint or the business of the corporation may require.

ARTICLE II - SEAL

Section 1. The corporate seal shall have inscribed thereon the name of the corporation, the year of its organization and the words

ARTICLE III - STOCKHOLDERS' MEETINGS

Section 1. Meetings of stockholders shall be held at the registered office of the corporation in this state or at such place, either within or without this state, as may be selected from time to time by the Board of Directors.

Section 2. Annual Meetings: The annual meeting of the stockholders shall be held on the   of

in each year if not a legal holiday, and if a legal holiday, then on the next secular day following at   o'clock when they shall elect a Board of Directors and transact such other business as may properly be brought before the meeting. If the annual meeting for election of directors is not held on the date designated therefor, the directors shall cause the meeting to be held as soon thereafter as convenient.

Section 3. Election of Directors: Elections of the directors of the corporation will   be by

Section 4. Special Meetings: Special meetings of the stockholders may be called at any time by the President, or the Board of Directors, or stockholders entitled to cast at least one-fifth of the votes which all stockholders are entitled to cast at the particular meeting. At any time, upon written request of any person or persons who have duly called a special meeting, it shall be the duty of the Secretary to fix the date of the meeting, to be held not more than sixty days after receipt of the request, and to give due notice thereof. If the Secretary shall neglect or refuse to fix the date of the meeting and give notice thereof, the person or persons calling the meeting may do so.

Business transacted at all special meetings shall be confined to the objects stated in the call and matters germane thereto, unless all stockholders entitled to vote are present and consent.

Written notice of a special meeting of stockholders stating the time and place and object thereof, shall be given to each stockholder entitled to vote thereat at least ten days before such meeting, unless a greater period of notice is required by statute in a particular case.

Section 5. Quorum: A majority of the outstanding shares of the corporation entitled to vote, represented in person or by proxy, shall constitute a quorum at a meeting of stockholders. If less than a majority of the outstanding shares entitled to vote is represented at a meeting, a majority of the shares so represented may adjourn the meeting from time to time without further notice. At such adjourned meeting at which a quorum shall be present or represented, any business may be transacted which might have been transacted at the meeting as originally noticed. The stockholders present at a duly organized meeting may continue to transact business until adjournment, notwithstanding the withdrawal of enough stockholders to leave less than a quorum.

Section 6. Proxies: Each stockholder entitled to vote at a meeting of stockholders or to express consent or dissent to corporate action in writing without a meeting may authorize another person or persons to act for him by proxy, but no such proxy shall be voted or acted upon after three years from its date, unless the proxy provides for a longer period

A duly executed proxy shall be irrevocable if it states that it is irrevocable and if, and only as long as, it is coupled with an interest sufficient in law to support an irrevocable power. A proxy may be made irrevocable regardless of whether the interest with which it is coupled is an interest in the stock itself or an interest in the corporation generally. **All proxies** shall be filed with the Secretary of the meeting before being voted upon.

Section 7. <u>Notice of Meetings</u>: Whenever stockholders are required or permitted to take any action at a meeting, a written notice of the meeting shall be given which shall state the place, date and hour of the meeting, and, in the case of a special meeting, the purpose or purposes for which the meeting is called.

Unless otherwise provided by law, written notice of any meeting shall be given not less than ten nor more than sixty days before the date of the meeting to each stockholder entitled to vote at such meeting.

Section 8. <u>Consent in Lieu of Meetings</u>: Any action required to be taken at any annual or special meeting of stockholders of a corporation, or any action which may be taken at any annual or special meeting of such stockholders, may be taken without a meeting, without prior notice and without a vote, if a consent in writing, setting forth the action so taken, shall be signed by the holders of outstanding stock having not less than the minimum number of votes that would be necessary to authorize or take such action at a meeting at which all shares entitled to vote thereon were present and voted. Prompt notice of the taking of the corporate action without a meeting by less than unanimous written consent shall be given to those stockholders who have not consented in writing.

Section 9. <u>List of Stockholders</u>: The officer who has charge of the stock ledger of the corporation shall prepare and make, at least ten days before every meeting of stockholders, a complete list of the stockholders entitled to vote at the meeting, arranged in alphabetical order, and showing the address of each stockholder and the number of shares registered in the name of each stockholder. No share of stock upon which any installment is due and unpaid shall be voted at any meeting. The list shall be open to the examination of any stockholder, for any purpose germane to the meeting, during ordinary business hours, for a period of at least ten days prior to the meeting, either at a place within the city where the meeting is to be held, which place shall be specified in the notice of the meeting, or, if not so specified, at the place where the meeting is to be held. The list shall also be produced and kept at the time and place of the meeting during the whole time thereof, and may be inspected by any stockholder who is present.

ARTICLE IV - DIRECTORS

Section 1. The business and affairs of this corporation shall be managed by its Board of Directors,
The directors need not be residents of this state or stockholders in the corporation. They shall be elected by the stockholders at the annual meeting of stockholders of the corporation, and each director shall be elected for the term of one year, and until his successor shall be elected and shall qualify or until his

earlier resignation or removal.

Section 2.   Regular Meetings: Regular meetings of the Board shall be held without notice

at   at the registered office of the corporation, or at such other time and place as shall be determined by the Board.

Section 3.   Special Meetings: Special Meetings of the Board may be called by the President on   days notice to each director, either personally or by mail or by telegram; special meetings shall be called by the President or Secretary in like manner and on like notice on the written request of a majority of the directors in office.

Section 4.   Quorum: A majority of the total number of directors shall constitute a quorum for the transaction of business.

Section 5.   Consent in Lieu of Meeting: Any action required or permitted to be taken at any meeting of the Board of Directors, or of any committee thereof, may be taken without a meeting if all members of the Board or committee, as the case may be, consent thereto in writing, and the writing or writings are filed with the minutes of proceedings of the Board or committee.   The Board of Directors may hold its meetings, and have an office or offices, outside of this state.

Section 6.   Conference Telephone: One or more directors may participate in a meeting of the Board, of a committee of the Board or of the stockholders, by means of conference telephone or similar communications equipment by means of which all persons participating in the meeting can hear each other; participation in this manner shall constitute presence in person at such meeting.

Section 7. <u>Compensation</u>: Directors as such, shall not receive any stated salary for their services, but by resolution of the Board, a fixed sum and expenses of attendance, if any, may be allowed for attendance at each regular or special meeting of the Board PROVIDED, that nothing herein contained shall be construed to preclude any director from serving the corporation in any other capacity and receiving compensation therefor.

Section 8. <u>Removal</u>: Any director or the entire Board of Directors may be removed, with or without cause, by the holders of a majority of the shares then entitled to vote at an election of directors, except that when cumulative voting is permitted, if less than the entire Board is to be removed, no director may be removed without cause if the votes cast against his removal would be sufficient to elect him if then cumulatively voted at an election of the entire Board of Directors, or, if there be classes of directors, at an election of the class of directors of which he is a part.

ARTICLE V - OFFICERS

Section 1. The executive officers of the corporation shall be chosen by the directors and shall be a President, Secretary and Treasurer. The Board of Directors may also choose a Chairman, one or more Vice Presidents and such other officers as it shall deem necessary. Any number of offices may be held by the same person.

Section 2. <u>Salaries</u>: Salaries of all officers and agents of the corporation shall be fixed by the Board of Directors.

Section 3. <u>Term of Office</u>: The officers of the corporation shall hold office for one year and until their successors are chosen and have qualified. Any officer or agent elected or appointed by the Board may be removed by the Board of Directors whenever in its judgment the best interest of the corporation will be served thereby.

Section 4. <u>President</u>: The President shall be the chief executive officer of the corporation; he shall preside at all meetings of the stockholders and directors; he shall have general and active management of the business of the corporation, shall see that all orders and resolutions of the Board are carried into effect, subject, however, to the right of the directors to delegate any specific powers, except such as may be by statute exclusively conferred on the President, to any other officer or officers of the corporation. He shall execute bonds, mortgages and other contracts requiring a seal, under the seal of the corporation. He shall be EX-OFFICIO a member of all committees, and shall have the general power and duties of supervision and management usually vested in the office of President of a corporation.

Section 5. <u>Secretary</u>: The Secretary shall attend all sessions of the Board and all meetings of the stockholders and act as clerk thereof, and record all the votes of the corporation and the minutes of all its transactions in a book to be kept for that purpose, and shall perform like duties for all committees of the Board of Directors when required. He shall give, or cause to be given, notice of all meetings of the stockholders and of the Board of Directors, and shall perform such other duties as may be prescribed by the Board of Directors or President, and under whose supervision he shall be. He shall keep in safe custody the corporate seal of the corporation, and when authorized by the Board, affix the same to any instrument requiring it.

Section 6. _Treasurer_: The Treasurer shall have custody of the corporate funds and securities and shall keep full and accurate accounts of receipts and disbursements in books belonging to the corporation, and shall keep the moneys of the corporation in a separate account to the credit of the corporation. He shall disburse the funds of the corporation as may be ordered by the Board, taking proper vouchers for such disbursements, and shall render to the President and directors, at the regular meetings of the Board, or whenever they may require it, an account of all his transactions as Treasurer and of the financial condition of the corporation.

ARTICLE VI - VACANCIES

Section 1. Any vacancy occurring in any office of the corporation by death, resignation, removal or otherwise, shall be filled by the Board of Directors. Vacancies and newly created directorships resulting from any increase in the authorized number of directors may be filled by a majority of the directors then in office, although less than a quorum, or by a sole remaining director. If at any time, by reason of death or resignation or other cause, the corporation should have no directors in office, then any officer or any stockholder or an executor, administrator, trustee or guardian of a stockholder, or other fiduciary entrusted with like responsibility for the person or estate of a stockholder, may call a special meeting of stockholders in accordance with the provisions of these By-Laws.

Section 2.   <u>Resignations Effective at Future Date</u>:   When one or more directors shall resign from the Board, effective at a future date, a majority of the directors then in office, including those who have so resigned, shall have power to fill such vacancy or vacancies, the vote thereon to take effect when such resignation or resignations shall become effective.

ARTICLE VII - CORPORATE RECORDS

Section 1.   Any stockholder of record, in person or by attorney or other agent, shall, upon written demand under oath stating the purpose thereof, have the right during the usual hours for business to inspect for any proper purpose the corporation's stock ledger, a list of its stockholders, and its other books and records, and to make copies or extracts therefrom. A proper purpose shall mean a purpose reasonably related to such person's interest as a stockholder.   In every instance where an attorney or other agent shall be the person who seeks the right to inspection, the demand under oath shall be accompanied by a power of attorney or such other writing which authorizes the attorney or other agent to so act on behalf of the stockholder.   The demand under oath shall be directed to the corporation at its registered office in this state or at its principal place of business.

ARTICLE VIII - STOCK CERTIFICATES, DIVIDENDS, ETC.

Section 1.   The stock certificates of the corporation shall be numbered and registered in the share ledger and transfer books of the corporation as they are issued.   They shall bear the corporate seal and shall be signed by the

Section 2.   Transfers: Transfers of shares shall be made on the books of the corporation upon surrender of the certificates therefor, endorsed by the person named in the certificate or by attorney, lawfully constituted in writing.   No transfer shall be made which is inconsistent with law.

Section 3.   Lost Certificate: The corporation may issue a new certificate of stock in the place of any certificate there-tofore signed by it, alleged to have been lost, stolen or destroyed, and the corporation may require the owner of the lost, stolen or destroyed certificate, or his legal representative. to give the corporation a bond sufficient to indemnify it against any claim that may be made against it on account of the alleged loss, theft or destruction of any such certificate or the issu-ance of such new certificate.

Section 4.   Record Date: In order that the corporation may determine the stockholders entitled to notice of or to vote at any meeting of stockholders or any adjournment thereof, or to express consent to corporate action in writing without a meet-ing, or entitled to receive payment of any dividend or other dis-tribution or allotment of any rights, or entitled to exercise any rights in respect of any change, conversion or exchange of stock or for the purpose of any other lawful action, the Board of Directors may fix, in advance, a record date, which shall not be more than sixty nor less than ten days before the date of such meeting, nor more than sixty days prior to any other action.

If no record date is fixed:

(a)   The record date for determining stockholders entitled to notice of or to vote at a meeting of stockholders shall be at the close of business on the day next preceding the day on which notice is given, or, if notice is waived, at the close of business on the day next preceding the day on which the meeting is held.

(b)   The record date for determining stockholders entitled to express consent to corporate action in writing without a meeting, when no prior action by the Board of Directors is necessary, shall be the day on which the first written consent is expressed.

(c)   The record date for determining stockholders for any other purpose shall be at the close of business on the day on which the Board of Directors adopts the resolution relating thereto.

(d)   A determination of stockholders of record entitled to notice of or to vote at a meeting of stockholders shall apply to any adjournment of the meeting; provided, however, that the Board of Directors may fix a new record date for the adjourned meeting.

Section 5.   Dividends: The Board of Directors may declare and pay dividends upon the outstanding shares of the corporation, from time to time and to such extent as they deem advisable, in the manner and upon the terms and conditions provided by statute and the Certificate of Incorporation.

Section 6.   Reserves: Before payment of any dividend there may be set aside out of the net profits of the corporation such sum or sums as the directors, from time to time, in their absolute discretion, think proper as a reserve fund to meet contingencies, or for equalizing dividends, or for repairing or maintaining any property of the corporation, or for such other purpose as the directors shall think conducive to the interests of the corporation, and the directors may abolish any such reserve in the manner in which it was created.

ARTICLE IX - MISCELLANEOUS PROVISIONS

Section 1. <u>Checks</u>: All checks or demands for money and notes of the corporation shall be signed by such officer or officers as the Board of Directors may from time to time designate.

Section 2. <u>Fiscal Year</u>: The fiscal year shall begin on

Section 3. <u>Notice</u>: Whenever written notice is required to be given to any person, it may be given to such person, either personally or by sending a copy thereof through the mail, or by telegram, charges prepaid, to his address appearing on the books of the corporation, or supplied by him to the corporation for the purpose of notice. If the notice is sent by mail or by telegraph, it shall be deemed to have been given to the person entitled thereto when deposited in the United States mail or with a telegraph office for transmission to such person. Such notice shall specify the place, day and hour of the meeting and, in the case of a special meeting of stockholders, the general nature of the business to be transacted.

Section 4. <u>Waiver of Notice</u>: Whenever any written notice is required by statute, or by the Certificate or the By-Laws of this corporation a waiver thereof in writing, signed by the person or persons entitled to such notice, whether before or after the time stated therein, shall be deemed equivalent to the giving of such notice. Except in the case of a special meeting of stockholders, neither the business to be transacted at nor the purpose of the meeting need be specified in the waiver of notice of such meeting. Attendance of a person either in person or by proxy, at any meeting shall constitute a waiver of notice of such meeting, except where a person attends a meeting for the express purpose of objecting to the transaction of any business because the meeting was not lawfully called or convened.

Section 5. <u>Disallowed Compensation</u>: Any payments made to an officer or employee of the corporation such as a salary, commission, bonus, interest, rent, travel or entertainment expense incurred by him, which shall be disallowed in whole or in part as a deductible expense by the Internal Revenue Service, shall be reimbursed by such officer or employee to the corporation to the full extent of such disallowance. It shall be the duty of the directors, as a Board, to enforce payment of each such amount disallowed. In lieu of payment by the officer or employee, subject to the determination of the directors, proportionate amounts may be withheld from his future compensation payments until the amount owed to the corporation has been recovered.

Section 6. <u>Resignations</u>: Any director or other officer may resign at anytime, such resignation to be in writing, and to take effect from the time of its receipt by the corporation, unless some time be fixed in the resignation and then from that date. The acceptance of a resignation shall not be required to make it effective.

ARTICLE X - ANNUAL STATEMENT

Section 1. The President and Board of Directors shall present at each annual meeting a full and complete statement of the business and affairs of the corporation for the preceding year. Such statement shall be prepared and presented in whatever manner the Board of Directors shall deem advisable and need not be verified by a certified public accountant.

ARTICLE XI - AMENDMENTS

Section 1. These By-Laws may be amended or repealed by the vote of stockholders entitled to cast at least a majority of the votes which all stockholders are entitled to cast thereon, at any regular or special meeting of the stockholders, duly convened after notice to the stockholders of that purpose.

Form 2.8

7.   Minutes of the Corporation

Minutes are the formalized records of the corporation reflecting the major decision-making of the company in written form. Standardized corporate kits usually have blank minutes pages and other specialized minutes formats. Examples of these minutes documents are included in the exercises below. As in all record keeping, the minutes should be an accurate image of the business activities of the corporation. Minutes can be formally transcribed from audio or video sources, can be the result of some shorthand technique of transcription or a composite narrative as long as the picture painted is accurate. Minutes are kept, not only of board activities, special meetings and other matters, but also of the original incorporators.

A.   Objectives

   (1)   To learn about the requirements of minutes and the general standards which accompany their reproduction; and

   (2)   To make a list of companies that make standardized minutes forms available.

B.   Student Obligations

   (1)   To complete standardized minutes forms employing specific fact patterns.

C.   Instructor Obligations

   (1)   To provide local forms if necessary; and

   (2)   To point out jurisdictional differences.

D.   Time Allotted: 1.5 hours

E.   Value of Assignment: 15.0 points

ASSIGNMENT #7 — PART 1
MINUTES OF INCORPORATORS

FACT PATTERN

Date of Organizational Meeting: April 15, 1989, at 10 a.m.
Meeting Location: The Hayward Building, Packard and Bell Sts., Philadelphia, PA 19006
Chairman: John F. Lewindowski
Secretary: Anthony Robertson
Incorporators: John F. Lewindowski; Jacqueline Casper
Elected Board Members: Anthony Antonelli; Michelle Eyler; Kristin Kretzler; John Michalka

COMPLETE THE STANDARDIZED MINUTES AT *FORM 2.9*.

MINUTES OF ORGANIZATION MEETING OF
INCORPORATORS

The organization meeting of the incorporators was held on the   day of   at   o'clock . M.,

pursuant to a written waiver of notice, signed by all the incorporators fixing said time and place.

The following incorporators were present in person:

being all of the incorporators of the corporation.

acted as Chairman and

was appointed Secretary of the meeting.

The Chairman announced that a Certificate of Incorporation had been issued to this corporation by the Department of State and that a certified copy of the Certificate had been forwarded for recording in the Office of the Recorder of Deeds and instructed the Secretary to cause a copy of the Certificate of Incorporation to be prefixed to the minutes.

Upon motion, duly made, seconded and carried, it was

RESOLVED, That the Certificate of Incorporation of the corporation be and it hereby is accepted and that this corporation proceed to do business thereunder.

The Secretary presented a form of By-Laws for the regulation of the affairs of the corporation, which were read article by article.

Upon motion, duly made, seconded and carried, said By-Laws were unanimously adopted and the Secretary was instructed to cause the same to be inserted in the minute book immediately following the copy of the Certificate of Incorporation.

The Chairman stated that the next business before the meeting was the election of a Board of Directors.

were nominated for directors of the corporation, to hold office for the ensuing year and until others are chosen and qualified in their stead. No other nominations having been made, the vote was taken and the aforesaid nominees declared duly elected.

Upon motion, duly made, seconded and carried, it was

RESOLVED, That the Board of Directors be and they are hereby authorized to issue the capital stock of this corporation to the full amount or number of shares authorized by the Certificate of Incorporation, in such amounts and proportions as from time to time shall be determined by the Board, and to accept in full or in part payment thereof such property as the Board may determine shall be good and sufficient consideration and necessary for the business of the corporation.

Upon motion, duly made, seconded and carried, the meeting thereupon adjourned.

_____
Secretary of the meeting

Form 2.9

ASSIGNMENT #7 — PART 2
MINUTES OF INITIAL MEETING OF BOARD OF DIRECTORS

FACT PATTERN

Date: May 29, 1989, at 10 a.m.
Present: Barthold Brizee; James Denane; Lewis Algonquin; Charles P. Nemeth, Esquire
Chairman: Charles P. Nemeth, Esquire
Secretary: Michelle Kretzler
Officers: President, Michael Kapilli; Vice President, Douglas McDonald; Treasurer, Joseph Graff; Secretary, Robert Aluski
Seal: Nembar Enterprises
Paid in Capital in Exchange for Shares: $25,000; split evenly amongst all directors

COMPLETE THE STANDARDIZED MINUTES AT *FORM 2.10*.

MINUTES OF FIRST MEETING OF

THE BOARD OF DIRECTORS

The first meeting of the Board of Directors was held

at

on the   day of   at   o'clock   M.

          Present:

constituting a quorum of the Board.

                              acted as Chairman and

was appointed temporary Secretary of the meeting.

          The Secretary presented and read a waiver of notice of

the meeting, signed by all the directors.

The minutes of the organization meeting of incorporators were read and approved.

The following persons were nominated to the offices set opposite their respective names, to serve for one year and until their successors are chosen and qualify:

All the directors present having voted, the Chairman announced that the aforesaid had been unanimously chosen as said officers, respectively.

The President thereupon took the chair and the Secretary thereupon entered upon the discharge of his duties.

Upon motion, duly made, seconded and carried, it was

RESOLVED, That the stock certificates of this corporation shall be in the form submitted at this meeting.

Upon motion, duly made, seconded and carried, it was

RESOLVED, That the
seal, an impression of which
is herewith affixed, be adopted
as the corporate seal of this
corporation.

The Secretary was authorized and directed to procure the proper corporate books.

Upon motion, duly made, seconded and carried, it was

RESOLVED, That the officers of this corporation be authorized and directed to open a bank account in the name of the corporation, in accordance with a form of bank resolution attached to the minutes of this meeting.

Upon motion, duly made, seconded and carried, the following preambles and resolutions were unanimously adopted:

WHEREAS, The following offer has been made to the corporation in consideration of the issuance of full paid and non-assessable shares of the corporation:

WHEREAS, In the judgment of this Board of Directors of this corporation, said offer is good and sufficient consideration for the shares demanded therefor and necessary for the business of this corporation,

Now, therefore, be it

RESOLVED, That the aforesaid offer be and hereby accepted and that the President and Secretary of this corporation be and they hereby are authorized and directed to execute in the name and on behalf of this corporation, and under its corporate seal, such agreement or agreements as may be necessary in accordance with said offer

FURTHER RESOLVED, That the President and Secretary be and they hereby are authorized and directed to issue and deliver in accordance with said offer certificates of full paid and non-assessable shares of this corporation to the said

Upon motion, duly made, seconded and carried, it was

RESOLVED, That in compliance with the laws of the

State of Delaware, this corporation have and continuously maintain a registered office within the State of Delaware and have an agent at all times in charge thereof, upon which agent process against this corporation may be served, and that the books and records of the corporation shall be available for examination by any stockholder for any proper purpose as provided by law.

Upon motion, duly made, seconded and carried, it was

RESOLVED, That the proper officers of the corporation be and they hereby are authorized and directed on behalf of the corporation, and under its corporate seal, to make and file such certificate, report or other instrument as may be required by law to be filed in any state, territory, or dependency of the United States, or in any foreign country, in which said officers shall find it necessary or expedient to file the same to authorize the corporation to transact business in such state, territory, dependency or foreign country.

Upon motion, duly made, seconded and carried, it was

RESOLVED, That the Treasurer be and hereby is authorized to pay all fees and expenses incident to and necessary for the organization of the corporation.

There being no further business, the meeting upon motion adjourned.

_____
                                    Secretary

Form 2.10

ASSIGNMENT #7 — PART 3
QUESTIONS REGARDING INFORMATION IN MINUTES

TO INSURE A CLOSE READING OF THE STANDARDIZED MINUTES FORMS, STU-DENTS ARE REQUIRED TO ANSWER THE QUESTIONS AT *FORM 2.11* AND SUBMIT THOSE ANSWERS TO THE INSTRUCTOR.

MINUTES QUESTIONNAIRE

Regarding the minutes of the organizational meeting of incorporators, answer the following:

1. Can notice of the organizational meeting of the incorporators be waived?
    ☐ Yes   ☐ No

2. What is the term of office for the board of directors?
    _____

3. Who is authorized to issue capital stock?
    _____

4. What does it mean that capital stock can serve as good and sufficient consideration?
    _____

5. What party generally signs and attests to the validity of the minutes?
    _____

- -

Regarding the Board of Directors initial meeting, answer the following:

1. Do minutes need to be approved?   ☐ Yes   ☐ No

2. What is done with stock certificates at the original meeting?
    _____

3. What is a seal or impression of a corporation?_____
    _____

4. Who is in charge of the corporate books?_____
    _____

5. What is paid in exchange for shares?_____
    _____

6. Who is authorized to formalize and execute agreements?_____
    _____

7. At what location will the records of the corporation be provided for the purposes of examination?
    _____
    _____

8. Who is empowered to pay all fees and expenses?_____
    _____

Form 2.11

ASSIGNMENT #7 — PART 4
SPECIAL MEETING OF THE BOARD OF DIRECTORS: MINUTES

Special meetings are permissible under the by-laws of most corporations. With notice or appropriate waiver, a special meeting can be held to discuss specialized forms of business of the enterprise.

REVIEW THE MINUTES AT *FIGURE 2.7* AND RESPOND TO THE QUESTIONS BELOW.

MINUTES OF A SPECIAL MEETING OF
THE BOARD OF DIRECTORS

A special meeting of the Board of Directors was held on the   day of   , at   o'clock .M., at

pursuant to written waiver of notice thereof signed by all the directors, fixing said time and place.

acted as Chairman and served as Secretary of the meeting.

The Chairman announced that the following Directors constituting the full Board of Directors of this corporation, were present:

The Chairman stated that the purpose of the meeting was to consider the adoption of a resolution to authorize the proper officers of the corporation to take the necessary steps to implement the election of the shareholders to have the corporation taxed under Subchapter S of the Internal Revenue Code.

Upon, motion, duly made, seconded and carried, the following preamble and resolution were unanimously adopted:

WHEREAS it is deemed advisable and to the advantage of the shareholders that this corporation be taxed under Subchapter S of the Internal Revenue Code,

Now, therefore, be it

RESOLVED, That the proper officer or officers of the corporation are hereby authorized and directed to obtain the necessary consents from the shareholders and file the same, together with such other papers and forms as may be required with the District Director of Internal Revenue, in order to permit the corporation to be taxed under Subchapter S of the Internal Revenue Code.

There being no further business, the meeting upon motion adjourned.

_____
                                            Secretary

Figure 2.7

1. Why is this special meeting being held?_____
    _____
    _____

2. Why would a corporation choose to become Subchapter S?_____
    _____
    _____

3. If the choice to become Subchapter S is affirmative, what steps must be taken?_____
    _____
    _____

4. Do these minutes reflect any other form of business?_____
    _____
    _____

5. How can you prove this was the chosen course of corporate action?_____
    _____
    _____

8. Waivers and Resolutions

Much of the work of a business corporation is very formal. This is especially evident in larger corporations where annual meetings, shareholder meetings and special meetings are required by internal regulation and statute. Some of the forms and documentation in the exercises below are regularly completed by practitioners in the area of business law. Included is the documentation necessary to waive notice of the attendance as well as the forms necessary if the decision is to hold no meeting at all. The similarities between these forms and documents is obvious, but the corporate record books must reflect adherence to the regulatory environment. Parties, such as shareholders who question this extraordinary corporate act, should be satisfied with these standardized, yet fully legal waivers.

Resolutions are evidence of specific board action. The board RESOLVES, usually in written form, that which it chooses to do. Some examples of resolution problems are included in these exercises as well.

- A. Objectives

    - (1) To learn about the techniques of waiver and notice of the holding of meetings; and

    - (2) To see the impact of a resolution upon board action.

- B. Student Obligations

    - (1) To prepare waivers; and

    - (2) To prepare resolutions.

- C. Instructor Obligations

    - (1) To point out local differences; and

    - (2) To provide whatever forms necessary to adhere to local guidelines.

- D. Time Allotted: 1.5 hours

- E. Value of Assignment: 10.0 points

ASSIGNMENT #8 — PART 1
WAIVER OF NOTICE: FIRST MEETING OF BOARD OF DIRECTORS

FACT PATTERN

Date: July 18, 1989
Place of Meeting: Luau Hotel, Honolulu, Hawaii 99888
Time of Meeting: December 23, 1989, at 4 p.m.

COMPLETE *FORM 2.12* BASED ON THE ABOVE FACTS.

WAIVER OF NOTICE
FIRST MEETING OF THE BOARD OF DIRECTORS

WE, THE UNDERSIGNED, being the directors elected by the incorporators of the above named corporation, DO HEREBY WAIVE NOTICE of the time, place and purpose of the first meeting of the Board of Directors of said corporation.

We designate the   day of   at   o'clock   .M. as the time and

as the place of said meeting; the purpose of said meeting being to elect officers, authorize the issue of the capital stock, authorize the purchase of property if necessary for the business of the corporation, and the transaction of such other business as may be necessary or advisable to facilitate and complete the organization of said corporation, and to enable it to carry on its contemplated business.

Dated:

Form 2.12

ASSIGNMENT #8 — PART 2
WAIVER OF NOTICE: SPECIAL MEETING OF THE BOARD OF DIRECTORS

FACT PATTERN

Date: July 29, 1989
Designation of Special Meeting Date: November 11, 1989, at 9 a.m.
Place of Meeting: Fort Dodge Rd., Fort Dodge, Kansas 66666

COMPLETE *FORM 2.13*.

WAIVER OF NOTICE

SPECIAL MEETING OF THE BOARD OF DIRECTORS

WE, THE UNDERSIGNED, being the directors elected by the stockholders of the above named corporation, DO HEREBY WAIVE NOTICE of the time, place and purpose of a special meeting of the Board of Directors of said corporation.

We designate the   day of   at   o'clock   M. as the time, and

as the place of said meeting; the purpose of said meeting being the adoption of a resolution providing for the corporation to elect to be taxed as a tax option corporation under Subchapter S of the Internal Revenue Code.

Dated:

Form 2.13

ASSIGNMENT #8 — PART 3
UNANIMOUS CONSENT WITH RESOLUTIONS
IN LIEU OF FIRST MEETING OF BOARD OF DIRECTORS

FACT PATTERN

Officers Appointed: President, John Regina; Vice President, Joseph Aloysius; Secretary, Anne Marie Hugonot; Treasurer, Stephen Charles
Impression: Nembar Seal
Shares Issued: 2,250 to John Regina; 2,250 to Joseph Aloysius; 750 to Anne Marie Hugonot; 750 to Stephen Charles
Date: April 15, 1989

COMPLETE *FORM 2.14.*

UNANIMOUS CONSENT IN LIEU OF
FIRST MEETING OF BOARD OF DIRECTORS

THE UNDERSIGNED, being all of the directors of the above named corporation,   hereby adopt the following resolutions:

RESOLVED, That the following persons be appointed to the offices set opposite their respective names, to serve for one year and until their successors are chosen and qualify:

RESOLVED, That the stock certificates of this corporation shall be in the form submitted.

RESOLVED, That the seal, an impression of which is herewith affixed, be adopted as the corporate seal of this corporation.

RESOLVED, That the Secretary is hereby authorized and directed to procure the proper corporate books, and the Treasurer be and is hereby authorized and directed to pay all fees and expenses incident to and necessary for the organization of the corporation.

WHEREAS any individual or partnership holding original issue common shares in a domestic small business corporation will benefit under the provisions of Section 1244 of the Internal Revenue Code in the event that their shares are disposed of at a loss or become worthless, by having the loss considered an ordinary loss up to $50,000.00 per taxable year ($100,000.00 on a joint return), and

WHEREAS a small business corporation is defined as one in which the aggregate amount of money and other property received by the corporation for stock, as a contribution to capital and as paid in surplus, does not exceed $1,000,000.00; and the corporation has derived more than 50% of its gross income for the five most recent taxable years from sources other than royalties, rents, dividends, interest, annuities or gains from the sale of securities;

RESOLVED, That in order for the shareholders of the corporation to enjoy the benefits of Section 1244 of the Internal Revenue Code of 1954, the proper officers of the corporation are hereby directed to issue the shares of the corporation in such manner as to comply with the conditions of Section 1244 and to see that all the required records are maintained and the share certificates are marked "Section 1244 Shares."

RESOLVED, That the officers of this corporation be authorized and directed to open a bank account in the name of the corporation, in accordance with a form of bank resolution attached to these minutes.

RESOLVED, That full paid and non-assessable shares of the corporation be issued as follows:

which is good and sufficient consideration for the shares demanded therefor and necessary for the business of this corporation

FURTHER RESOLVED, That the President and Secretary be and they are hereby authorized and directed to issue and deliver certificates of full paid and non-assessable shares of this corporation to the said parties.

RESOLVED, That in compliance with the laws of the State of Delaware, this corporation have and continuously maintain a registered office within this state and have an agent at all times in charge thereof, upon which agent process against this corporation may be served, and that the books and records of the corporation shall be available for examination by any stockholder for any proper purpose as provided by law.

RESOLVED, That the proper officers of the corporation be and they hereby are authorized and directed on behalf of the corporation, and under its corporate seal, to make and file such certificate, report or other instrument as may be required by law to be filed in any state, territory, or dependency of the United States, or in any foreign country, in which said officers shall find it necessary or expedient to file the same to authorize the corporation to transact business in such state, territory, dependency or foreign country.

Dated:

ASSIGNMENT #8 — PART 4
ANNUAL MEETING FOR SHAREHOLDERS: RESOLUTION

FACT PATTERN

Purposes: To determine the acquisition of Beezer Enterprises

Notice: Secretary of corporation to give: not less than 10 days nor more than 40 days before date of meeting.

Name of Corporation: Airlog Enterprises, Inc.

Date of Meeting: September 1, 1989

Location: 402 Monument Street, Baltimore, MD 20111

Record Date of Shareholder Voting Rights: August 1, 1989

Notice Requirement for Shareholder Voting Rights: August 10, 1989

COMPLETE THE RESOLUTION AT *FORM 2.15.*

RESOLUTION

RESOLVED, that the annual meeting of the shareholders of _____ will be held at _____ on, 19_____, at _____ _____.M.

RESOLVED FURTHER, that the record date for determination of shareholders entitled to vote at the meeting is _____, 19_____.

RESOLVED FURTHER, that the purposes of such meeting of which the shareholders should be notified are:

_____
_____
_____
_____

RESOLVED FURTHER, that_____is hereby instructed to send the shareholders a notice of the annual meeting not later than _____, 19_____.

RESOLVED FURTHER, that a call of the annual meeting, a copy of which is attached to these minutes as Exhibit A and incorporated herein, be sent to the Secretary of the corporation.

CALL OF ANNUAL SHAREHOLDERS' MEETING

TO: _____

Secretary of _____

The 19_____ annual meeting of the shareholders of_____is hereby called by the Board of Directors to be held at_____, on _____, 19_____, at _____ _____.M., for the purposes of _____

The record date for determination of shareholders entitled to vote at the meeting is _____ _____, 19_____. Notice of the meeting should be sent to the shareholders of record on that date not later than _____, 19_____.

Dated: _____, 19_____.

Form 2.15

ASSIGNMENT #8: PART 5
RESOLUTION: PAYMENT OF SHARES FOR LAND

FACT PATTERN

Time of Transaction: November 10, 1987
Tract of Land: Burrus Land Tract, Lot 1, Lot 2, Buxton, NC
Transferred To: Hatteras Storms, Inc.
Amount of Shares: 2,000
Chairman of the Board: President of Hatteras Storms, Inc.
Signatories: Chairman of the Board and Secretary

COMPLETE THE RESOLUTION AT *FORM 2.16*.

RESOLUTION

Form 2.16

ASSIGNMENT #8 — PART 6
RESOLUTION: CHECKING ACCOUNT

FACT PATTERN

Corporate Name: King of Nails, Inc., 1418 Sampson St., Arco, TX 55533
Signatories: Secretary, Treasurer
Date: Use today's date
Purpose: To open up a checking account

COMPLETE THE RESOLUTION AT *FORM 2.17*.

<u>RESOLUTION</u>

Form 2.17

ASSIGNMENT #8 — PART 7
RESOLUTION: APPOINTMENT OF OFFICER

FACT PATTERN

Company: E.I. Dravo Corporation

Purpose of Resolution: To appoint Bartholomew Jacobs as Chief Executive Officer and Vice President of Corporation

Term of Years: 2

Compensation: $60,000 per annum

COMPLETE THE RESOLUTION AT *FORM 2.18.*

RESOLUTION

Form 2.18

9.   Stock Record Keeping

Professionals in business administration and record keeping must safeguard the distribution of shares since the documents manifest an enforceable ownership in the corporation. Additionally, those in-house shares must be rigorously accounted for. A share is a fractional portion of ownership in a corporation. A share certificate is below at *Figure 2.8*.

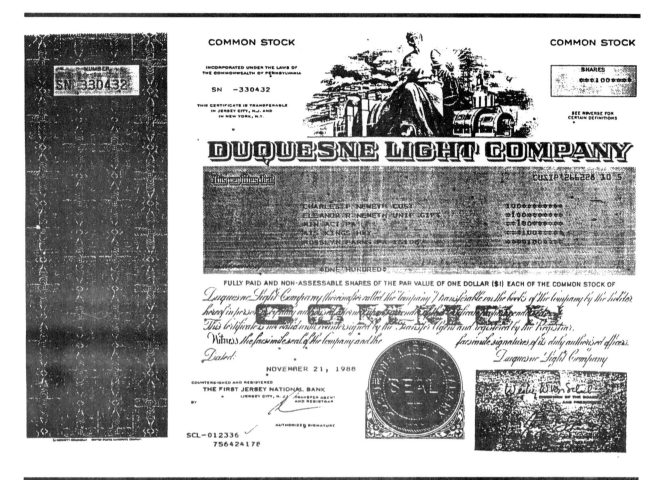

Figure 2.8

A.   Objectives

   (1)   To become familiar with the components of a share stock certificate; and

   (2)   To become aware of the transfer and ledger formats available for tracking the issuance and retention of shares.

B.   Student Obligations

   (1)   To fill out a share certificate, transfer ledger and cancelled certificate; and

   (2)   To become familiar with the abbreviations utilized in the authorship of shares.

C.   Instructor Obligations

   (1)   To point out local differences in the completion of share certificates and transfer ledgers; and

   (2)   To insure that students have correct forms given the local jurisdiction.

D.   Time Allotted: 1.0 hours

E.   Value of Assignment: 10.0 points

ASSIGNMENT #9 — PART 1
SHARE CERTIFICATE

FACT PATTERN

Owner of Certificate: William R. O'Donnell
President of Corporation: Adeline Formosa
Secretary: Bridgette Nelson
Date of Corporate Attestation: February 12, 1989
*Amount of Shares: 4,000
*Note that there are two locations for that notation.

COMPLETE THE SHARE CERTIFICATE AT *FORM 2.19*.

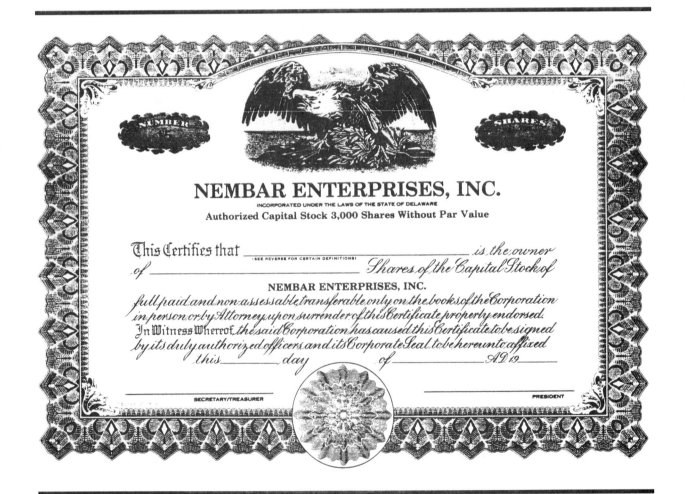

Form 2.19

ASSIGNMENT #9 — PART 2
TRANSFER OF SHARE CERTIFICATE

FACT PATTERN

Social Security No.:   222-33-3333
Date: July 1, 1994
Witnessed By: Anna Connelly
Transfer Agent: Continental Trust
Transferred To: Regina Romulus

COMPLETE THE REVERSE SIDE OF A STOCK CERTIFICATE AT *FORM 2.20.*

The following abbreviations, when used in the inscription on the face of this certificate, shall be construed as though they were written out in full according to applicable laws or regulations:

TEN COM—as tenants in common
TEN ENT —as tenants by the entireties
JT TEN —as joint tenants with right of survivorship
    and not as tenants in common

UNIF GIFT MIN ACT—..........Custodian..........under
            (Cust)   (Minor)
Uniform Gifts to Minors Act..............
               (State)

Additional abbreviations may also be used though not in the above list.

For Value Received,____ hereby sell, assign and transfer unto

PLEASE INSERT SOCIAL SECURITY OR OTHER
IDENTIFYING NUMBER OF ASSIGNEE

Shares represented by the within Certificate, and do hereby irrevocably constitute and appoint _____ Attorney to transfer the said Shares on the books of the within named Corporation with full power of substitution in the premises.
Dated _____ 19 ___
In presence of

NOTICE. THE SIGNATURE OF THIS ASSIGNMENT MUST CORRESPOND WITH THE NAME AS WRITTEN UPON THE FACE OF THE CERTIFICATE, IN EVERY PARTICULAR, WITHOUT ALTERATION OR ENLARGEMENT, OR ANY CHANGE WHATEVER.

Form 2.20

ASSIGNMENT #9 — PART 3
ADDITIONAL QUESTIONS

1. Assume that Gerald Connelly was married to Marie Connelly and wished to share equally the value of these shares. How would his and her names be so designated?_____

_____

What initials would be employed?_____

_____

2. Assume that two brothers, William and Stephen Shopley wish to own the shares jointly. What designations would be appropriate?_____

_____

What initials would be employed?_____

_____

3. Assume that stock had been given to a child six years of age. The child's name is Anna Reynolds. How would evidence of her ownership be so designated?_____

_____

What abbreviations would be employed?_____

_____

ASSIGNMENT #9 — PART 4
RECORDING CANCELLED CERTIFICATES

Shares which are transferred to others as evidenced in the assignment above eventually come back to the corporate secretary for record keeping. The form at *Form 2.21* is the customary and efficient way of affixing cancelled certificates.

FACT PATTERN

Amount of Shares: 2,000
Originally Issued to: Roberta Flaunders
Date Originally Issued: September 1, 1956
Original Certificate No.: 49
Number of Original Shares: 2,000
Number of Shares Transferred: 2,000
Transferror: Roberta Flaunders
Date of Transfer: July 1, 1987
Corporate Receives Back: Same certificate
Certificate Issued To: Wanda Fleming, 1189 Rondo Way, Rondo, NC 88844

ASSUME THESE FACTS TO COMPLETE *FORM 2.21*.

PASTE CANCELLED CERTIFICATE IN THIS SPACE

CERTIFICATE No. **15**_____

FOR _____ SHARES

ISSUED TO

_____

_____

_____

DATED_____ 19 ___

RECEIVED CERTIFICATE No._____

FOR _____ SHARES

THIS _____ DAY OF_____ 19___

_____

_____

_____

_____

TRANSFER FROM ORIGINAL ISSUE BELOW		
FROM WHOM TRANSFERRED:		

DATED _____ 19___

NO. ORIGINAL CERTIFICATE	NO. ORIGINAL SHARES	NO. OF SHARES TRANSFERRED

TRANSFER DETAILS FOR SURRENDERED CERTIFICATES		
NEW CERTIFICATES ISSUED TO:	NO. OF SHARES TRANSFERRED	NO. OF NEW CERTIFICATES

Form 2.21

10.   Dissolution and Liquidation

Corporations can be perpetual in nature but, due to economic, political and human circumstances, frequently need to be dissolved or liquidated. Dissolution can be voluntary or involuntary. Dissolution often occurs as a result of a judicial order or because the parties who originally founded the business have no further desire to continue it. Change of economic circumstances often causes this event to take place. The exercises below highlight the documentation and statutory requirements of a decision to dissolve.

A.   Objectives

   (1)   To become familiar with the dissolution process of the corporation.

B.   Student Obligations

   (1)   To prepare a certificate of election to dissolve;

   (2)   To prepare articles of dissolution; and

   (3)   To prepare a resolution of shareholders to dissolve the corporation.

C.   Instructor Obligations

   (1)   To provide guidance and insight into local aspects of a dissolution process; and

   (2)   To provide whatever forms are necessary to complete these tasks.

D.   Time Allotted: 1.0 hours

E.   Value of Assignment: 10.0 points

ASSIGNMENT #10 — PART 1
CERTIFICATE OF ELECTION TO DISSOLVE

FACT PATTERN

Registered Agent's Office: CRC, Inc., 946 Bathwain, Avella, NY 14666

Names and Addresses of Officers: John Jacobs, 11 Tenway St., New York, NY, President; Phillip Harris, 139 Longstreth Rd., Long Island, NY, Vice President; Mary Dickerson, 14 Sewickley Ave., St. Johns, NY, Treasurer; Artemis Johnson, 46 Bodin St., Syracuse, NY, Secretary.

Names and Addresses of Directors: same

Outstanding Number of Shares: 12,000

Dissolution decided by: Resolution

Name of Corporation: Jamestown Enterprises, Inc.

COMPLETE THE CERTIFICATE OF ELECTION TO DISSOLVE AT *FORM 2.22*.

CERTIFICATE OF ELECTION TO DISSOLVE

Filing Fee: $ _____

Filed this _____ day of _____
_____, 19_____

CORPORATION BUREAU
DEPARTMENT OF STATE

This undersigned corporation desiring to elect to dissolve, hereby certifies that:

1. The name of the corporation is:

_____

2. The address of the registered office of the corporation is:

_____

(Number)   (Street)

_____

(City)   (State)   (Zip Code)

3. The names and addresses including street and number and official title of its officers are:

NAME   ADDRESS   OFFICIAL TITLE

_____

_____

_____

_____

4. The names and addresses, including street and number of its directors are:

NAME   ADDRESS

_____

_____

_____

5. (Check, and if appropriate, complete one of the following):

_____ All shareholders of record signed personally or by their duly authorized attorneys an agreement consenting to the dissolution.

_____ A resolution recommending that the corporation be dissolved was adopted by the shareholders at a meeting held in accordance with law.

(1) At the time of the action of the shareholders
(i) The total number of shares outstanding was:

_____

Form 2.22

ASSIGNMENT #10 — PART 2
ARTICLES OF DISSOLUTION

FACT PATTERN

Secretary: Mary Allison
Name of Corporation: Rondo Enterprises, Inc.
President: Harvey Popile
Current State of Litigation: None
Current State of Debt: Not sufficient equity to satisfy and discharge debts
Certificate of Election Filed: June 1, 1989
Registered Office: CTI International, 1115 Shumway St., Marietta, GA 44406

COMPLETE THE ARTICLES OF DISSOLUTION AT *FORM 2.23*.

CERTIFICATE OF ELECTION TO DISSOLVE

Filing Fee: $_____

Filed this _____ day of _____, 19 _____

CORPORATION BUREAU
DEPARTMENT OF STATE

This undersigned corporation desiring to dissolve, does hereby certify that

1. The name of the corporation is:

_____

2. The address of the registered office of the corporation is:

_____
(Number)   (Street)

_____
(City)   (State)   (Zip Code)

3. The corporation has heretofore delivered to the Department of State a Certificate of Election to Dissolve, which was filed by the Department on_____.

4. (Check one the following):

_____ All debts, obligations and liabilities of the corporation have been paid and discharged.

_____ Adequate provision has been made for the payment of the debts, obligations and liabilities of the corporation.

_____ The property and assets of the corporation are not sufficient to satisfy and discharge its debts, obligations and liabilities, and all the property and assets of the corporation have been fairly and equitably applied, as far as they will go, to their payment.

5. All remaining property and assets of the corporation have been distributed among its shareholders, in accordance with their respective rights and interests.

6. (Check one of the following):

_____ There are no actions pending against the corporation in any court.

_____ Adequate provision has been made for the satisfaction of any judgment or decree which may be obtained against the corporation in each action pending against the corporation.

7. Notice of the winding-up proceedings of the corporation was mailed by certified or registered mail to each municipality in which the corporation's registered office or principal place of business is located.

IN TESTIMONY WHEREOF, the undersigned corporation has caused these Articles of Dissolution to be signed by a duly authorized officer and its corporate seal, duly attested by another such officer, to be hereunto affixed this _____ day of _____, 19_____.

_____
(Name of Corporation)

By: _____
(Signature)

_____
(Title)

Attest

_____
(Signature)

_____
(Title)

(Corporate Seal)

INSTRUCTIONS FOR COMPLETION OF FORM

A. Proof of advertising required and tax clearance certificates from the Department of Revenue and from the Bureau of Employment Security of the Department of Labor and Industry (evidencing payment of all taxes and charges) must be submitted with this form.

B. Any necessary governmental approvals shall accompany this form.

Form 2.23

ASSIGNMENT #10 — PART 3
SHAREHOLDERS' RESOLUTION TO DISSOLVE

FACT PATTERN

Name of Corporation: Reston Corporation
Address of Corporation: 4562 Boulder Lane, Salem, Ohio 45362
Signatories: John Lewis, President; Nancy Conners, Secretary
Resolution Matters: Submit a complete plan of liquidation; authorize plan of distribution of
        assets; approve plan of liquidation; approve dissolution of the corporation.
Address of Meeting: Same as corporate address
Date of Meeting: December 1, 1989

COMPLETE THE RESOLUTION AT *FORM 2.24* USING THE FOLLOWING FACT PATTERN.

RESOLUTION OF SHAREHOLDERS TO DISSOLVE CORPORATION

WHEREAS, at a meeting of the Board of Directors of _____ _____, a _____ corporation, held on _____ _____, 19____, at _____, the Board of Directors adopted resolutions recommending:

By their signatures, the responsible parties acknowledge these actions.

Witness

President

Witness

Secretary

Form 2.24

PRACTICUM EXERCISES NO. 3
CAREERS IN THE LAW

	Time Allotted (hours)	Point Value
Evaluating the Legal Environment: Assignment #1	3.0	30.0
Opportunities in the Legal Environment: Assignment #2 (7 parts)	2.0	20.0
Agencies and Institutions of the Law: Assignment #3 (3 parts)	3.0	30.0
Ethical Concerns and Considerations: Assignment #4 (7 parts)	2.0	20.0
	10.0	100.0

I.
INTRODUCTION

The purpose of this set of exercises is to afford any party who wishes a career in law to become familiar with the environment of a legal practice. Studying from textbooks can never totally or accurately reflect the nature of the legal environment. These exercises will give insight into what the student is getting into if they eventually choose to enter into this career. Additionally, these exercises provide a window to view their career choice — a confirmation or verification of vocational direction. This practice is not uncommon. Other disciplines, including teaching, policing or medical, give the beginning student a preview of the day-to-day work of the profession. After completing this unit, the student will be able to make a more education and intelligent judgment regarding career choice. Prospective paralegals, legal assistants, law clerks, legal secretaries, lawyers and judicial personnel should find these exercises most illuminating.

II.
CAREERS IN THE LAW

1. Evaluating the Legal Environment

To acquire a taste and understanding for the nature of law and its practice, an undertaking essential to choosing the right career path or direction, an extended visitation to a specific legal environment is of great utility. Paralegals and legal assistants, law clerks, legal secretaries, attorneys and persons in related occupations will benefit from an on-site inspection. For various reasons, students may initially balk at the visitation requirement citing workload and the fact that this activity can only be conducted during the day. While there are certain tactical and logistical problems, students should find lawyers, agencies of state, local and federal governments, hospitals and other medical facilities, corporate legal departments, and a whole host of other entities which engage in the practice of law to be cooperative in the after-hours. As an example, students might set up an appointment to visit a law firm or law office during any evening office hours which the firm conducts. Students will also find that the majority of people who are involved in the practice of law are very cooperative and helpful to individuals who desire a career in it. Students will be hard pressed to assert that no agency, entity, law firm or lawyer exists who is willing to assist in the completion of the assignment.

The assignment requires both a visual and analytical evaluation of the legal environment, the place in which career selections become reality, the place in which dreams and ambitions come to the forefront. By reviewing and completing the following document entitled, "Survey of the Legal Environment," the student should leave the experience with a representative idea of what is involved in the practice of law, both from a human and administrative perspective.

Students must exhibit common courtesy when making appointments and follow up any appointments that are granted with written confirmation. It is a good idea as well to call a day or so before the visitation. Students who have ongoing and continuous trouble setting up their visitation schedule should consult directly with the instructor. Permission forms might be needed in certain circumstances, and your institution will provide them. Strongly advised is the pairing of students or the creation of small teams who will work together on the survey outlined below.

Visitations can be conducted at any location that is involved in the practice of law from the law firm and law office to a government agency or even a prison legal staff. Be creative and do not feel constrained in choice of location or area of practice.

A. Objectives

    (1) To become familiar with and comfortable with some typical legal environments; and

    (2) To determine whether or not career choice and direction is a sensible choice after an examination of a law firm, government agency or other entity which engages in the practice of law.

B. Student Obligations

    (1) To identify a specific legal environment which will cooperate in the completion of this assignment;

    (2) To set up an appointment and visitation schedule for the purposes of examining a legal environment; and

    (3) To complete the "Survey of the Legal Environment" questionnaire.

C. Instructor Obligations

    (1) To assist students in locating a firm, agency, business or industrial legal department or other entity which will permit students both a visitation and the opportunity to complete the "Survey of the Legal Environment";

    (2) To provide whatever permission forms are needed; and

    (3) To provide whatever correspondence, in conjunction with the educational institution, that might be needed to meet the requirements of this assignment.

D. Time Allotted: 3.0 hours

E. Value of Assignment: 30.0 points

ASSIGNMENT #1

COMPLETE THE "SURVEY OF THE LEGAL ENVIRONMENT" AT *FORM 3.1.*

SURVEY OF THE LEGAL ENVIRONMENT

Upon visitation to the legal environment you have selected, please answer the following and submit to your instructor.

1. Name of legal environment:_____

_____

2. Address:_____

_____

3. Phone number:_____

4. Contact person:_____

5. Date of Visitation:_____

6. Time Spent in Visitation:_____

7. Areas of Specialization or Practice:_____

_____

_____

8. Write out impressions of law office or legal environment layout (desk location, file cabinet locations, general environment of the office). Please also draw a diagram of the office.

_____

_____

_____

_____

_____

_____

_____

_____

_____

_____

_____

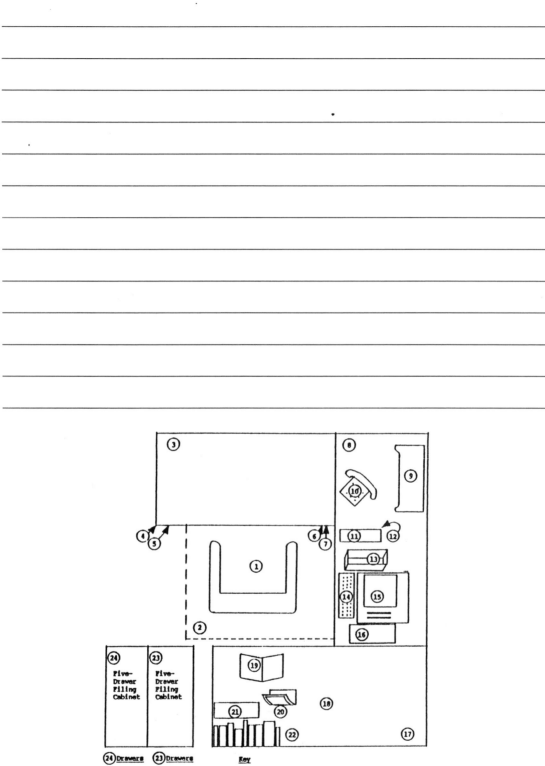

Sample Diagram

Student Diagram

9. Describe in two paragraphs or less what filing system is employed. If possible, attach an example of the filing mechanism.

_____

_____

_____

_____

_____

_____

_____

_____

_____

_____

_____

_____

10. Is there any special equipment employed in the mailing process?_____

_____

_____

11. Does the firm have a technique for reminding itself of special dates? Explain._____

_____

_____

_____

_____

_____

12. What are the areas of practice this agency or firm engages in?_____

_____

_____

_____

_____

_____

_____

_____

_____

_____

_____

_____

13. Is there a coding system that is employed to highlight those areas of practice? If so, provide an outline of that system in the space below.

14. Make a list of all major legal publications at your visitation site. Number each one and give the full name of the series. (Example: Corpus Juris Secundum)_____

15. Ask the interviewee which reference materials are most useful in their daily practice. Also ask why._____

16.   Ask the interviewee for two or three words of wisdom regarding the practice of law. In other words, what does the person you are interviewing perceive to be the most important skills, characteristics or traits in the practice of law?

_____

_____

_____

_____

_____

17.   Does the firm or agency have an initial client information form? If so and if permitted, attach.   ☐ Yes   ☐ No

18.   How are fees calculated?_____

_____

_____

_____

19.   If applicable, does the firm have standardized fee arrangement forms? If so and if permitted, attach.☐ Yes   ☐ No

20.   How are clients billed?_____

21.   Does the firm have standardized forms? If so and if permitted, attach.   ☐ Yes   ☐ No

22.   How does the firm or agency account for time? For example, does it punch all correspondence in? If so, have a punch or rubber stamp placed upon the space provided below.

23.   Does the firm or agency have rubber stamps? If so, and if provided, please name at least five.   ☐ Yes   ☐ No

_____

_____

_____

_____

_____

24. Ask the interviewee, if applicable, how difficult it is to collect fees from clients._____

_____

_____

25. Does it make any difference whether the client wins or loses as regards the collection of fees?_____

_____

_____

26. How are phone calls routinely handled in the firm or agency?_____

_____

_____

_____

27. Devise an administrative flow chart outlining all principal parties and players in the law firm, agency or other entity. List all employees in terms of their hierarchy, commencing with the owners or partners, all the way to the mail clerk.

28. Does the firm or agency have concerns or problems with malpractice claims?   ☐ Yes   ☐ No

29. How costly are malpractice premiums?_____

_____

30. Does the firm, agency or other entity have to be concerned about the fraud or corruptions of other lawyers? How
     so?_____

_____

_____

_____

_____

_____

31. What role does technology play in the general functions of this law firm, agency or other entity? How has it
     assisted?

_____

_____

_____

_____

_____

32. List all high technology equipment currently in use.

_____

_____

_____

_____

_____

_____

_____

_____

_____

_____

33. How are personnel handled in this firm, agency or other entity?_____

_____

_____

_____

34. Who is primarily responsible for the hiring, firing, retention and training of individuals?_____

_____

_____

_____

MISCELLANEOUS

35. Is the interviewee a member of the American Bar Association's Economics of Law Practice Section? ☐ Yes   ☐ No

36. Does the interviewee have a business card file?   ☐ Yes   ☐ No

If so, how is it of use?_____

_____

37. What goes in the in and out box?_____

_____

_____

38. Are file cabinets differentiated by topic or other subject matter?   ☐ Yes   ☐ No

39. Does the firm find useful expandable files?   ☐ Yes   ☐ No

40. Does the firm employ current matter folders?   ☐ Yes   ☐ No

41. Is there a daily letter file?   ☐ Yes   ☐ No

42. Is there a master file?   ☐ Yes   ☐ No

43. What types of activities are deemed non-billable?_____

_____

_____

_____

44. Does the firm, agency or other entity possess a trial manual?   ☐ Yes   ☐ No

45. Does the firm, agency or other entity possess a standard letter binder?   ☐ Yes   ☐ No

46. Does the firm, agency or other entity engage in continuing legal education?   ☐ Yes   ☐ No

47. How are problems of confidentiality handled?_____

_____

_____

_____

48. What system exists to insure adherence to the Statute of Limitations?_____

_____

_____

49. How is billing time kept? By quarters, tenths or other fractional basis?_____

_____

50. Does the interviewee have a business card? If so, attach.

51. Does the firm, agency or other entity have stationery? If so, attach.

SUMMARY:

52. What are the most difficult demands the interviewee indicated in the practice of law?_____

_____

_____

_____

53. What does the interviewee like most about his or her professional activities?_____

_____

_____

_____

54. What does he or she like least?_____

_____

_____

_____

55. Can the interviewee cite any specific ethical concerns he or she has about the legal profession and what roles paralegals and legal assistants play within that ethical scheme?_____

_____

_____

_____

_____

_____

_____

_____

_____

_____

_____

_____

_____

_____

_____

_____

_____

Form 3.1

2. Opportunities in the Legal Environment

The law makes available a whole array of different career opportunities from being a paralegal or legal assistant to a law clerk for a federal district judge. The choice of law as a profession is not a narrow one since there are many lateral and horizontal opportunities within the profession, numerous opportunities to grow, expand and enlarge one's career horizons and certainly avoid severe career track boredom that is common in many positions. To educate the student about the multiple avenues of career pursuit in the law is the function of the exercises that follow. Many things will be accomplished but none more obvious than an awareness, an education, an enlightenment about where positions might exist and what they entail.

A. Objectives

   (1) To become familiar with the many career tracks that are available in the law from paralegalism to judicial personnel;

   (2) To become aware of the various sources that exist for the identification of and tracking of career opportunities in the law; and

   (3) To enumerate and enunciate those factors which make a job more or less attractive after consideration of its requirements and description.

B. Student Obligations

   (1) To research local newspapers identifying specific career positions;

   (2) To perform a self-assessment on a job description to determine whether or not the job meets the needs of the applicant;

   (3) To make a list, chart or diagram which outlines law firms in the area and their level of legal employment; and

   (4) To make a list, chart or diagram which outlines government agencies in the area which employ paralegals and other legal specialists.

C. Instructor Obligations

   (1) To assist the student in identifying agencies, firms, business and industrial concerns and other entities which have interest in the employment of paralegals, legal assistants and other legal specialists; and

   (2) To give some insight into local associations and groups which would assist in career professionalism.

D. Time Allotted: 2.0 hours

E. Value of Assignment: 20.0 points

ASSIGNMENT #2 — PART 1
INVESTIGATING THE NEWSPAPERS

USING A LOCAL NEWSPAPER, CUT OUT AND DESCRIBE IN AS CLOSE DETAIL AS POSSIBLE THE POSITIONS LISTED ON *FORM 3.2.*

POSITION TITLE: Paralegal

CUT OUT
DESCRIPTION
AND ATTACH HERE

Educational Requirements:_____

_____

_____

Experience Requirements:_____

_____

_____

Pay Offered:_____

Other Unique Requirements:_____

_____

_____

_____

POSITION TITLE: Legal Secretary

CUT OUT
DESCRIPTION
AND ATTACH HERE

Educational Requirements:_____

_____

_____

Experience Requirements:_____

_____

_____

_____

Pay Offered:_____

Other Unique Requirements:_____

_____

_____

_____

POSITION TITLE: Law Clerk

CUT OUT
DESCRIPTION
AND ATTACH HERE

Educational Requirements:_____

_____

_____

Experience Requirements:_____

_____

_____

_____

Pay Offered:_____

Other Unique Requirements:_____

_____

_____

_____

POSITION TITLE: Attorney

CUT OUT
DESCRIPTION
AND ATTACH HERE

Educational Requirements:_____

_____

_____

Experience Requirements:_____

_____

_____

_____

Pay Offered:_____

Other Unique Requirements:_____

_____

_____

_____

POSITION TITLE: Court Personnel

CUT OUT
DESCRIPTION
AND ATTACH HERE

Educational Requirements:_____

_____

_____

Experience Requirements:_____

_____

_____

Pay Offered:_____

Other Unique Requirements:_____

_____

_____

_____

POSITION TITLE: Judge or Other Judicial Personnel

CUT OUT
DESCRIPTION
AND ATTACH HERE

Educational Requirements:_____

_____

_____

Experience Requirements:_____

_____

_____

Pay Offered:_____

Other Unique Requirements:_____

_____

_____

_____

Form 3.2

ASSIGNMENT #2 — PART 2

LOCATE A JOB DESCRIPTION FROM ANY SOURCE WHICH IS MOST ATTRACTIVE TO YOU AFTER INITIAL READING. ANALYZE THAT JOB BY COMPLETING THE QUESTIONNAIRE AT *FORM 3.3.*

ATTACH JOB DESCRIPTION TO QUESTIONNAIRE.

1. Has the position description outlined the duties clearly and explicitly?   ☐ Yes ☐ No

2. Does the position appear to be interesting and provide for long-term growth?   ☐ Yes ☐ No

3. Does the position afford one the opportunity to be involved in various legal aspects?   ☐ Yes ☐ No

4. Is the salary sufficient to meet your economic needs?   ☐ Yes ☐ No

5. Does the position afford any opportunity for financial growth?   ☐ Yes ☐ No

6. Are there any benefits payable?   ☐ Yes ☐ No

7. Will the position provide you with high levels of supervision or permit some significant delegation of responsibility?

_____

_____

8. What are the working hours?_____

_____

9. What level of education is required?_____

_____

10. How will you get there?_____

_____

11. Can you outline any advantages or other issues which would make this position more or less attractive?_____

_____

_____

Form 3.3

ASSIGNMENT #2 — PART 3

PROFESSIONAL ASSOCIATIONS AND GROUPS AND THEIR LITERATURE

In your quest for employment, professional associations and groups as well as their literature are most helpful in finding a career position.

USING *FORM 3.4*, LOCATE AT LEAST THREE OF THOSE PROFESSIONAL ORGANIZATIONS

IN YOUR GEOGRAPHIC AREA, THEIR ADDRESSES AND PHONE NUMBERS AND WHETHER OR NOT THEY PROVIDE PLACEMENT ASSISTANCE OR ADVISORY SERVICE OR PROFESSIONAL PUBLICATIONS WHICH WILL ASSIST YOU IN OBTAINING A CAREER POSITION.

PROFESSIONAL ORGANIZATIONS AND GROUPS

Name of Organization:_____

Address:_____

Phone Number:_____

Placement Service?   ☐ Yes   ☐ No

Advisory Information on Career Tracks?   ☐ Yes   ☐ No

Professional Publications Listing Jobs?   ☐ Yes   ☐ No

Name of Publication:_____

Name of Organization:_____

Address:_____

Phone Number:_____

Placement Service?   ☐ Yes   ☐ No

Advisory Information on Career Tracks?   ☐ Yes   ☐ No

Professional Publications Listing Jobs?   ☐ Yes   ☐ No

Name of Publication:_____

Name of Organization:_____

Address:_____

Phone Number:_____

Placement Service?   ☐ Yes   ☐ No

Advisory Information on Career Tracks?   ☐ Yes   ☐ No

Professional Publications Listing Jobs?   ☐ Yes   ☐ No

Name of Publication:_____

Does your local bar association or group have a committee or subcommittee on your particular area of legal endeavor?   ☐ Yes   ☐ No

Name of Organization:_____

Address:_____

Phone Number:_____

Form 3.4

ASSIGNMENT #2 — PART 4

In the field of paralegalism, there is increasing talk about the free-lance aspects of the profession. Free-lancers work for many firms, organizations and entities. Do you think this is a feasible exercise?

POINT OUT FIVE ADVANTAGES AND FIVE DISADVANTAGES OF BEING A FREE-LANCE LEGAL SPECIALIST. *FORM 3.5* IS PROVIDED FOR YOUR USE.

ADVANTAGES:

1. _____

2. _____

3. _____

4. _____

5. _____

DISADVANTAGES:

1. _____

2. _____

3. _____

4. _____

5. _____

Form 3.5

ASSIGNMENT #2 — PART 5
EDUCATION AND TRAINING

OUTLINE IN A LIST AT LEAST THREE ACADEMIC PROGRAMS WHICH PROVIDE THE OPPORTUNITY TO STUDY VARIOUS ASPECTS OF LAW IN YOUR GEOGRAPHIC REGION. USE *FORM 3.6.*

Name of Institution:_____

Address:_____

Field of Study:_____

Name of Institution:_____

Address:_____

Field of Study:_____

Name of Institution:_____

Address:_____

Field of Study:_____

Form 3.6

ASSIGNMENT #2 — PART 6

The diversity of professional opportunities in the law, especially for paralegals and legal assistants, is quite staggering.

COMPLETE THE SURVEY AT *FORM 3.7* INDICATING WHETHER OR NOT JOB OPPORTUNITIES EXIST IN YOUR REGION IN THOSE AGENCIES AND ENTITIES SPECIFIED.

Legal Clinics: ☐ Yes   ☐ No

(For example, Legal Services Corporation)

Name_____

Address_____

Administrative Agencies: ☐ Yes   ☐ No

Name_____

Address_____

Hospitals and Other Medical Facilities: ☐ Yes   ☐ No

Name_____

Address_____

Correctional Facilities: ☐ Yes   ☐ No

Name_____

Address_____

Federal Government: ☐ Yes   ☐ No

Name three agencies.

Name_____

Address_____

Name_____

Address_____

Name_____

Address_____

Office of the Attorney General or District Attorney: ☐ Yes   ☐ No

Name_____

Address_____

State Civil Service Positions: ☐ Yes   ☐ No

Name_____

Address_____

Financial Institutions: ☐ Yes   ☐ No

Name_____

Address_____

Name_____

Address_____

Name_____

Address_____

Businesses and Industrial Concerns: ☐ Yes   ☐ No

Name_____

Address_____

Name_____

Address_____

Name_____

Address_____

Real Estate Companies: ☐ Yes   ☐ No

Name_____

Address_____

Name_____

Address_____

Name_____

Address_____

Prepaid Legal Services: ☐ Yes   ☐ No

Name_____

Address_____

Name_____

Address_____

Name_____

Address_____

Form 3.7

ASSIGNMENT #2 — PART 7

Before you embark in a career in paralegalism it is important to note your expectations. *Form 3.8* is a type of diary which you may wish to come back to repeatedly as you grow and develop in your professional career track.

COMPLETE *FORM 3.8.*

Comment below on what your expectations are as you enter into the field of law.

_____

_____

_____

_____

_____

Name 10 specific expectations you have regarding your chosen career track on matters involving compensation, responsibility, promotion, bonuses or issues of professionalism.

1. _____

2. _____

3. _____

4. _____

5. _____

6. _____

7. _____

8. _____

9. _____

10. _____

Name exactly what positions your initial entry-level position could or should mature into. In other words, will a paralegal or legal assistant eventually become another position, and if so, what?

_____

_____

_____

_____

_____

Form 3.8

3.   Agencies and Institutions of the Law

Persons choosing a legal endeavor for a career should become familiar with the different agencies and institutions of the law. First and foremost, some exposure to the American court system will be of significant interest to legal specialists. To most of the citizenry, the American court is shrouded in mystery and pompous formality. Courts are agencies of the people, places in which civilized men and women choose to adjudicate their claims. They are merely buildings, locations, facilities where people meet and put the law to work.

This series of exercises goes a little bit further since other agencies are highlighted, such as:

— Local, state or federal police departments
— Correctional facilities
— Local, state and federal agencies given the power to enforce law

At the end of these exercises the student should have some appreciation for not only the place and location of agencies or institutions involved in the law but also a sense or feeling of comfort that these institutions exist to serve society and not themselves. Of most importance in these exercises is the opportunity actually to visualize, inspect and visit a courtroom, to see it in action and to gain awareness of how the adversarial system in American justice operates.

A.   Objectives

(1)   To become familiar with the local agencies and institutions of law.

B.   Student Obligations

(1)   To perform a site visitation at a selected agency or institution of law;

(2)   To become familiar with the judicial system presently in place in the student's jurisdiction; and

(3)   To observe, analyze and write about the adversarial system in actual operation.

C.   Instructor Obligations

(1)   To assist the students in finding and locating local courts of jurisdiction; and

(2)   To provide students with permission slips and other forms and documents necessary for admittance into institutions or agencies of the law.

D.   Time Allotted: 3.0 hours

E.   Value of Assignment: 30.0 points

ASSIGNMENT #3 — PART 1
CHARTING THE COURT SYSTEM

USING *FIGURE 3.2*, THE WYOMING COURT SYSTEM, AS AN EXAMPLE, TRACK AND CHART THE COURT SYSTEM OF YOUR JURISDICTION. DO NOT FEEL THAT THE SYSTEM OF BLOCKS, NAMES OR DESIGNATIONS MUST BE ADHERED TO GIVEN LOCAL AND JURISDICTIONAL DIFFERENCES. USE YOUR OWN STATIONERY TO COMPLETE THIS ASSIGNMENT.

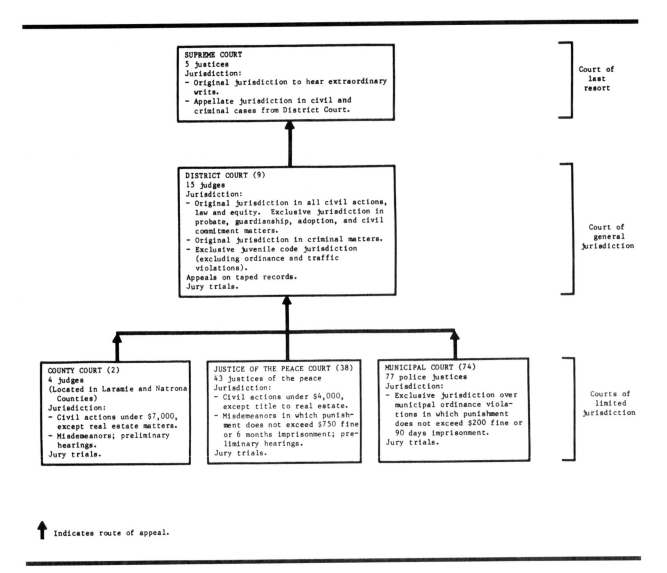

SUPREME COURT
5 justices
Jurisdiction:
- Original jurisdiction to hear extraordinary writs.
- Appellate jurisdiction in civil and criminal cases from District Court.

Court of last resort

DISTRICT COURT (9)
15 judges
Jurisdiction:
- Original jurisdiction in all civil actions, law and equity. Exclusive jurisdiction in probate, guardianship, adoption, and civil commitment matters.
- Original jurisdiction in criminal matters.
- Exclusive juvenile code jurisdiction (excluding ordinance and traffic violations).
Appeals on taped records.
Jury trials.

Court of general jurisdiction

COUNTY COURT (2)
4 judges
(Located in Laramie and Natrona Counties)
Jurisdiction:
- Civil actions under $7,000, except real estate matters.
- Misdemeanors; preliminary hearings.
Jury trials.

JUSTICE OF THE PEACE COURT (38)
43 justices of the peace
Jurisdiction:
- Civil actions under $4,000, except title to real estate.
- Misdemeanors in which punishment does not exceed $750 fine or 6 months imprisonment; preliminary hearings.
Jury trials.

MUNICIPAL COURT (74)
77 police justices
Jurisdiction:
- Exclusive jurisdiction over municipal ordinance violations in which punishment does not exceed $200 fine or 90 days imprisonment.
Jury trials.

Courts of limited jurisdiction

↑ Indicates route of appeal.

Figure 3.2

ASSIGNMENT #3 — PART 2

VISITATION TO A COURTROOM

For the most part, courtrooms and their proceedings are open to the public. There are exceptional cases involving child abuse, sexual molestation and the like which forbid a public presence. However, most American citizens are not aware that the activities of adjudication are open to spectators. For those of you who work during business hours, please know that most major urban and other metropolitan areas have 24-hour courts. Many courts of limited or rural jurisdiction are open on Saturdays and Sundays. District magistrates and justices of the peace often operate on an on-call basis, 24 hours a day, seven days a week. To be sure, those students who do not have to work on a nine-to-five basis have better access, but students with working obligations should not be fully excused from this activity. As a result, only in special circumstances will a waiver of this assignment be granted and only after consultation with the instructor.

Visitation serves many purposes: first, to make familiar to the student the nature of a courtroom and its physical structure; second, to allow the chance to observe and analyze the adversarial process at work;

and finally, to see theory translate into legal reality. The conceptions of the media, the public press and the stereotypical impressions of lawyering and related occupations quickly coalesce into a more realistic appraisal. Activities can range from the mundane to the incredibly fascinating.

COMPLETE THE QUESTIONNAIRE AT *FORM 3.9* WHICH WILL HIGHLIGHT AND MEMORIALIZE YOUR EXPERIENCE AS AN OBSERVER IN AN AMERICAN COURTROOM.

COURTROOM QUESTIONNAIRE

1. Draw a pictorial representation of the courtroom that you visited. (If permitted to take a picture, please do so. That is just as acceptable.)

2. Designate the personnel who were present during your visitation to the courtroom. Name their positions and give a brief job description.

Position:_____

Description:_____

_____

Position:_____

Description:_____

_____

Position:_____

Description:_____

_____

Position:_____

Description:_____

_____

Position:_____

Description:_____

_____

3. If possible, name the exact case which you observed (e.g., People v. John Stevens)._____

_____

4. If possible, name the attorneys who represented plaintiffs and defendants.

Plaintiff's Attorney:_____

Address:_____

Defendant's Attorney:_____

Address:_____

5. Was there a jury present?   ☐ Yes   ☐ No

6. What was your impression of the jury and its conduct during your observation?_____

_____

_____

_____

7. What impressions did you form regarding the conduct of the judge during this adjudication?_____

_____

_____

_____

8. What was your impression of the attorneys as they advocated their positions?_____

_____

_____

_____

9. How do all of the above impressions differ from your previous expectations and perceptions?_____

_____

_____

_____

_____

_____

10. What was the issue of the case being adjudicated before you?_____

_____

_____

_____

11. Do you think that the attorneys presented clear, concise arguments regarding that issue?_____

_____

_____

_____

12. If the judge gave instructions to a jury or ruled on a matter of law or other motion, do you think the judge presented a clear and legally correct position?_____

_____

_____

13. It is often said that advocacy is more theatrics then a direct application of law. Is there any truth in this comment?

_____

_____

_____

14. If you were present for more than one proceeding, make a list of other matters that came before the court during your visitation.

_____

_____

_____

_____

_____

_____

_____

_____

_____

_____

_____

_____

_____

15. What is your general impression of the justice that was meted out during your visitation to the courtroom? Give your opinions freely but base them, not on personalities, but on the conduct of the legal professionals in light of the law they were to apply._____

_____

_____

Form 3.9

ASSIGNMENT #3 — PART 3
SECONDARY VISITATION

The second exercise under this heading requires that you visit, make contact with or perform some form of research on a secondary agency that is charged with substantial responsibility in matters of enforcing the law. You may choose or select any of the following entities for your secondary visitation. They are:

1. A local, state or federal police department.

2. Public defender's office.

3. District Attorney's office

4. The Office of the Attorney General

5. The office of a city or county solicitor.

6. A government agency responsible for enforcing the law.
    a. OSHA
    b. Unemployment Compensation
    c. Workers' Compensation
    d. Insurance Commissioner
    e. Interstate Commerce Commission
    f. Revenue Department

This list should not be considered exhaustive, but it is advisable that you propose your location to the instructor to make certain that it is an agency which is involved in an ongoing and continuous application of the law.

COMPLETE THE QUESTIONNAIRE AT *FORM 3.10.*

SECONDARY VISITATION QUESTIONNAIRE

If not on the list of agencies, please so designate the agency selected:_____

Instructor Approval:_____

1. Please take a photograph of the agency chosen to complete your secondary visitation.

2. What is the name, address and phone number of the contact person at the site you have selected?_____

    _____

    _____

3. Does the location you have selected have police powers?   ☐ Yes   ☐ No

4. Does it have detention powers?   ☐ Yes   ☐ No

5. What statute or law is the agency you have selected empowered to enforce? (Attach a copy of the statute or representative piece of legislation.)_____

    _____

    _____

6. What is the manpower of this agency?_____

    _____

    _____

7. What is the budget of this agency?_____

    _____

    _____

8. What are the most common litigation problems which take place in this agency? Name at least three difficulties.

    1._____

    2._____

    3._____

9. What types of career opportunities are available for paralegals and legal assistants?_____

_____

_____

_____

10. List five career track positions available in this agency or institution of the law.

    1._____

    2._____

    3._____

    4._____

    5._____

11. Do you have any desire to enter into a career track position within this agency or institution? Explain._____

_____

_____

_____

Form 3.10

4. Ethical Concerns and Considerations

Anyone who enters into a career in law will be faced with an amazing array of ethical concerns and considerations. Ethics is a much trumpeted term in these times, and there are those who would say that ethics cannot be taught, but is something inherent in a personal value structure. This author advises students and practitioners alike that no ethical code or series of rules can possibly replace a strong foundation in spiritual, human and religious-based values. A common rule of thumb to employ is if it feels wrong, it probably is. Unfortunately, many aspects of lawyering have gray areas, especially in the coverage of unauthorized practice, fee splitting, contingent fee agreements and the legitimate advocacy of meritorious claims. The exercises completed below using the newly adopted *Model Rules of Professional Responsibility* should focus prospective paralegals, legal assistants, lawyers and other legal specialists on the innumerable ethical dilemmas that arise each and every day. Students are strongly advised to purchase a copy of the *Model Code of Professional Responsibility* and *Code of Judicial Conduct* as well as the *Model Rules of Professional Conduct* propounded by the American Bar Association. They are an investment worth making. The series of exercises that follow will highlight some of the often recurring difficulties.

A. Objectives

   (1) To review and assess recurring ethical problems which crop up in various careers in law; and

   (2) To become familiar with some relevant provisions of the *Model Rules of Professional Conduct*.

B. Student Obligations

   (1) To analyze, assess and author an opinion on ethical problems and dilemmas.

C. Instructor Obligations

   (1) To monitor and oversee students' reviews of ethical problems.

D. Time Allotted: 2.0 hours

E. Value of Assignment: 20.0 points

ASSIGNMENT #4 — PART 1

DISQUALIFICATION AND THE PARALEGAL

As a general principle, lawyers have an obligation to keep confidential all communications relating to representation of a client. If a lawyer changes firms and the client does not follow, the problems of conflicting representation and breach of confidentiality become obvious.

What if a paralegal has worked on a case for a law firm and that paralegal changes law firms, now employed by a law firm that is not in direct conflict with the previous client's position, though employed by a law firm that will want and desire access to all confidential information that the paralegal possesses. Does the law firm of the newly hired paralegal, who once represented the former client, have an obligation to disqualify itself?

DISCUSS THE ETHICAL RAMIFICATIONS OF THIS ISSUE. USE YOUR OWN STATIONERY TO COMPLETE THIS ASSIGNMENT.

ASSIGNMENT #4 — PART 2

Sally Stevens has hired a third-year law student to assist her in the function of law clerk and legal researcher. The law student is not licensed or granted any special permissions or exemptions to practice before any tribunal, administrative agency or other entity. Consider the following tasks that the law student has performed.

COULD ANY CAUSE THE ATTORNEY TO BE DISCIPLINED FOR A VIOLATION OF THE *CODE OF PROFESSIONAL RESPONSIBILITY?*
1. DRAFTING RELEASE FORMS FOR PERSONAL INJURY CASES.
2. INTERVIEWING EYEWITNESSES TO ACCIDENTS.
3. ADVISING ON WHETHER OR NOT A CLIENT SHOULD TAKE A SETTLEMENT AGREEMENT IN AN INSURANCE CASE.

USE YOUR OWN STATIONERY TO COMPLETE THIS ASSIGNMENT.

ASSIGNMENT #4 — PART 3

Review Model Rule of Professional Responsibility 5.5 below:

A lawyer shall not:

(a)   practice law in a jurisdiction where doing so violates the regulation of the legal profession in that jurisdiction; or

(b)   assist a person who is not a member of the bar in the performance of activity that constitutes the unauthorized practice of law.

How do paralegals fit within this unauthorized practice provision? Think hard and fast about this since the delegation of responsibilities for paralegals and legal assistants can sometimes border on unauthorized practice.

THINK CREATIVELY HERE AND LIST FIVE EXAMPLES OF A DELEGATION OF RESPONSIBILITY WHICH MIGHT VIOLATE THESE PROVISIONS. *FORM 3.11* IS PROVIDED FOR YOUR USE.

Write out examples of the unauthorized practice of law. Be precise and thoroughly identify the conduct which might breach this standard.

1. _____

2. _____

3. _____

4. _____

5. _____

Form 3.11

ASSIGNMENT #4 — PART 4

MERITORIOUS CLAIM

John Fortunato comes to the law offices of Bark and Clark. John has asked the attorney to file a civil action against a long-time business competitor and enemy. After reviewing the file and assessing the merits of the claim, the attorney advises the client that it is a complete waste of time to file such a suit. The client responds by stating that he does not care if it is a waste of time but will spend any amount of money to harass and make difficult the life of this long-time business competitor. The attorney eventually acquiesces and files the lawsuit.

USE YOUR OWN STATIONERY TO COMPLETE THIS ASSIGNMENT.

ASSIGNMENT #4 — PART 5

FEES

Paralegals who are given the responsibility of accounting for fees, their collection and ledgering often come across an ethical dilemma considering the following facts.

Attorney and client have a contingent fee agreement for the total sum of $25,000 or twenty-five percent of any eventual settlement in a negligence case. At trial, the judgment results in an award of $20,000. The client is immediately dissatisfied with the amount since all of this friends and relatives have advised him that he should have received at least double. The client objects to the fee and insists that the attorney gets nothing. What should the attorney do with the proceeds totalling $20,000 when they arrive? Can he or she do the following:

1. Send the entire amount of $20,000 to the client; or

2. Send $15,000 to the client and deposit $5,000 in his client's trust account; or

3. Send $15,000 to the client and deposit $5,000 in the attorney's own personal account.

USE YOUR OWN STATIONERY TO COMPLETE THIS ASSIGNMENT.

ASSIGNMENT #4 — PART 6

SAFEGUARDING PROPERTY

In an estate case, jewelry worth a substantial amount of money has been entrusted to the law firm. A paralegal has been asked by an associate in the law firm to safekeep the jewelry. The jewelry is placed in an unlocked desk drawer though the paralegal has indicated that he will take better care of the property the next day. Assume that the jewelry has been stolen. Can the attorney be subject to discipline?

ASSIGNMENT #4 — PART 7

Review Model Rule 5.3 below.

With respect to a nonlawyer employed or retained by or associated with a lawyer:

(a)   a partner in a law firm shall make reasonable efforts to ensure that the firm has in effect measures giving reasonable assurance that the person's conduct is compatible with the professional obligations of the lawyer;

(b)   a lawyer having direct supervisory authority over the nonlawyer shall make reasonable efforts to ensure that the person's conduct is compatible with the professional obligations of the lawyer; and

(c)   a lawyer shall be responsible for conduct of such a person that would be a violation of the rules of professional conduct if engaged in by a lawyer if:

(1)   the lawyer orders or, with the knowledge of the specific conduct, ratifies the conduct involved; or

(2)   the lawyer is a partner in the law firm in which the person is employed, or has direct supervisory authority over the person, and knows of the conduct at a time when its consequences can be avoided or mitigated but fails to take reasonable remedial action.

ANSWER THE QUESTIONS AT *FORM 3.12.*

---

1. Who else might be a nonlawyer assistant in a typical law firm or agency. List at least five other occupations.

_____

_____

_____

_____

_____

2. Who is ultimately responsible for the misconduct of a paralegal?_____

_____

3. List three programs which might be in place which insures reasonable supervision over a paralegal in a law firm.

_____

_____

_____

_____

_____

Form 3.12

PRACTICUM EXERCISES NO. 4
TORTS AND PERSONAL INJURY

	Time Allotted (hours)	Point Value
Product Liability:		
Assignment #1 (4 parts)	3 1/3	33 1/3
Medical Negligence:		
Assignment #2 (5 parts)	3 1/3	33 1/3
Auto Accidents:		
Assignment #3 (6 parts)	3 1/3	33 1/3
	10.0	100.0

I.
INTRODUCTION

These field exercises involve an examination of certain events, conditions, products or services which cause injury and harm to the person. More specifically, the student who completes the following assignments will become more attuned to the wide range of environmental, social, and cultural forces which form the causal basis for injury itself. After completing the required assignments, the student should have a better understanding of the inherent and manmade dangers that people confront on a daily basis. The assignments are definitely oriented towards field work and do require extensive inquiry, visitation, photography, charting, diagramming, or other means of pictorial representation. The three specific areas of coverage will be:

Product Liability Action
Medical Negligence and Malpractice
Auto Accident Analysis

Few logistical or practical problems exist while completing these assignments since students can work on the weekends, nights or even set up and arrange visitations at institutions that operate on a 24-hour basis. The only additional burden imposed on the student is his or her ability to operate a camera. Any type of camera is acceptable from a 35mm to an inexpensive Polaroid.

II.
PRODUCT LIABILITY

A. Objectives

   (1) To investigate the home, the workplace or other selected environment for specific products and services that may cause injury to another; and

   (2) To apply product liability legal principles to a personal injury case.

B. Student Obligations

   (1) To complete all questionnaires involving product liability;

   (2) To conduct a survey or search of product liability problems in a specific environment; and

   (3) To photograph and document actual product liability problems.

C. Instructor Obligations

   (1) To assist and give guidance to the student as he or she prepares all required assignments.

D. Time Allotted: 3 1/3 hours

E. Value of Assignment: 33 1/3 points

ASSIGNMENT #1 — PART 1
TREASURE HUNT: DEFECTIVE PRODUCTS

Perform an exhaustive search in your own residence to determine whether or not there are products which you can identify as defective. Find at least three products in your domicile which have the potential to cause injuries.

COMPLETE THE QUESTIONNAIRE AT *FORM 4.1.*

PRODUCT LIABILITY QUESTIONNAIRE

PRODUCT #1

1. Name of Product:_____

2. Manufacturer of Product:_____

_____

_____

3. Pictorial representation of product (either diagram or provide a photograph).

4. Explain the exact nature of the defect (Where is it broken? Why did it malfunction? What part malfunctioned?)

_____

_____

_____

_____

5. Did any injuries result from usage of the product?_____

_____

_____

_____

_____

6. Can you predict reasonably, or as the law requires, foreseeably, any injuries that might result?_____

_____

_____

_____

_____

7. Who is legally responsible for this product damage or defect?_____

_____

_____

_____

8. Name the manufacturer._____

_____

_____

9. Name the retailer (if applicable)._____

_____

_____

_____

10. Name the distributor (if applicable)._____

_____

_____

_____

11. Name the salesperson or other agent of company who sold that product (if applicable)._____

_____

_____

_____

12. Name a party who is responsible for the supervision of the product's use (if applicable)._____

_____

_____

_____

13. Is there any possibility that the product was used for a purpose other than that for which it was manufactured? If so, explain._____

_____

_____

_____

14. Was the product subject to owner abuse?   ☐ Yes   ☐ No

If yes, why?_____

_____

_____

15. Give specific recommendations on how the product could have been made safer._____

_____

_____

_____

_____

PRODUCT #2

1. Name of Product:_____

2. Manufacturer of Product:_____

_____

_____

3. Pictorial representation of product (either diagram or provide a photograph).

4. Explain the exact nature of the defect (Where is it broken? Why did it malfunction? What part malfunctioned?)_

_____

_____

_____

_____

5. Did any injuries result from usage of the product?_____

_____

_____

_____

_____

6. Can you predict reasonably, or as the law requires, foreseeably, any injuries that might result?_____

_____

_____

_____

_____

7. Who is legally responsible for this product damage or defect?_____

_____

_____

_____

8. Name the manufacturer._____

_____

_____

9. Name the retailer (if applicable)._____

_____

_____

10. Name the distributor (if applicable)._____

_____

_____

_____

11. Name the salesperson or other agent of company who sold that product (if applicable)._____

_____

_____

_____

12. Name a party who is responsible for the supervision of the product's use (if applicable)._____

_____

_____

_____

13. Is there any possibility that the product was used for a purpose other than that for which it was manufactured? If so, explain._____

_____

_____

_____

14. Was the product subject to owner abuse?   ☐ Yes   ☐ No

    If yes, why?_____

_____

_____

15. Give specific recommendations on how the product could have been made safer._____

_____

_____

_____

_____

PRODUCT #3

1. Name of Product:_____
2. Manufacturer of Product:_____

_____

_____

3. Pictorial representation of product (either diagram or provide a photograph).

4. Explain the exact nature of the defect (Where is it broken? Why did it malfunction? What part malfunctioned?)

_____

_____

_____

_____

5. Did any injuries result from usage of the product?_____

_____

_____

_____

_____

6. Can you predict reasonably, or as the law requires, foreseeably, any injuries that might result?_____

_____

_____

_____

_____

7. Who is legally responsible for this product damage or defect?_____

_____

_____

_____

8. Name the manufacturer._____

_____

_____

9. Name the retailer (if applicable)._____

_____

_____

_____

10. Name the distributor (if applicable)._____

_____

_____

_____

11. Name the salesperson or other agent of company who sold that product (if applicable)._____

_____

_____

_____

12. Name a party who is responsible for the supervision of the product's use (if applicable)._____

_____

_____

_____

13. Is there any possibility that the product was used for a purpose other than that for which it was manufactured? If so, explain._____

_____

_____

_____

14. Was the product subject to owner abuse?   ☐ Yes   ☐ No

If yes, why?_____

_____

_____

15. Give specific recommendations on how the product could have been made safer._____

_____

_____

_____

_____

Form 4.1

ASSIGNMENT #1 — PART 2
TRACKING RECURRING CLAIMS OF PRODUCT DEFECTS

Merchandise or products seem to be repeatedly the subject of product liability lawsuits. The following series of exercises calls for the student to perform some investigative and deductive inquiry. Be prepared to go beyond your immediate geographic area. Since we live in an extremely mobile society, it is important for the future practitioner to go beyond his or her immediate environment to discover potential product and service liability activities. In this exercise, you must look to the farm and the highway.

COMPLETE THE QUESTIONNAIRE AT *FORM 4.2.*

PRODUCT #1 — FARM MACHINERY

1. Why do so many product liability problems emerge on the farm?_____

_____

_____

_____

2. What type of equipment is commonly utilized by the agricultural community, equipment which has the potential to cause great injury or harm? Name at least three._____

_____

_____

_____

3. Take a photo of at least two forms of farm equipment (or draw if you prefer).

4. What types of injuries might result from the use of such equipment? (The fact that injuries take place does not imply that the manufacturer is negligent.)_____

    _____

    _____

    _____

    _____

5. Select either of the two pieces of equipment above and by close visual inspection, answer the following questions.

    a. Does the equipment appear old or outdated?   ☐ Yes   ☐ No

    b. Does the equipment have the capacity to work on all types of terrains and topographies?   ☐ Yes   ☐ No

        Explain:_____

        _____

        _____

    c. Are there any parts of the equipment where hands, feet or clothing can be caught in power-driven parts?
                                                                                            ☐ Yes   ☐ No

        Explain:_____

        _____

        _____

d. Does the equipment produce a large amount of dust or other airborne particles?   ☐ Yes   ☐ No

Explain:_____

_____

_____

e. Are there any parts of the machinery that would appear to be an attractive nuisance for a child?

☐ Yes   ☐ No

Explain:_____

_____

_____

f. Are there any chains, blades, cutting devices which could cause serious and substantial injury?☐ Yes   ☐ No

Explain:_____

_____

_____

6. Do you have any specific recommendations on how this equipment could be safer? Outline in words or draw pictorially your suggested improvements.

PRODUCT #2 — MOTORCYCLE

1. Discuss your own perceptions of motorcycles and product liability problems. What types of problems continually are discussed in the media?_____

_____

_____

_____

2. Is there something inherently dangerous about the use of a motorcycle?   ☐ Yes   ☐ No

3. Does its inherent dangerousness (if it exists at all) make it impossible for the manufacturer, retailer and distributor to prevent all accidents?   ☐ Yes   ☐ No

    Explain:_____

_____

_____

4. Consumer advocates have been calling upon manufacturers of motorcycles to make them more crash-worthy. Give five suggestions as to how a motorcycle might be made more crash-worthy.

    1._____

    2._____

    3._____

    4._____

    5._____

5. If your firm or agency is contending with a case of injury resulting from the operation of a motorcycle, who are the potential defendants?_____

_____

_____

_____

6. Take a picture of a motorcycle. Give a few recommendations on how a motorcycle could be improved to make it a safer product. If you have no recommendations, the converse of this assignment is also acceptable. If you perceive the motorcycle as being a perfectly safe instrument of travel, give a few reasons as to how the product has been made safer by the manufacturer. Point out the particular location of product improvements in your photograph.

_____

_____

_____

_____

_____

Form 4.2

ASSIGNMENT #1 — PART 3
PRODUCT LIABILITY AND THE SMALL BUSINESS

The implications of product liability on business planning and decision making is a regular influence. This assignment requires a short, brief visitation to a small business, such as a service station or convenience store, eliciting responses to the questionnaire at *Form 4.3*.

COMPLETE THE QUESTIONNAIRE AT *FORM 4.3*.

_____

SMALL BUSINESS QUESTIONNAIRE

1. Name of Business (Insure the owner or proprietor of complete confidence or anonymity if he or she prefers.):___

_____

_____

2. Type of Business (describe products and services):_____

_____

_____

3. What products have been recalled due to a defective design or nature in the last year (if any)?_____

_____

_____

4. What product is most frequently returned to the enterprise due to its defective design or construction?_____

_____

_____

5. What product or service does this small business provide which causes the owner or proprietor the most concern about liability?_____

_____

_____

*You may have difficulty getting responses to these questions. You must insure the small business proprietor that your intention is to discover those products or services which cause daily consternation for the small business owner. The small business owner may prefer to speak in more general or hypothetical terms which is thoroughly acceptable.

Form 4.3

ASSIGNMENT #1 — PART 4
PRODUCT LIABILITY: TOBACCO

The recent case of *Cippollone v. Liggett Group, Inc.* (83-2864) District Court of New Jersey (1988) manifests how product liability is an evolving legal action since it held that a damage award against a tobacco industry for the injury and death of people who smoke cigarettes is appropriate.

COMPLETE THE QUESTIONNAIRE AT *FORM 4.4.*

PRODUCT LIABILITY: TOBACCO QUESTIONNAIRE

1. What arguments could the cigarette company make regarding its non-liability in a suit regarding the injurious nature of tobacco?_____

_____

_____

_____

_____

2. What arguments do you think the estate of the deceased smoker made regarding the tortious tobacco product lines?_____

_____

_____

_____

_____

_____

3. How does the notice or warning applied to the side of a cigarette package affect a product liability case?_____

_____

_____

_____

_____

4. Use of warnings and notices on the packaging of products plays a key role, at least from the manufacturer's perspective, in limiting liability. Place in the spaces provided below five examples of notices, warnings and limitations of responsibility for specific products.

Name of Product:_____

Notice or Warning Label:

Name of Product:_____

Notice or Warning Label:

Name of Product:_____

Notice or Warning Label:

Name of Product:_____

Notice or Warning Label:

Name of Product:_____

Notice or Warning Label:

_____

Form 4.4

III.
MEDICAL NEGLIGENCE

Most people are not aware of how extensive the problems of medical negligence and malpractice are. Increasingly, suits are being filed against medical practitioners, from doctors and physicians to surgeons, anesthesiologists, to secondary personnel of hospitals and emergency rooms as well as the traditional family physician. Great debate exists on the merits of such claims, but after completing these exercises the student should have some appreciation of the ramifications, the implications and the nature of a misdiagnosis, an error in medical judgment and the resulting injuries and damages that are caused. One does not have to be a medical expert to see the effects, and one, as a rule, need not go any further than his or her own family to appreciate the nature of medical negligence. This series of assignments will require investigative questioning amongst family or friends as well as a visitation to a hospital, emergency room, family physician or other medical setting. Additionally, the assignments call for the documentation of a specific medical injury with the analysis of charts and diagrams which anatomically portray injury.

A. Objectives

(1) To discern and discover examples of personal injury resulting from medical negligence or malpractice;

(2) To appreciate the regularity of medical negligence and malpractice; and

(3) To learn skills of interpretation when analyzing charts and diagrams that graphically portray medical injuries.

B. Student Obligations

(1) To complete questionnaires involving medical negligence and malpractice;

(2) To complete an exercise matching injuries to a pictorial representation; and

(3) To visit a physician, emergency room or hospital or other medical setting and complete a questionnaire which determines the nature of negligence problems.

C. Instructor Obligations

(1) To provide students with whatever permission forms are necessary to complete the visitation; and

(2) To assist and give general guidance to the student regarding the completion of all assignments.

D. Time Allotted: 3 1/3 hours

E. Value of Assignment: 33 1/3 points

ASSIGNMENT #2 — PART 1
A CASE OF MEDICAL NEGLIGENCE

Most students are initially surprised that medical negligence, malpractice, misdiagnosis and other errors on the part of medical personnel affect almost all families. Your task under this first assignment is to discover, either in your own personal medical history or in that of a family member, some error or mistake in judgment. To be sure, these exercises and assignments do not call for an absolute finding of medical malpractice but an awareness and appreciation for the common errors in judgment exhibited by certain medical personnel. Of course, this assignment should not lead the student to conclude that all medical specialists and personnel have made these types of mistakes. As in all professions, only a minority of individuals carry out their responsibilities incompetently. At any rate, if you have difficulty finding in either your own history or that of your family some example of medical mistake or error, extend your search beyond the nuclear family to friends, acquaintances or work associates.

COMPLETE THE QUESTIONNAIRE AT *FORM 4.5.*

Your task is to identify a specific diagnosis, treatment given or therapeutic regimen recommended which apparently was incorrect. Again, either you, a relative, close friend or business associate will satisfy.

1. Describe the facts which lead up to the injury in question:_____

    _____

    _____

    _____

    _____

    _____

2. Describe the exact nature of the injury:_____

    _____

    _____

    _____

3. What was the diagnosis provided to you by the medical professional?_____

    _____

    _____

4. Were you advised to seek a second opinion?   ☐ Yes   ☐ No

5. Did you get a second opinion?   ☐ Yes   ☐ No

    With what result?_____

    _____

    _____

6. Were you suspicious of the original diagnosis given by the physician or other medical provider?   ☐ Yes   ☐ No

    If so, why?_____

    _____

    _____

7. Did the therapy or curative regimen recommended to you seem to accomplish or hinder in the rehabilitation of the injury?_____

_____

_____

8. Given the lack of progress and the underlying suspicion of the diagnosis and restorative suggestions, did you seek out other medical assistance?   ☐ Yes   ☐ No

   What was the result of that secondary visitation?_____

_____

_____

9. Did the original diagnosis change or was a new therapeutic, restorative or rehabilitative regimen suggested?_____

_____

_____

_____

10. Was the original diagnosis and therapeutic suggestion a cause of further injury and harm?_____

_____

_____

11. Point out, exactly, what was negligent about the first interpretation of the injury._____

_____

_____

12. Did the secondary physician indicate that the initial provider or physician made a mistake in his or her diagnosis or suggested treatment?   ☐ Yes   ☐ No

   Give some details:_____

_____

_____

13. Was the mistake in the diagnosis and the suggested treatment a mistake of judgment that a reasonable doctor in similar circumstances with a reasonable level of background and preparation should have been aware of?
                                                      ☐ Yes   ☐ No

   Why?_____

_____

_____

14. Comments (Give any other comments or feelings you have regarding this experience, either yours or another party's.):_____

_____

_____

_____

_____

_____

Form 4.5

ASSIGNMENT #2 — PART 2
THE VALUE OF EXPERT TESTIMONY

One of the critical functions of legal specialists engaged in medical negligence and malpractice analysis is in the proof that the medical specialist has given substandard care. Paralegals and legal assistants frequently assist the trial attorney in preparing a series of questions which attack the credibility of the medical personnel, which cause an impeachment favorable to the plaintiff. Various techniques exist which impeach the credibility and experiential foundation of a medical witness.

REVIEW THE SERIES OF QUESTIONS AND ANSWERS AT *FORM 4.6* AND POINT OUT IN RESPONSE THE STRATEGY OR TACTIC EMPLOYED BY THE DIRECT OR CROSS-EXAMINER.

Q. Dr. James, are you familiar with Dr. John Stevens?

A. I am.

Q. How about Dr. Jacob Dennison?

A. I am.

Q. Are you familiar with a book entitled, *Leg Fractures and Possible Complications*?

A. I am.

Q. Are you aware that this book was written by Drs. Stevens and Dennison?

A. That is correct. I am aware of that.

Q. Would you agree that this book is considered a seminal work on the setting of leg fractures?

A. It is, but it only provides general guidelines.

Q. Would you agree that in the setting of a leg fracture, no more than a 45-degree angle relative to knee flection and hypertension is permissible?

A. No, I do not agree.

Q. Doctor, I would like to ask you whether or not you are familiar with Chapter 9, Page 1, of the textbook, *Leg Fractures and Possible Complications*.

A. Yes, I am familiar.

Q. In it, it states exactly, "No more than a 45-degree angle relative to knee flection and hypertension is permissible." How do you resolve your opinion and that of the book?

A. It is their opinion, and mine is different.

_____

1. This seeming contradiction of positions between the doctor and the scholarly textbook produces what result?____

_____

_____

2. How do you think jurors feel about such a difference of opinion?_____

_____

_____

_____

Point out the purposes of the following cross-examination.

Q. Is it reasonable, Dr. Stevens, when a physician has been trained at the Johns Hopkins Medical Center, has studied extensively at Harvard and Yale Universities, and has performed numerous research studies on the type of blood analysis that is the subject of this lawsuit, to rely upon that training in the prescription of a particular drug?

A. The doctor should take into consideration many factors including research, the work of educational institutions, papers written and presented and the standard practice in his or her community.

Q. In other words, Doctor, are there not times when a decision rendered, a medication prescribed or a medical regimen advised is in a gray area?

A. Very few things in life are totally black and white, and this is so in medical practice as well. There are frequently minority opinions and new research studies. It is my general philosophy that the minority view, the exception to the rule, is not the first course of action.

_____

3. What is the attorney trying to accomplish with this series of questions?_____

_____

_____

4. If he succeeds in showing that the doctor employed a minority, non-traditional means of attacking a medical problem, what might he be able to show?_____

_____

_____

5. Does it make any difference where the doctor was trained and educated?_____

_____

_____

_____

In a case in which a doctor is challenged for his negligent prescription of the drug Valium, what do the following questions accomplish?

Q. Doctor, you have indicated the importance of weighing and evaluating numerous variables in an individual prescription.

A. That is correct.

Q. One of the reasons that you have given for not prescribing the drug Valium is that the data available to you indicates that normal individuals have widely varying responses to the drug.

A. That is correct.

Q. In the process of treating the patient, the physician then is under an obligation to acquire whatever data is reasonably available to make a correct decision regarding medications.

A. That is correct.

Q. One of the considerations is the relative risk of irrevocable, substantial harm. Is it not?

A. Correct.

Q. So then, a physician should adopt a medication alternative that would decrease the possibility of irrevocable substantial harm. Is this correct?

A. Correct.

_____

   Assume you have a case in which a patient has suffered severe, irrevocable harm from the administration of the drug Valium.

6. What would this cross-examination demonstrate?_____

_____

_____

7. If there is a likelihood of irrevocable harm, would it be more or less negligent for the doctor not to prescribe the drug at all, assuming that there is an alternative medication?_____

_____

_____

_____

8. Is there another way of responding to this series of questions that might be more advantageous to the defendant doctor? Explain._____

_____

_____

_____

Form 4.6

ASSIGNMENT #2 — PART 3
PHOTOGRAPHING A MEDICAL INJURY

A photographic record is often the best evidence that can be presented to a jury regarding the medical injury. You are not required to find a specific case of medical negligence to complete this assignment. However, you are required to portray visually or photograph an injury and to write out a set of facts which might explain a case of medical negligence or malpractice.

COMPLETE *FORM 4.7.*

PHOTOGRAPHING AN INJURY

1. Nature of injury (describe):_____

_____

_____

2. Photograph or pictorial representation of injury:

3. Statement of facts which lead to injury:_____

_____

_____

_____

_____

a. What was the original diagnosis?_____

_____

b. Did the diagnosis or treatment prescribed cause this specific injury? Explain._____

_____

_____

_____

c. What could have been done differently that would have prevented this specific injury?_____

_____

_____

_____

Form 4.7

ASSIGNMENT #2 — PART 4
EVALUATING MEDICAL DIAGRAMS

The evaluation of medical diagrams, charts and pictorial representations of injuries is an important component in the nature of medical negligence or malpractice. Some general familiarity with medical terms is an important part of developing expertise. More to the point is translating a pictorial display, medical chart or diagram into an exposition. Paralegals and legal assistants must become comfortable with a description of injuries in narrative form. The four exercises that follow call upon the student to write such descriptions.

Part 4(a)

Chest Injuries: Traumatic Wet Lung

Review the picture and corresponding chart below at *Figures 4.1* and *4.2* made available from the *Attorney's Textbook of Medicine* by Matthew Bender and Company. Create a fact pattern which would explain how the air passages became filled with blood and secretions. Again, make sure the facts relate to a case of medical negligence or malpractice.

USE YOUR OWN STATIONERY TO COMPLETE THIS ASSIGNMENT.

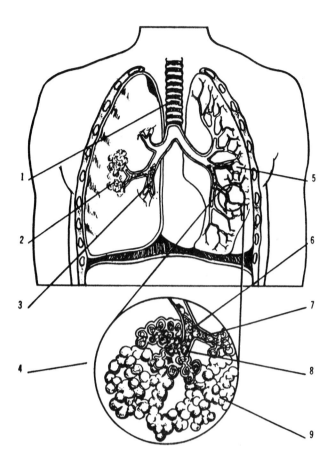

Figure 4.1

Nomenclature

(The numbers and anatomical references identify the corresponding numbers on the facing illustration.)

1. Trachea
2. Pulmonary Contusion
3. Interstitial Hemorrhage and Transudation of Fluid
4. Blood and Mucus in Gas Exchange Structures
5. Bronchial Tree
6. Air Passages Become Filled With Blood and Secretions
7. Terminal Bronchiole
8. Respiratory Bronchiole
9. Alveoli

Figure 4.2

Copyright ©1989 by Matthew Bender & Co., Inc., and reprinted with permission from *Attorney's Textbook of Medicine*.

Write a narrative of facts leading up to the medical condition of Traumatic Wet Lung.

Part 4(b)

Knee Injuries: Fracture of Spine of Tibia

Based on the diagram and key nomenclature at *Figures 4.3* and *4.4* below, write out a narrative report on what the nature of this injury is. (Students as well as instructors should be aware that there is no perfectly correct response and that this is an exercise more for the purposes of becoming familiar with medical terminology.)

USE YOUR OWN STATIONERY TO COMPLETE THIS ASSIGNMENT.

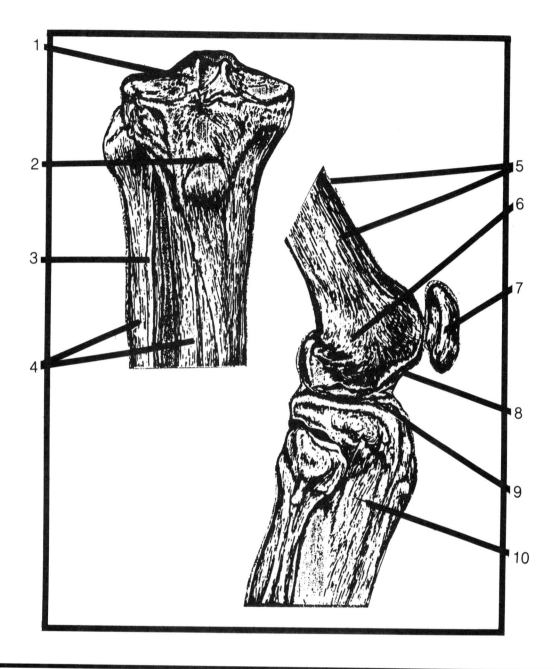

Figure 4.3
Copyright ©1989 by Matthew Bender & Co., Inc., and reprinted with permission from *Attorney's Textbook of Medicine.*

Nomenclature

(The numbers and anatomical references identify the corresponding numbers on the facing illustration.)

1. Fracture of Tibial Spine
2. Tibia
3. Fibula
4. Anterior Aspect
5. Medial Aspect
6. Femur (Posterior Displacement)
7. Patella
8. Knee Flexed
9. Avulsion of Tibial Spine
10. Tibia (Fixed)

Figure 4.4

Copyright ©1989 by Matthew Bender & Co., Inc., and reprinted with permission from *Attorney's Textbook of Medicine.*

Write a narrative of facts leading up to the medical condition of fracture of the spine of the tibia.

USE YOUR OWN STATIONERY TO COMPLETE THIS ASSIGNMENT.

Part 4(c)

Match the diagrams and pictures (*Figures 4.5 through 4.9*) with the narrative descriptions that follow those figures.

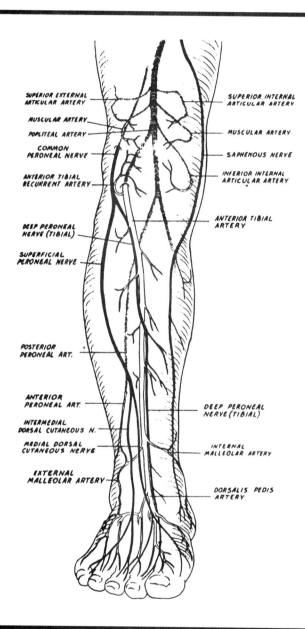

Figure 4.5

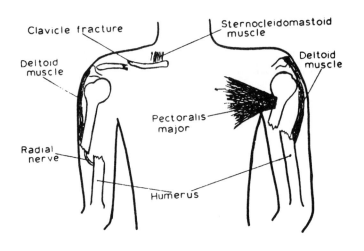

Figure 4.6
Copyright ©1989 by Matthew Bender & Co., Inc., and reprinted with permission from *Attorney's Textbook of Medicine.*

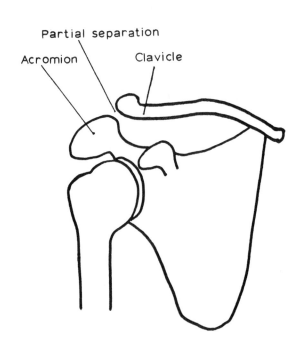

Figure 4.7
Copyright ©1989 by Matthew Bender & Co., Inc., and reprinted with permission from *Attorney's Textbook of Medicine.*

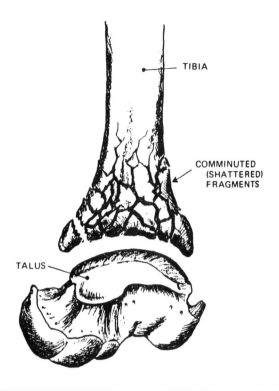

Figure 4.8

Copyright ©1989 by Matthew Bender & Co., Inc., and reprinted with permission from *Attorney's Textbook of Medicine.*

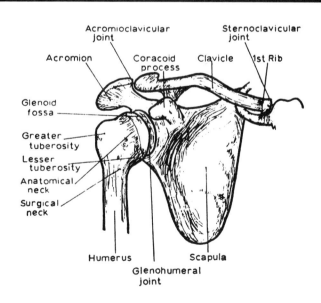

Figure 4.9

Copyright ©1989 by Matthew Bender & Co., Inc., and reprinted with permission from *Attorney's Textbook of Medicine.*

Description A: Comminuted fracture of distal tibia involving ankle joint. ANSWER: Figure _____.

Description B: Diagrammatic representation of anterior view of bones and joints in a normal shoulder. ANSWER: Figure _____.

Description C: Anterior view of right leg showing major nerves and major arteries. ANSWER: Figure _____.

Description D: Diagrammatic representation of fractured humerus below deltoid muscle as well as radial nerve laceration from bone fragments. ANSWER: Figure _____.

Description E: Acromioclavicular subluxation; representing a partial separation of the acromioclavicular joint. ANSWER: Figure _____.

ASSIGNMENT #2 — PART 5
VISITATION TO MEDICAL SETTING

Practitioners in medical negligence and malpractice will spend extended periods of time working with medical personnel. An open-ended assignment calling for a visitation or on-site review with an employee in a medical setting is a most functional exercise. Don't be surprised if a certain reticence or even fear crops up when questioning medical specialists about legal issues. If you have difficulty, ask your instructor to provide you with a letter of introduction and a signed permission slip which evidences the educational purposes of your interview. The thrust of the exercise is for you to become attuned to the legal implications of medical practice in a realistic medical setting. Using a questionnaire and interview format as your chief mechanisms, visit a medical location. A phone consultation may be just as appropriate. Again, assure the interviewed party that if he or she so desires, anonymity will be honored and that this activity is strictly for educational purposes. The medical facility or specialist may insist on this form of confirmation. In any event, if there are serious problems in completing this assignment, please consult with your instructor.

COMPLETE *FORM 4.8.*

MEDICAL SITE VISITATION QUESTIONNAIRE

1. Name of site:_____

_____

2. Person responsible (unless anonymity requested):_____

_____

3. Nature of location (describe the nature of the facility):_____

_____

_____

4. Tasks, duties and obligations of the facility or carrier:_____

_____

_____

5. How has this medical facility responded to the continuous and ongoing matter of medical negligence and malpractice?_____

_____

_____

_____

6. Does it employ or use any forms upon patient entry? ☐ Yes   ☐ No

7. Does it advise patients and secure consents? ☐ Yes   ☐ No

8. If there is a case with very complex medical considerations, does it recommend second opinions?
☐ Yes   ☐ No

9. Are patients and admittees fully advised of their rights regarding the nature of their medical treatment?
☐ Yes   ☐ No

10. What is the most pressing legal dilemma that this medical carrier currently faces?_____

_____

_____

_____

_____

11. Where does the negligence begin and end at this medical site?_____

_____

_____

_____

_____

12. Can physicians, surgeons and other high-level personnel be held accountable for malpractice? ☐ Yes   ☐ No

13. How about nurses? ☐ Yes   ☐ No

14. What about secondary tier employees such as janitorial staff, clerks, or administrators? ☐ Yes   ☐ No

15. What is the nature of the emergency room relative to the rest of the hospital? Explain._____

_____

_____

_____

16. Has the interviewee ever witnessed a case of pure medical negligence or malpractice? ☐ Yes   ☐ No

17. If the interviewee so desires and, again, insuring anonymity, can he or she give a generic broad-based description of what took place?_____

_____

_____

_____

18. What is the interviewee's perception of the legal community as relates to medical negligence and malpractice litigation?_____

_____

_____

_____

19. What does he or she think her colleagues' perception is of the legal profession?_____

_____

_____

_____

20. In general, what recommendations does the interviewee have regarding the alleviation of ongoing malpractice and negligence problems in the medical community?_____

_____

_____

_____

NOTE: Students should be aware that this questionnaire can be tailored outside of the hospital or emergency room setting. Students must feel free to reconstruct the questions to direct them towards specific physicians, nurses or other medical personnel. There is no absolute requirement that a visitation take place at a hospital or other agency. Be mindful that the questions are often very delicate and may not be answered at all, but the very asking of the questions indicates the seriousness and liability implications of medical malpractice.

Form 4.8

IV.
AUTO ACCIDENTS

The auto accident exercises require a great deal of independent action and thought. Students are not required under these series of assignments to attend actual accidents, since the assignments can be completed by factual reconstruction. Use your imagination. The skills that result from this series of exercises are applicable to any auto case, often the meat and potatoes portion of a typical law practice.

Auto accident cases are multi-faceted involving negligence, product or strict liability. Criminal negligence may also be germane depending on the facts.

A. Objectives

    (1) To gain some understanding of the steps that must be taken to insure the preservation of the record in an auto accident case.

B. Student Obligations

    (1) To prepare forms, diagrams and photographic expositions as required in the assignments;

    (2) To produce narrative reports or other documentation as is called for; and

    (3) To compile a list of governmental agencies that serve as a repository for auto accident and vehicular records.

C. Instructor Obligations

    (1) To assist the student and monitor the progress of these assignments; and

    (2) To provide permission slips, letters of introduction or other matter to assist in the completion of these exercises.

D. Time Allotted: 3 1/3 hours

E. Value of Assignment: 33 1/3 points

ASSIGNMENT #3 — PART 1
PRESERVING THE ACCIDENT SCENE

Accident scenes can be preserved either through an actual diagram or photographic display. Students, if they do have the opportunity and, of course, do not interfere or obstruct the proper and lawful duties of the police community, can complete this assignment by visiting an actual accident site. Many people are used to locating accident sites by simply listening to sirens, contacting the local police stations, listening to a scanner or other public radio tracking system or making contact with a specific insurance company whose claims adjuster will call you when he or she is asked to visit an accident site. Contacts play a crucial part in gaining access.

Using the example at *Figure 4.10* below, create a diagram of an auto accident as well as hypothetical information that you may feel comfortable with. No evaluation will take place on the student's artistic skill, but attention to detail, adherence to graphic scale and understandability will be the key factors in the assessment of your final work.

USE YOUR OWN STATIONERY TO COMPLETE THIS ASSIGNMENT.

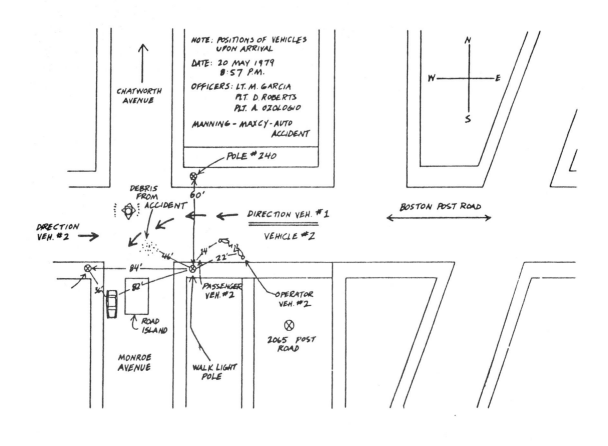

Figure 4.10

ASSIGNMENT #3 — PART 2
PHOTOGRAPHING THE ACCIDENT SCENE

Photographs of an accident scene should be taken from many angles including the following: points of entrance, points of exit, diverse directions, from victim's perspective, from defendant's perspective, complete overview, emphasis from a damage perspective. Some of the pictures you see below are good, solid examples of photography at an accident scene.

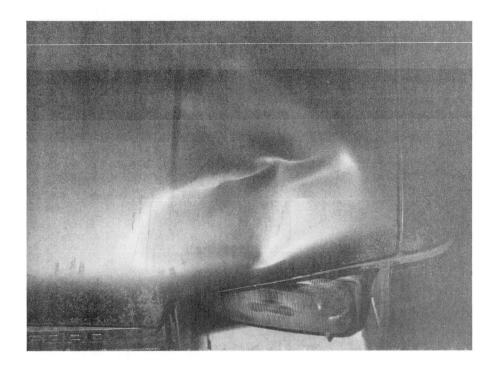

For posterity, photography of the accident scene is mandatory. Again, remember that you are not mandatorily required to visit an actual accident site; however, all students are required to either actually or hypothetically recreate an accident scene. Of course, do not take this suggestion literally, claiming that your instructor has required that you cause an accident fact pattern. With all seriousness, you are required to take pictures of the following and to provide a corresponding narrative.

COMPLETE *FORM 4.9*.

PHOTOGRAPHING THE ACCIDENT SCENE

PHOTO 1: Location of Intersectional Collision

Description of collision (why, where, how and when):

_____

_____

_____

_____

_____

_____

_____

_____

_____

_____

PHOTO 2: Location of Victim's Vehicle

Description (who and to what extent injured/damaged; describe vehicle, serial number and license tag):

_____

_____

_____

_____

_____

_____

_____

_____

_____

_____

PHOTO 3: View of Defendant's Vehicle

Description (who and to what extent injured/damaged; describe vehicle, name, serial number and license tag):

_____

_____

_____

_____

_____

_____

_____

_____

_____

_____

PHOTO 4: Evidence of Stopping, Speeding, Impact or Other Matter

(Any photographic representation indicating tire tracks, oil or other fluids spilled or damaged parts is required.)

Description:_____

_____

_____

_____

_____

_____

_____

_____

_____

_____

PHOTO 5: BODY DAMAGE

(Take a picture of any vehicle you know that has minor or even major body damage. The picture does not have to relate to the accident scene outlined above. Describe in detail that body damage.)

Description:_____

_____

_____

_____

_____

_____

_____

_____

_____

PHOTO 6:

(Outside of body damage, are there any other points or locations on the vehicle or any other person's vehicle which would indicate a point of impact? For example: Are there broken seats? Are there scrapes and tears in the fabric of the vehicle? Are there broken seatbelts? Is there an impact or intrusion mark in the lower chassis of the vehicle? If there are no easily seen pieces of evidence which show impact, skip this requirement.)

Description:_____

_____

_____

_____

_____

_____

_____

_____

_____

Form 4.9

ASSIGNMENT #3 — PART 3
WORKING WITH AGENCIES

Legal practitioners in auto negligence must become adept at collecting records and documentation. The requirements under this section call for either phone inquiry or actual visitation at the following sites:

— Hospital or emergency room
— Physician's office
— Police station or department
— Insurance company

This assignment should make the paralegal or legal assistant more comfortable in the collection of records. Courtesy and discretion go a long way in opening up doors.

Part 3(a)
POLICE REPORT

COMPLETE THE QUESTIONNAIRE AT *FORM 4.10.*

POLICE REPORTS QUESTIONNAIRE

Contact your local police agency and ask what is the procedure and cost involved in acquiring a vehicular accident report.

1. Name of Police Department:_____

_____

2. Procedure for acquiring a copy of a police report:_____

_____

_____

_____

_____

_____

3. Cost of acquiring a police report:_____

4. Ask for a sample of a police report if at all possible and attach.

Form 4.10

Part 3(b)
MEDICAL RECORDS

COMPLETE THE QUESTIONNAIRE AT *FORM 4.11.*

MEDICAL RECORDS QUESTIONNAIRE

Call a local hospital, physician or other medical setting and ask how medical records on a specific patient can be acquired.

1. Name of physician, hospital or medical care provider (if possible and appropriate):_____

    _____

    _____

2. What is the procedure for acquiring copies of medical records?_____

    _____

    _____

    _____

    _____

3. Are there any specific forms or authorizations that this agency publishes for this purpose?   ☐ Yes   ☐ No

    Attach a copy if possible.

Form 4.11

Part 3(c)
INSURANCE COMPANIES

Part 3(c)(1)
DAMAGE ESTIMATES

Insurance companies are the dominant force in the settlement of auto accident claims and predictably require much documentation. For property damages, they will require a minimum of one and usually two estimates.

Visit your local body shop. Take with you a picture of a damaged auto. Ask them to write up an estimate, though not in scientific terms, but a rough estimate as to what it would cost to fix the vehicle. Make sure that the photo outlines the damages clearly or that you provide the body shop with a sufficient written description. Also be sure that you know the name, make and year of the vehicle.

ATTACH A WRITTEN ESTIMATE AS EVIDENCE OF YOUR COMPLETION OF THIS ASSIGNMENT.

Part 3(c)(2)
DOCUMENTATION

In dealing with insurance companies, many forms and other documentation are necessary. Call your local insurance agent, introduce yourself and ask what types of forms and documents are repeatedly used in the evaluation and adjustment of auto accident claims.

MAKE A LIST OF THE FORMS THAT THEY USE ON A STANDARDIZATION BASIS AND ATTACH COPIES IF AT ALL POSSIBLE. USE YOUR OWN STATIONERY FOR THE LIST.

Part 3(c)(3)
POLICY DECLARATIONS

LIBERTY MUTUAL FIRE INSURANCE COMPANY-LIBERTYGUARD AUTO POLICY
BOSTON MASSACHUSETTS

REWRITE   10/16/87

ITEM 1 NAMED INSURED AND ADDRESS	POLICY NUMBER	TD	CD
	AO2-281-362813-007 RT	02	0

For Service Call or Write Your Liberty Service Office At:

ROBINSON PLAZA TWO RT 60
ROBINSON TOWNSHIP PA 15205
412-787-7375

ITEM 2 POLICY PERIOD 12:01 A.M. Standard Time (At The Address of The Named Insured As Stated In The Policy)

FROM: 10/16/87   TO: 10/16/88

This policy shall expire on the date shown except that it may be continued in force for successive policy periods by the payment of the required renewal premium. Each such policy period shall be for the period specified in the renewal declarations.

ITEM 3 COVERAGES, LIMITS OF LIABILITY AND ANNUAL PREMIUM CHARGES

Coverage is provided only where a premium or limit of liability is shown for the coverage.
Limits of liability are expressed in thousands of dollars.

A. LIABILITY			A B C UNDER-INSURED ANNUAL PREMIUM	A U T O	D. COVERAGE FOR DAMAGE TO YOUR AUTO			D ANNUAL PREMIUM	NO FAULT		TOTAL ANNUAL PREMIUM
SINGLE LIMIT Each Accident	SEPARATE LIMITS Bodily Injury Ea. Person/Ea. Accident	Property Damage Ea. Accident			Cov. For Loss Caused By Collision Included	Deductible Amount Applicable to Each Loss In Dollars: Loss Caused By Collision	Loss Other Than Loss Caused By Collision				
[X] 50	[ ]		277.	1	YES	250	100	249.			526.
B. MEDICAL PAYMENTS Each Person	C. UNINSURED MOTORIST Ea. Person/Ea. Accident	UNDERINSURED MOTORIST Ea. Person/Ea. Accident									
5	20/40 10 PD	20/40 10 PD									
OPTIONAL COVERAGES	PP0302 6/80 ENDORSEMENT NUMBER	10. PREMIUM	ENDORSEMENT NUMBER		PREMIUM	ENDORSEMENT NUMBER		PREMIUM	TOTAL PREMIUM		536.

RENT REIMB VEH 1

ENDORSEMENTS PP0467 04 86,PP0453 11/82,AS1080,PP0305 8/83,
ATTACHED   PP0303 04 86,PP0002 04 86,AS1046 7/80,
            PP0302 6/80

ITEM 4 DESCRIPTION OF AUTOMOBILE OR TRAILER

AUTO	YEAR	MAKE	VEHICLE IDENTIFICATION NUMBER	RATING CLASS	DISC CODE	SAFE DRIVER PLAN MODIFICATION	OWNERSHIP OF AUTOMOBILE OTHER THAN NAMED INSURED
1	84	FORD	1FABP2837EF163558	13	0	VIOL-SC 0 ACC-SC 0	

GARAGING (If Other Than Named Insured's Address)

ITEM 5 LOSS PAYEE	1 MOBAY FCU	041

SECRETARY   PRESIDENT

This policy, including all endorsements attached is countersigned by:

AUTHORIZED REPRESENTATIVE

AUTO 2888 5/86

COMPLETE THE QUESTIONNAIRE AT *FORM 4.12*.

INSURANCE POLICY DECLARATIONS QUESTIONNAIRE

A policy declaration page lists those coverages available under an insurance contract. Review the policy declaration **page above. Answer the following questions.**

1. Are there any funeral benefits payable under this policy?   ☐ Yes   ☐ No

    If yes, what are they?_____

    _____

2. Is there any underinsurance or uninsured motorist coverage under this policy?   ☐ Yes   ☐ No

    What are the limits?_____

    Is there a limitation per accident?   ☐ Yes   ☐ No

    If yes, what is the limitation?_____

    _____

3. What is the premium payable under this policy?_____

    _____

4. What vehicles are covered under the policy?_____

    _____

    _____

    _____

    _____

5. If you have a car insurance policy or you have access to another party's policy, compare and contrast that policy declaration page with this example. What are the significant differences?_____

    _____

    _____

    _____

    _____

Form 4.12

Part 3(c)(4)
INSURANCE QUESTIONNAIRE

In auto accident analysis, the attorneys for plaintiffs and the insurance carrier frequently find themselves in hardened, adversarial positions. Unfortunately, perceptions on both sides of the legal fence are often exaggerated and stereotypical. Assure the insurance company of confidentiality and anonymity and ask for their general perception of the legal profession when handling an auto accident case. If you have difficulty with this assignment, ask your instructor for a permission form or other letter of introduction.

COMPLETE THE QUESTIONNAIRE AT *FORM 4.13.*

INSURANCE AGENCY QUESTIONNAIRE

1. What is your agency's general position on the validity of auto accident claims?_____

_____

_____

_____

2. Do you think they are credible as a rule or is your agency suspicious of their integrity?_____

_____

_____

_____

3. What role do you see lawyers playing in the insurance adjustment process, that is, from a plaintiff's perspective?

_____

_____

_____

4. How do lawyers benefit or cause detriment to the insurance adjustment process?_____

_____

_____

_____

_____

5. As an agent, what is your general impression of lawyers in personal injury practice?_____

_____

_____

6. Think of your own company's ability to pay claims. Does your company make an honest, good faith effort to resolve auto accident claims?   ☐ Yes   ☐ No

Explain:_____

_____

_____

7. Do you see any better means or methods for the adjudication of auto accident claims than the one that presently exists? Take your time since your thoughts are most appreciated._____

_____

_____

_____

_____

_____

_____

_____

_____

_____

_____

Thank you very much for your cooperation.

Form 4.13

ASSIGNMENT #3 — PART 4
HUMAN DAMAGES

The human damage in auto accidents reaches staggering proportions. Medical bills, loss of human lives and pain and suffering are almost too immeasurable to calculate. This assignment calls for the legal specialist to interview people on the street who deal directly with the types of injuries often the subject matter of an auto accident. You have some choices in this matter, but you are required to conduct either a phone or personal interview with any of the following agencies or entities:
1. Hospital emergency room
2. Family physician or other medical personnel
3. EMT or paramedic personnel
4. Police officer
5. Insurance adjuster

COMPLETE THE QUESTIONNAIRE AT *FORM 4.14.*

HUMAN DAMAGES QUESTIONNAIRE

In any of those entities listed, you are to pose the following questions seeking to gauge the extent of damages that people suffer in auto accidents.

NAME OF AGENCY OR ENTITY:_____

1. What is the chief cause of auto accidents in your view?_____

_____

_____

_____

2. Is the make and design of automobiles in the contemporary marketplace partially responsible for the injury or destruction?_____

_____

_____

3. What types of injuries affect you most when you see them?_____

_____

_____

_____

4. Do seatbelts play an important role in the minimization of damages?   ☐ Yes   ☐ No

   Explain your position:_____

_____

_____

5. Surely you have seen many injuries. Who is most severely injured in auto accident cases, children or adults?____

_____

6. Give an example of a miracle accident, that which should have produced death, but everyone walked away unscathed. Outline the facts as closely as you can._____

_____

_____

_____

_____

_____

7. Have you ever seen lawyers acting as ambulance chasers?   ☐ Yes   ☐ No

   Explain:_____

_____

_____

Thank you for your cooperation.

Form 4.14

ASSIGNMENT #3 — PART 5
MAKING CONTACTS

Auto accident analysis and litigation requires the development of many good contacts. Previously mentioned were insurance companies, police departments and hospital and emergency room personnel. However, there are other, often overlooked, contacts that can provide insight into the nature of your case.

USING *FORM 4.15*, COMPILE A LIST OF CONTACTS AND WRITE OUT A RATIONALE AS TO WHY THEY MAY BE OF ASSISTANCE TO YOU.

LIST OF CONTACTS

1. Towing Dealer:

   Name_____

   Address_____

   Rationale_____

   _____

   _____

2. Private Security Companies (list 3):

   Name_____

   Address_____

   Name_____

   Address_____

   Name_____

   Address_____

   Rationale_____

   _____

   _____

3. United States Army/State/Local Pathologists:

   Name_____

   Address_____

   Rationale_____

   _____

   _____

4. Engineering Firms (specializing in accident reconstruction):

Name_____

Address_____

Name_____

Address_____

Rationale_____

_____

_____

5. Engineering Firms (specializing in highway design, construction, and corresponding defects):

Name_____

Address_____

Name_____

Address_____

Rationale_____

_____

_____

6. Types of expert witnesses that are useful in a case of auto litigation (list 3):

Name_____

Address_____

Name_____

Address_____

Name_____

Address_____

Rationale_____

_____

7. Product liability specialists. Auto litigation often involves product liability problems. From your own personal knowl-edge, what types of vehicles, the particular components thereof, have had a defective design or construction? You may remember the case of the automobile fuel tank problem in the Ford Pinto during the 1970s. Can you list two or three other examples of product liability actions brought against automobile manufacturers? If you cannot remem-ber the exact names of the cases or companies, a brief narrative description will suffice.

Product liability problem 1:_____

_____

_____

_____

Product liability problem 2:_____

_____

_____

_____

_____

Product liability problem 3:_____

_____

_____

_____

*You may also find an auto dealer or service repairman who would be most helpful in indicating to you chronic and ongoing product liability problems in automobile construction. Secondly, consumer agencies in your local community may also be of help.

Form 4.15

ASSIGNMENT #3 — PART 6
SURVEYING THE LANDSCAPE FOR TORTIOUS CONDUCT

This final exercise is pure field work. You are asked to provide examples of the following tortious conduct by photographing or diagramming its existence. The assignment requires that you adhere to the elements required in the proof of the given cause of action and that you state why your pictorial representation meets that standard.

COMPLETE *FORM 4.16*.

TORTIOUS CONDUCT

The following tortious conduct should be photographed and documented.

1. A case of trespass

Description:_____

_____

_____

_____

_____

_____

_____

_____

_____

_____

2.   Violation of Toxic Waste Legislation, Emissions Standards or Pollution Control Activities

Description:_____

_____

_____

_____

_____

_____

_____

_____

_____

_____

3.   Zoning Ordinance Violation

Description:_____

_____

_____

_____

_____

_____

_____

_____

_____

_____

_____

4. Assault (a hypothetical injury is acceptable)

Description:_____

_____

_____

_____

_____

_____

_____

_____

_____

5.   Conversion of Property (stolen property)

Description:_____

_____

_____

_____

_____

_____

_____

_____

_____

_____

_____

Form 4.16

PRACTICUM EXERCISES NO. 5
LITIGATION AND PLEADINGS

	Time Allotted (hours)	Point Value
Preliminary Investigation:		
Assignment #1	2.0	20.0
Summons and Service of Process:		
Assignment #2	0.5	5.0
Preparation of Pleadings:		
Assignment #3	4.0	35.0
Discovery: Interrogatories:		
Assignment #4	2.0	25.0
Special Pleadings from the Defendant's Perspective:		
Assignment #5 (3 parts)	1.5	15.0
	10.0	100.0

I.
INTRODUCTION
The Case of an Elevator Accident

The major function of paralegals and legal assistants regarding litigation and pleadings is client consultation and the preparation of pleadings documents themselves under the supervision of an attorney. The fact pattern provided in this series of exercises involves an elevator shaft accident. The instructor may substitute another fact pattern and call for the completion of the same documentation.

The series of exercises should produce the typical and standardized forms, pleadings and other litigation materials. At times, certain facts and issues may be left out and the student should feel free to fill in such information with hypothetical data. Therefore, for purposes of these exercises, the following fact pattern governs the entire series of assignments.

FACT PATTERN

Parties: Plaintiff — Victim Edward Robinson, 1811 Library Road, Saginaw, Michigan 46668

Age: 17

Location of Accident: Jayco's Discount Stores and Warehouse, 1215 Guelph Street, Detroit, Michigan 45555

Nature of Accident: Victim caught between elevator shaft and elevator itself and crushed to death. Severe internal injuries of extreme complexity, resulting in fatality. (See *Photo 5.1* below.)

Photo 5.1

Elevator Manufacturer: Robert's Elevator Design, 14 Park Avenue, New York, New York 10010
Elevator Distributor: ODO Elevator Company, 12 Rayon Avenue, Salem, New Jersey 08888
Elevator Installer: Harvey Construction Company, 9004 Miller Lane, Indianapolis, Indiana 66610
Details of Incident:

After an exhaustive investigation by both civil and criminal authorities, the following details are an accurate reflection of the incident. First, plaintiff/victim entered into Jayco's warehouse at 9:30 p.m. on June 1, 1989, for purposes of purchasing tools at bargain basement prices. As he was wandering around the store, he inadvertently entered into an employee area that traditionally is off-limits. However, there were no signs or other warnings posted which would indicate that this location of the store was for employees only. After a short period of time, the plaintiff/victim apparently wandered into the wrong location of the store, clearly on the wrong floor. Seeing an elevator at the northwesterly corner of the building, it is assumed he decided to enter it to go up to the next floor.

Unknown to the plaintiff/victim, the elevator was currently being repaired for faulty switches. As a result, the elevator was located in a stationary position five feet below floor level. Without any warning tapes, signs, barriers or other evidence, the plaintiff/victim walked into the shaft and fell 15 feet down. Remember also that the elevator carriage portion of the entire elevator mechanism was below, though the internal walls and barriers appeared to be normal, thereby creating an illusion that the shaft had stopped in the proper place. While no serious injuries had yet been inflicted outside of a broken ankle, plaintiff/victim was definitely in a precarious situation. This was especially true when the elevator started to rise again as the maintenance personnel were performing electrical switching functions below. In the plaintiff's/victim's efforts to get out of the shaft as it moved upward, seeing that there was a severe and imminent danger of being crushed to death, his clothing became caught between the shaft walls and the operating mechanism of the elevator itself. So forceful was the draw on the material of his clothing that his leg was pulled between the wall of the shaft and the shaft itself. The other leg was soon thereafter pulled. As the shaft continued its climb of 15 feet, the plaintiff/victim, crudely put, was sucked in between the elevator shaft and the wall itself and crushed to death.

Plaintiff's/victim's family seeks representation from your law firm. Upon initial consultation, it is determined that certain actions will lie against various parties. Those actions are: wrongful death, negligence, product liability. Other actions may exist, but for purposes of these exercises, students should only be concerned with the above three causes.

II.
ANATOMY OF A LAWSUIT: AN ELEVATOR ACCIDENT

The series of exercises below commence with the initial interview of a client or, as in this case, the client's representative, to collect information for case preparation and analysis. For purposes of these assignments, the following will apply:

Case Number: 89-68841

Action: Civil

Jurisdiction: Local trial court (Instructor will give specifics.)

Law Firm Representing Plaintiff/Victim: Arnold and Palkowski, 1139 Byrne Street, Decatur, Georgia 44488

Firm Representing Manufacturer: Larry Gaitlin, Professional Associates, 34 Wilson Street, Wilson, Michigan 68111

Construction Company Counsel: Lucinda Davis, 39 Argon Avenue, Aurora, Michigan 61133

Firm Representing Retailer/Distributor of Elevator: Wilson, Pickett and Jones, 84 Lanny Lane, Ann Arbor, Michigan 66613

Counsel for Jayco Manufacturing: Armitage and Arbutis, P.C., 400 Davis Way, Detroit, Michigan 66111

Estate Administrator: Edward Robinson, Sr., same address as victim

*Additional facts will be made available as each assignment is completed.

A. Objectives

(1) To learn about the specific causes of action which might exist in an elevator shaft accident;

(2) To sort, discern and translate narrative facts into litigation, pleadings and other documentation; and

(3) To follow and track an adjudication of an elevator shaft claim from initial interview to commencement of trial.

B. Student Obligations

(1) To complete all litigation checklists, interview sheets, diagrammatic or photographic assignments;

(2) To prepare all pleadings documents as required under these series of exercises; and

(3) To prepare a series of interrogatories focusing on the nature of an elevator shaft accident.

C. Instructor Obligations

    (1) To provide students with whatever local forms are necessary to complete assignments appropriately;

    (2) To give local guidance and input which highlights jurisdictional differences from the generic fact patterns provided;

    (3) To make certain that all forms and documents that students complete reflect local practice and custom.

D. Time Allotted: 10 hours*

E. Value of Assignment: 100 points*

*Time allotment and point value to be distributed exercise by exercise.

ASSIGNMENT #1
PRELIMINARY INVESTIGATION

Time Allotted: 2.0 hours
Point Value: 20.0 points

COMPLETE THE QUESTIONNAIRE AT *FORM 5.1.*

PRELIMINARY INVESTIGATION QUESTIONNAIRE

Information Regarding Elevator:

1. There are many types of elevators from passenger to freight. What type of elevator is this more likely to be given the set of facts above?_____

    _____

2. Go into the field and take a picture of at least one form of elevator. If at all possible, take pictures of both the exterior and the interior. Place the photographs below.

3. As you analyze the nature of the elevator, what types of accidents appear most likely and possible. List at least three types.

    1._____

    2._____

    3._____

4. After inspecting an actual elevator, do you see how the injury and death occurred in the facts outlined?

    ☐ Yes   ☐ No

5. The investigators in this case deduced that this was the only way that this could have happened. Do you have another explanation?_____

_____

_____

6. In any elevator you have inspected, is there some type of license or authority to operate that elevator?

☐ Yes ☐ No

Explain exactly what:_____

_____

7. Look closely at the license. Is there a reference to a statute, ordinance or other piece of legislation which guides the safe operation of elevators? ☐ Yes ☐ No

8. Do you think it makes any difference if a statute exists? ☐ Yes ☐ No

Explain:_____

_____

_____

9. Does it bear on the question of standard of care or possible negligence? ☐ Yes ☐ No

Why?_____

_____

_____

Status of Plaintiff/Victim:

How a plaintiff/victim is classified in an elevator shaft accident is an extremely important element. If he is a business invitee, a higher standard of care is owed, but if a trespasser, a lower standard applies. In the facts described above, how would you classify the plaintiff/victim?

10. Is the plaintiff/victim a business invitee? ☐ Yes ☐ No

Why?_____

_____

11. Is the plaintiff/victim a licensee? ☐ Yes ☐ No

Why?_____

_____

12. Is the plaintiff/victim a trespasser? ☐ Yes ☐ No

Why?_____

_____

13. Does the type of establishment where the elevator is located have any bearing on the nature of the cause of action? ☐ Yes ☐ No

Why?_____

_____

14. Would it be important to acquire a copy of the repair history on the elevator? ☐ Yes ☐ No

Why?_____

_____

15. Would it be important to track or confirm repairs that have taken place on the elevator since the date of the accident? ☐ Yes ☐ No

Why?_____

_____

16. Would an inspection schedule, mandated by ordinance or statute, be an important piece of information in the preparation of this cause of action? ☐ Yes ☐ No

Why?_____

_____

17. The physical and personal characteristics of the plaintiff/victim may play an important role in the preparation of these causes of actions. Why so?_____

_____

_____

_____

a. What difference does the age make?_____

_____

_____

b. What about substandard vision?_____

_____

_____

c. What if the plaintiff had physical handicaps?_____

_____

_____

d.   What if plaintiff was under the influence of alcohol or drugs?_____

_____

_____

18.   Who are the potential defendants in this case and on what theories of action (list five)?

Defendant #1:_____

Theory behind cause of action:_____

_____

_____

Defendant #2:_____

Theory behind cause of action:_____

_____

_____

Defendant #3:_____

Theory behind cause of action:_____

_____

_____

Defendant #4:_____

Theory behind cause of action:_____

_____

_____

Defendant #5:_____

Theory behind cause of action:_____

_____

_____

Form 5.1

ASSIGNMENT #2

SUMMONS AND SERVICE OF PROCESS

Time Allotted: 0.5 hours
Point Value: 5.0 points

To commence a cause of action, service of process is a necessary component of any litigation. Acquire from your instructor those forms that are unique to your local jurisdiction to complete this series of exercises. Before completing the localized versions, look at the documents below at *Figures 5.1* and *5.2* and complete using the facts stated above as well as these additional facts.

1. The case, for purposes of this exercise, is in the U.S. District Court.
2. Defendant: Jayco Warehouse
3. Response Time: 30 days
4. Clerk: Hypothetical data

COMPLETE YOUR OWN LOCALIZED VERSION OF A SUMMONS SUCH AS THAT SHOWN FOLLOWING.

AO 440 (Rev. 5/85) Summons In a Civil Action 3-12

United States District Court

__________________ DISTRICT OF __________________

SUMMONS IN A CIVIL ACTION

V.

CASE NUMBER:

TO: (Name and Address of Defendant)

YOU ARE HEREBY SUMMONED and required to file with the Clerk of this Court and serve upon

PLAINTIFF'S ATTORNEY (name and address)

an answer to the complaint which is herewith served upon you, within ______________ days after service of this summons upon you, exclusive of the day of service. If you fail to do so, judgment by default will be taken against you for the relief demanded in the complaint.

_______________________ CLERK

_______________________ DATE

_______________________ BY DEPUTY CLERK

Figure 5.1

In service of process, a return of service form of some type is usually employed in the jurisdiction.

COMPLETE YOUR OWN LOCALIZED VERSION OF THE RETURN OF SERVICE FORM BELOW WITH THE FOLLOWING INFORMATION.

1. Service made by: Anadaga County Sheriff's Department
2. Date: June 30, 1989
3. Place of Service: Business address
4. Service fees: $100
5. Travel expenditures: $20
6. Successful personal service
7. Address of server: Anadaga County, Michigan 66680

AO 440 (Rev. 5/85) Summons in a Civil Action

RETURN OF SERVICE

Service of the Summons and Complaint was made by me[1]	DATE
NAME OF SERVER	TITLE

Check one box below to indicate appropriate method of service

☐ Served personally upon the defendant. Place where served: _____
_____   _____

☐ Left copies thereof at the defendant's dwelling house or usual place of abode with a person of suitable age and discretion then residing therein.
Name of person with whom the summons and complaint were left: _____

☐ Returned unexecuted: _____
_____
_____

☐ Other (specify): _____
_____
_____

STATEMENT OF SERVICE FEES

TRAVEL	SERVICES	TOTAL

DECLARATION OF SERVER

I declare under penalty of perjury under the laws of the United States of America that the foregoing information contained in the Return of Service and Statement of Service Fees is true and correct.

Executed on _____   _____
            Date   *Signature of Server*

            _____
            Address of Server

1) As to who may serve a summons see Rule 4 of the Federal Rules of Civil Procedure.

Figure 5.2

ASSIGNMENT #3
PREPARATION OF PLEADINGS

The standard components of pleadings for an all-purpose litigation are the subject matter of these exercises.

Time Allotted: 4.0 hours
Point Value: 35.0 points

ASSIGNMENT #3 — PART 1
THE COMPLAINT

Part 1(a): Captions

Prepare a caption using the following formats for all parties involved. Plaintiff will always be *Estate of Edward Robinson v.* either singular or multiple defendants. Prepare first multiple causes of action. Assume also aside from the singular plaintiff-defendant caption that defendants have been joined in some fashion or determined, for efficiency in adjudication, to be designated multiple defendants.

CAPTION 1: Use as an example the model outlined below.

```
United States,                          )
plaintiff                               )
                                        )
v.                                      )
                                        )   Case No.
Harold Davis, E.I. Dupont               )
Corporation of America, Inc.,           )
defendant                               )
```

USE *FORM 5.2* TO COMPLETE THIS ASSIGNMENT.

CAPTION #1

```
                                        )
                                        )
                                        )
                                        )
                                        )
                                        )
                                        )
                                        )
                                        )
```

CAPTION #2

```
                                        )
                                        )
                                        )
                                        )
                                        )
                                        )
                                        )
                                        )
                                        )
```

CAPTION #3

)
)
)
)
)
)
)
)
)
)

CAPTION #4

)
)
)
)
)
)
)
)
)
)

CAPTION #5

)
)
)
)
)
)
)
)
)
)

CAPTION #6

)
)
)
)
)
)
)
)
)
)

Form 5.2

Depending on your local rules, place a statement of jurisdiction or venue either at the top or other location as your instructor advises. An example of such would be:

IN THE COURT OF COMMON PLEAS
VENANGO COUNTY, COMMONWEALTH OF PENNSYLVANIA

Fill in below where your jurisdictional or venue statement would be cited on the cover page of a complaint.

Outside of the jurisdictional heading and a caption, a complaint should outline in detail the following issues:

— Jurisdictional facts
— Status of the plaintiff/victim
— Facts upon which the complaint exists
— Status of the defendant
— The nature and manner of defendant's negligence
— Nature and extent of injuries suffered by plaintiff
— Type of damages
— Prayer for relief
— Signature
— Verification

Part 1(b)
Identification and Jurisdictional Paragraphs

A complaint requires a statement of identification of the parties as well as a reference to the jurisdictional and venue requirements of the court so selected.

COMPILE ONE EXAMPLE OF AN INITIAL TWO PARAGRAPHS FOR THIS ELEVATOR SHAFT ACCIDENT USING THE FOLLOWING FORMAT. SELECT PLAINTIFF AND ANY DEFENDANT YOU SO DESIRE TO COMPLETE THIS EXERCISE. USE LEGAL RULED PAPER.

Comes before this honorable court the plaintiff, _____, by and through his attorneys, _____, and therefore complains that the defendant, _____, a corporation _____:

1. That on _____ day of _____, 1989, the defendant owned, managed and controlled a building located at _____, City of _____, County of _____, State of _____.

Part 1(c)
Body of Complaint

At this stage of the complaint, the parties set forth those facts, conditions and theories of argument which provide a substantive basis for the cause of action. Read the sample complaint below, taken from 17 *Am. Jur. Model Trials,* at pages 772 through 774, for a standard complaint in an elevator shaft accident. This form is reproduced with the permission of the copyright owners, The Lawyers Co-operative Publishing Company, Rochester, New York.

Now comes the plaintiff, _____, by his attorneys, _____, and complains of the defendant, _____, a corporation, as follows:

1. That on and prior to the _____ day of _____, 1989, the defendant owned, managed and controlled a certain building located at _____ Streets in the City of _____, County of _____, State of _____.

2. That the defendant maintained a certain elevator in said building which defendant equipped, maintained, and operated for patrons and other business invitees of the defendant; that the defendant invited or permitted all such persons to ride and use said elevator.

3. That at the time and place, and immediately prior thereto, plaintiff was lawfully in said building.

4. That on the date and place above mentioned, and while plaintiff was attempting to enter said elevator car, he was caused to or did fall from the landing platform of the elevator shaft.

5. That _____ Elevator Co. had been engaged by the codefendant to care for, maintain, repair and otherwise keep the above-mentioned elevator in safe operating condition.

6. That by reason of the premises it became and at all times was the duty of the defendants, their agents, servants and employees, to exercise the highest degree of care in equipping, maintaining and operating said elevator so as to avoid injuring persons using said elevator in said building.

7. That the defendant, by and through its agents, servants and employees, was then and there guilty of one or more of the following acts of negligence or carelessness:

    (a) Failure to keep and maintain said elevator in a reasonably safe condition;

    (b) Failure to keep and maintain sufficient and suitable lights on or about said elevator;

    (c) Failure to keep gates, doors, and other safeguards on said elevator in a closed or proper position;

    (d) Failure to provide said elevator with proper and adequate safety devices;

    (e) Failure to place or spot said elevator at or on the first floor;

    (f) Failure to provide an operator, when defendant knew, or in the exercise of due care, could have known that plaintiff would have occasion to use said elevator;

    (g) Causing or permitting employees of an independent contractor to use faulty, inadequate, and improper tools or equipment while using said elevator;

    (h) Maintaining faulty and inadequate elevator hatchway doors;

    (i) Failure to properly inspect said elevator and hatchway doors;

    (j) Failure to comply with requirements of Chapter _____ of the Municipal Code of _____;

    (k) Failure to comply with Chapter _____, Section _____ of the Municipal Code of _____, which provides:

[Insert provisions of appropriate section or sections of applicable rules, regulations or laws.]

    (l) Negligent failure to warn the plaintiff that the elevator cage was in use on another floor;

    (m) Negligent failure to warn the plaintiff that the elevator was not on the floor level at that particular time.

8. That as a direct and proximate result of the negligence of the defendants in one or more of the above particulars, the plaintiff was caused to and did fall into said elevator shaft while attempting to enter, thereby sustaining serious injuries and fractures of his _____ shoulder, _____ elbow, _____ hip, _____ ankle and fracture of the spine, with incontinence of the bowel and bladder, all of which caused injuries and aggravation of pre-existing conditions of a permanent and lasting nature, and the plaintiff then and there suffered other injuries, both externally and internally, and as a result thereof the plaintiff became, was and is sick, sore, lame, and disordered, and has suffered and will continue to permanently suffer great pain and agony in body and mind, and plaintiff was caused to and did lay out and expend, in endeavoring to be cured of his certain injuries, and will in the future be compelled to lay out and expend divers sums of money for medical care, nursing care, and attention and for medicine in endeavoring to be cured of certain injuries, and plaintiff was greatly hindered and will be prevented in the future from

following his usual occupation, at which he earned divers large gains, and has lost divers other large gains which he would and could have made.

[Prayer for relief, signature, verification.]

USING THIS STANDARD COMPLAINT AS AN EXAMPLE, ASSUMING THAT YOUR COMPLAINT IS GOING TO BE FILED AGAINST MANUFACTURER AND DISTRIBUTOR OF THE ELEVATOR, PREPARE YOUR OWN DOCUMENT EMPLOYING THE FOLLOWING FACTUAL ALLEGATIONS. USE LEGAL RULED PAPER.

1. That the car had various operating devices and controls which were broken.
2. That there was no protective barrier between the floor level and the elevator shaft when plaintiff/victim fell into it.
3. That the elevator electrical components were defective, constructed of substandard wiring, rusted and corroded joints and bolts.
4. That the ropes of the elevator which guide the shaft up a vertical path were crushed, worn, broken and excessively in disrepair.
5. That all safety devices were improperly adjusted, corroded and not appropriately lubricated.
6. That the elevator mechanism did not include a safety device when a jam or other intrusion took place.

PREPARE A SECONDARY COMPLAINT BODY ALLEGING THESE FACTS AGAINST THE WAREHOUSE OWNER WHERE THE ELEVATOR WAS LOCATED. USE LEGAL RULED PAPER.

1. Knowing that the elevator was in a state of disrepair and was not available to the general public, the defendant did not appropriately post signs or other warning notices.
2. Knowing that the elevator could possibly be used by non-authorized personnel, the defendant did not take proper precautions in securing the area.
3. The elevator was not properly maintained as is required under legislation.
4. That the elevator area did not have appropriate lighting highlighting its dysfunctional state.
5. That the elevator was not equipped, updated or modernized according to current statutory standards.
6. That there were no warnings that the elevator could only be operated by authorized personnel.
7. That the warehouse was negligent in not providing appropriate security to discover the injury in time to possibly save a life.

PREPARE A THIRD COMPLAINT DIRECTED AT THE MANUFACTURER BASED ON A PRODUCT LIABILITY THEORY. WHAT TYPE OF PLEADING LANGUAGE WOULD BE NECESSARY TO PROVE A DEFECTIVE DESIGN OF THE PRODUCT? USE LEGAL RULES PAPER.

Can you think of any other parties a complaint can be directed to?_____

_____

_____

_____

Could a warranty theory possibly be alleged? How so?_____

_____

_____

_____

_____

DIVIDE EACH MATERIAL ALLEGATION IN THE BODY OF THE COMPLAINT BY ANY OF THE FOLLOWING SYSTEMS:
— COUNT I, THEN COUNT II
— ROMAN NUMERAL I, THEN ROMAN NUMERAL II
— FIRST CAUSE OF ACTION, THEN SECOND CAUSE OF ACTION

YOUR COMPLAINT SHOULD CONTAIN SOME ELEMENTARY ALLEGATIONS REGARDING NEGLIGENCE CAUSE OF ACTION, THAT IS, LACKING IN DUE CARE OR FAILURE TO ADHERE TO REASONABLE STANDARDS OF CONDUCT; A PRODUCT LIABILITY CLAIM, THAT IS, THAT THE MANUFACTURE, RETAIL AND DISTRIBUTION OF THIS PRODUCT IS A DEFECTIVE UNDERTAKING; AND THIRDLY, THAT BOTH THE NEGLIGENCE AND THE DEFECTIVE PRODUCT DESIGN CAUSED THE WRONGFUL DEATH OF A YOUNG MAN. BE SURE THESE THREE CAUSES OF ACTION ARE HIGHLIGHTED IN YOUR COMPLAINT BODY.

Part 1(d)
Prayer for Relief

After alleging specific theories of liability within the body of the complaint, the complainant then requests or prays for specific relief. A standardized relief clause might be:

Therefore, plaintiff requests judgment against defendant for the following:

1. All physical and mental pain and suffering, anguish present, past and future in the sum of $_____.

2. Any and all hospital and medical expenses, past, present and future in the sum of $_____.

3. Any loss of earnings, past, present and future, in the sum of $_____.

4. Any costs of the lawsuit incurred.

5. Other such relief that the court may deem just, proper and equitable.

DRAFT A PRAYER FOR RELIEF EMPLOYING THE FACT PATTERN AT HAND, AND DO NOT FORGET TO HIGHLIGHT THE WRONGFUL DEATH ASPECTS OF THIS CASE. LOOK TO THE AGE OF THE PLAINTIFF AND SEE THE INCREASED ECONOMIC IMPACT SUCH AN EARLY MORTALITY HAS, ESPECIALLY AS RELATES TO FUTURE EARNINGS. USE LEGAL RULED PAPER.

COMPLETE THE QUESTIONNAIRE AT *FORM 5.3* WHICH WILL ASSIST YOU IN DRAFTING THE PRAYER FOR RELIEF.

DAMAGES QUESTIONNAIRE

1. When analyzing the damage value of any case and stating so in the prayer for relief within the complaint document, consider the following issues:

   — What is the age of the plaintiff?

   — What is the life expectancy?

   — Is the plaintiff married?

   — Does the plaintiff have any dependents?

   — What is the educational level of the plaintiff?

   — What is the plaintiff's annual income for the last three to five years?

   — What would be the value of any lost benefits?

   — What is the total of the medical bills?

   — What are the physician's bills?

   — What are the medication and drug costs?

   — What are the costs of diagnostic tests — x-ray and diagnostic imaging?

   — What are the costs for any intensive or long-term care?

   — What are the funeral expenses?

   — What are the costs for any psychiatric or psychological counseling for either plaintiff or the plaintiff's family?

2. Describe below the more formidable arguments one might claim in a damage request against the defendants.___

   _____

   _____

   _____

   _____

   _____

3. What makes this case more valuable than another?_____

   _____

   _____

   _____

   _____

4. Does the brutality and grotesqueness of the case bear on the question of damages?   ☐ Yes   ☐ No

Discuss below:_____

_____

_____

_____

_____

_____

_____

_____

_____

_____

_____

_____

Form 5.3

Part 1(e)
Signature and Verification Clauses

The final components of a complaint include the signature and verification clauses which can be signed, depending on local practice and custom, either by the attorney representing the client or by the client himself or herself. Signature clauses are easy enough to complete.

IN THIS ASSIGNMENT, SIMPLY IMITATE THE SIGNATURE CLAUSE BELOW.

_____

Charles P. Nemeth, Esquire
402 E. Dickson St.
Midway, PA 15060
ATTORNEY FOR PLAINTIFF

INSERT YOUR SIGNATURE CLAUSE HERE:

The verification clause of a claimant is positive affirmation that the content of the complaint is true and correct to the best knowledge of the complainant or his attorney. Under the Federal Rules of Civil Procedure, Rule 11 requires that if an attorney signs a complaint that the attorney verify the truth or accuracy of the statements therein. Rule 11 has been the subject of some substantial academic commentary and litigation. At any rate, the verification clause completes the complaint and assures the court that the content within is not frivolous nor unmeritorious. An example of a verification clause is:

Samuel Davis, Attorney for Plaintiff, being duly sworn according to law hereby states and deposes that he is the attorney for the plaintiff in the foregoing matter and that all those facts set forth within this complaint and attached hereto are true and accurate to the best of his knowledge, information and belief.

_____

Samuel Davis
Attorney for Plaintiff

Sworn to and subscribed before me this _____ day of _____, 1989.

_____

Notary

My commission expires _____, 19____.

COMPLETE A VERIFICATION FORM USING COUNSEL FOR THE PLAINTIFF/VICTIM ESTATE REPRESENTATIVE TO FILL IN THE APPROPRIATE BLANKS. USE LEGAL RULED PAPER.

4.   Discovery: Interrogatories

Time Allotted: 2.0 hours
Value: 25.0 points

You are required under this section of the practicum exercises to draft a set of interrogatories. Interrogatories are generally in written form and are guided by state, local and federal rules and custom. As a general principle, interrogatories, as long as they are not too broad-based, too vague in nature or nothing more than fishing expeditions are reasonable questions the adversarial parties have posed to each other for purposes of case evaluation and trial preparation. In the case of an elevator shaft accident, a wide range of issues need preliminary resolution. Utilize the following issues to construct interrogatories in question-style format.

1. Distance of fall into the shaft.
2. Extent of injuries initially received after fall.
3. Complete explanation as to how plaintiff's body became caught between the shaft and the moving elevator.
4. First party on scene after injury.
5. Amount and type of witnesses.
6. First reporting officer.
7. Name of insurance company.
8. Name of claims adjuster.
9. Inspection report on elevator.
10. Historical problems with elevator.
11. Replacement records since date of accident.
12. Exact parts or mechanisms repaired or replaced.
13. Ownership of building where incident took place.
14. Landlord or leases involved.
15. Existence of elevator operators.
16. Tests and inspection records.
17. Licenses and certificates.
18. Last inspection date.
19. Inspection after date of accident.
20. Results of inspections after date of accident.
21. Defendants' reasons for malfunction.
22. Level of illumination and lighting.
23. Distance of warning or notices.
24. Total depth of elevator shaft or hoistway.
25. Type of lubricants used.
26. Authorization for operation.
27. Safety equipment and devices.
28. Construction of the frame of the elevator.
29. Construction of the elevator car floor.
30. Depth of elevator car platform.
31. Height of elevator car.
32. Emergency or safety devices.
33. Automatic stopping devices.
34. Emergency stopping devices.

35. Rated capacity in pounds.
36. Illumination in hoist or shaftway.
37. Safety devices — electrical, hydraulic or mechanical.
38. Slow down devices — buffers, auxiliary fastening devices, speed governors, product safety mechanism switch, slack rope switch.
39. Statutory guidance on operation.
40. Color of elevator shaft doors.
41. Elevator floor indicator's accuracy.
42. Security systems.
43. Speaker units.
44. Alarms.

COMPLETE A FULL SERIES OF INTERROGATORY QUESTIONS FOR PURPOSES OF DIS-COVERY IN THE ELEVATOR SHAFT INCIDENT. USE LEGAL RULED PAPER.

5. Special Pleadings from the Defendant's Perspective

Time Allotted: 1.5 hours
Value: 15.0 points

Thus far, the preparation of our case has been pro-plaintiff. Ponder for a second the task of defending either the warehouse, the manufacturer, distributor and retailer or the construction company that installed this elevator system. What types of arguments might cast a favorable light on defendants' conduct? Pose at least four different arguments.

1. _____

_____

2. _____

_____

3. _____

_____

4. _____

_____

Preparation of some of the following pleadings will highlight a defendant's perspective in an elevator shaft incident.

ASSIGNMENT #5 — PART 1
ANSWER

The response to a complaint is usually referred to as an answer. An answer is a form of pleading which admits or denies the allegations made in the plaintiff's complaint. Caption, jurisdiction and venue references, identification of the parties and headings are synonymous with the complaint components. A good answer will accomplish the following:

— It will analyze the complaint for any procedural or substantive defects.
— It will evaluate potential damage claims to both person and business concerns.
— It will provide an intellectual forum for determining affirmative defenses, motions pleadings, counterclaims or cross-claims that may be applicable.
— It will force an examination of who is ultimately responsible in multiple party litigation.

Each paragraph of the complaint will be directly addressed in the answer. An example of an answer might be as follows:

I, plaintiff/victim, individually and through my attorney, Charles Stone, Jr., Esquire, respond to the complaint as follows:

Count 1

Admitted or Denied.

Count 2

Admitted or Denied.

Or, the format of answer/response may be according to paragraph, such as:

I

Admitted or Denied.

II

Admitted or Denied.

The response or answer to the allegation should reflect the meat, the substance, of the claim. An example might be:

> *Defendant denies that the construction of the elevator equipment was defectively designed, engineered or operated.*

If the defendant is not capable of providing an answer, some of the following responses are customary:

> *Defendant lacks sufficient knowledge and/or information of the allegations set forth to respond.*

Or, if the complaint allegation is argumentative, defendant might respond that no answer is required.

The essence of any answer rests in its orderly response to the complaint paragraph posed.

For this exercise, let's assume that the lawsuit has been filed against the warehouse company on facts already indicated.

PREPARE A DEFENDANT'S ANSWER OUTLINING THE FOLLOWING RESPONSES. USE LEGAL RULED PAPER.

1. Defendant warned plaintiff about the currently defective and inoperable state of the elevator.
2. Defendant warned plaintiff that only authorized personnel were permitted to operate the elevator.
3. Defendant posted signs and warnings in well-illuminated locations.
4. Defendant alleges that plaintiff did not exercise reasonable care in entering into a business location that was declared off-limits.
5. Defendant alleges that all statutory ordinances, laws and statutes were adhered to in the maintenance of its elevator.
6. Defendant states that plaintiff should have or could have known that the elevator shaft was lower than the adjoining floor at the time he fell into it.
7. Defendant responds that it was foreseeable that a human being could be caught between a moving elevator and a shaft wall.
8. Defendant responds that it is not responsible for defects, if any at all, since it did not engineer, design or construct the elevator.

ASSIGNMENT #5 — PART 2
AFFIRMATIVE DEFENSES

Usually at the end of the response pattern of an answer, the defendant is provided with the opportunity to pose affirmative defenses, those defenses that must be raised under threat of forever being later barred. There are numerous defenses which could be posed by the defendants in the fact pattern above. Review the list of possible affirmative defenses below, especially the requirements for the proof thereof.

DEFENSE	ELEMENTS OF PROOF
Assumption of Risk	— Duty of reasonable care owed to plaintiff.
	— Injury or damage caused to plaintiff.
	— Plaintiff's information, knowledge and consent of dangers necessarily related to the act.
	— Plaintiff assumes risks by his actions.

Contributory Negligence	— Injury or damage to plaintiff. — Plaintiff's lack of reasonable care coinciding with defendant's negligence. — Plaintiff's own negligence is the proximate cause of the injury.
Laches	— Right or claim. — Plaintiff abandoned the right to make a claim or was negligent in asserting the claim. — The unexplained lapse of time in asserting the claim was unreasonable. — Adverse party's rights in the case prejudiced by this negligence and/or unreasonable lapse of time.
Release	— Right, claim or privilege. — One party's surrender of a right to one whom it might have been demanded, expected or enforced by law.
Statute of Limitations	— A right of action. — Statute or law prescribing time limitations to the right of action. — Right to the action is halted because time for bringing suit has expired.

Which of these would fit most aptly in the fact pattern? Think pro-defendant rather than pro-plaintiff in this exercise.

_____

_____

_____

PREPARE A SERIES OF MULTIPLE AFFIRMATIVE DEFENSES IN A PLEADING RESPONSE. AS NOTED ABOVE, THE AFFIRMATIVE DEFENSES ARE USUALLY LISTED AFTER THE PARAGRAPH-BY-PARAGRAPH ANSWER RESPONSE. AN EXAMPLE IS BELOW.

First Affirmative Defense

Plaintiff's case fails to state any claim upon which relief may be granted.

Second Affirmative Defense

Plaintiff assumed the risk of entry into an elevator which was inoperable and in the process of being repaired, and therefore was the cause of his own injury.

Third Affirmative Defense

Defendant is not responsible for the engineering design.

Fourth Affirmative Defense

Plaintiff caused his own injury due to his impermissible entry and operation of an inoperable elevator.

PLEASE USE THE CHART TO CREATE LANGUAGE THAT HIGHLIGHTS THE ORIGINAL FACT PATTERN AND SUBSEQUENT FACTS IN THESE EXERCISES. USE LEGAL RULED PAPER.

ASSIGNMENT #5 — PART 3

MOTIONS

From a defendant's perspective, certain motions may eliminate or refine the litigation. There are technical, substantive and procedural motions. Motions can deal with the nature of the pleadings or the jurisdictional elements. Motions can address the heart of the complaint alleging or demurring that there is no legal substance to the allegations made. Two examples of motions are required under this section of the assignment.

Part 3(a)

Motion for a Judgment on the Pleadings

An example of a motion for a judgment on the pleadings is below.

United States District Court
Eastern District of Pennsylvania

Ellen Stevens,	)
plaintiff	)
	)
v.	)
	) Civil Action No.
John Lewiston Coal Company,	)
a Pennsylvania Corporation,	)
defendant	)

Motion for Judgment on the Pleadings

Defendant respectfully moves this court to take notice and enter judgment on the pleadings in the above-captioned case in favor of the defendant and to dismiss the plaintiff's action and assess costs for the following reasons:

1. (State reason.)

2. (State reason.)

3. (State reason.)

(Date)

(Signature)
(Address of Attorney)
(Attorney Identification No.)

ATTORNEY FOR DEFENDANT

Assume in our elevator shaft fact pattern that the construction company who originally installed and did no repairs or regular service on the elevator, was sued for failure to post signs during a period of repair. However, the construction company named in the action is the wrong construction company with a similar name but a different address and in a different jurisdiction. On its face, the construction company has no liability on this theory.

PREPARE A MOTION FOR A JUDGMENT ON THE PLEADINGS CITING THE REASONS. USE LEGAL RULED PAPER.

Part 3(b)
Motion for a Summary Judgment

In a summary judgment case, the defendant might be able to argue that the plaintiff admits that the defendant has no liability yet still proceeds with a cause of action. A summary judgment request calls upon the court to dismiss the action since there are no material facts or issues that are subject to controversy. Assume the following facts:

FACT PATTERN

The elevator engineering firm has been sued for defective design of its product; however, the plaintiff's/victim's family's attorney has written to them indicating that they are certain, after consultation with their experts, that no defect in design can be found. The elevator company's own expertise has lead to that same conclusion. A letter from the attorney for the plaintiff/victim also describes the purpose of the continuing litigation, that is, to use as leverage multiple lawsuits to effect a favorable settlement. The letter from plaintiff's/victim's attorney to the elevator company states explicitly:

The estate of Edward Robinson is fully aware that there is no defect or problem in the elevator design. However, it will proceed with the case until all other matters have been resolved.

In an action for a summary judgment, the motion would outline those issues that are uncontroverted and supported by some form of attached evidence.

WHAT TYPE OF SUMMARY JUDGMENT FORM WOULD BE APPROPRIATE IN THIS FACT PATTERN? USE THE APPROPRIATE CAPTION AND HEADING AND USE THE SAME SIGNATURE CLAUSES AS BEFORE. USE LEGAL RULED PAPER.

PRACTICUM EXERCISES NO. 6
CRIMINAL LAW AND PROCEDURE

	Time Allotted (hours)	Point Value
Police Ledger: Assignment #1	0.5	5.0
Violent Crime Questions: Assignment #2	0.5	5.0
Comparing and Contrasting a Homicide: Assignment #3	0.5	5.0
Sexual Offenses: Terms and Definitions: Assignment #4	0.5	5.0
Enforcing a Law: Smoking in Public: Assignment #5	0.5	5.0
Firearms Regulation: Assignment #6	0.5	5.0
Matching Test: Conduct with Criminal Offenses: Assignment #7	0.5	5.0
An Imaginary Case of Arson: Assignment #8	0.5	5.0
Fingerprint Identification: Assignment #9	0.5	5.0
Diagrams from a Narrative: Assignment #10	0.5	5.0
Diagram of a Scene or Location: Assignment #11	0.5	5.0
Suspect Descriptions: Assignment #12	0.5	5.0
Crime Report: From Diagram to Narrative: Assignment #13	0.5	5.0
The Arrest: Assignment #14	0.5	5.0
The Criminal Complaint: Assignment #15	0.5	5.0
Initial Disposition of a Case: Assignment #16	0.5	5.0
Processing the Criminal Case: Jurisdictional Differences: Assignment #17	0.5	5.0
Defense Issues: Insanity: Assignment #18	0.5	5.0

Novel Defenses:		
Assignment #19	**0.5**	**5.0**
Technology in a Criminal Case:		
Assignment #20	**0.5**	**5.0**
	10.0	**100.0**

I.
INTRODUCTION

If men and women were perfect beasts, there would be no need for legal specialists in the fields of criminal law and procedure. Unfortunately, the evidence is indisputable that crime is a way of life in American society. Even more unfortunately, for those of us who have been victims, the effects of crime are very real. Legal specialists in criminal law and procedure, from district attorneys to legal assistants, are witnesses to the negative effects crime has on this society. Criminal law practitioners tend to develop a realistic, often hardened, view of the world. It is a notable reality of dealing with life's darker side.

In a sense, crime has many faces. Look at some of the faces below. First, in a sort of macabre criminal's hall of fame, we shall begin with John Wayne Gacy.

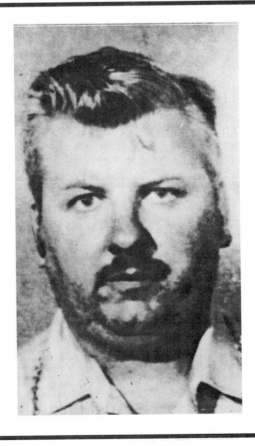

Photo 6.1
Portrait of a Mass Murderer

John Wayne Gacy, during a period from 1968 to 1978, sexually abused, sodomized and murdered more than 33 young men roughly between the ages of 13 and 20. His crimes were so heinous and despicable that he is considered one of America's premier mass murderers. Using drugs, alcohol and other entrapments, he essentially lured teenagers to their deaths, suffocating or asphyxiating them and committing acts of sodomy and other sexual misconduct while they were alive or after their deaths. So bizarre was his regimen of death that upon his arrest and subsequent investigation, 33 corpses were found in the cellar of his home, buried in rows one stacked upon another in plastic bags. Curiously, upon his arrest, his wife remarked that she had always noticed "a strange smell in the house."

A second example of a criminal of national repute is the recently executed Theodore Bundy. The six pictures below show almost six identities or six personalities of a man who was either under suspicion or proven guilty of the murder and sexual molestation of almost 30 college coeds throughout the United States during the decade of the 1970s.

Photo 6.2

Bundy's style of perpetration was brutally violent, and his eventual conviction resulted from the teethmark impressions that he left in his victims. The field of forensic odontology came into its own during Bundy's trial.

A third regrettable example of human existence was one of the first mass murderers to attain notoriety in American culture, namely, Richard Speck. His 1966 slaying of eight student nurses in an apartment complex near a Chicago university shocked the world. With little regret or remorse, and with the most repeated stabbings, clubbings and beatings, Richard Speck killed with wild abandon. He claimed, "I stabbed and choked them. If that one girl wouldn't have spit in my face, they'd all be alive today."

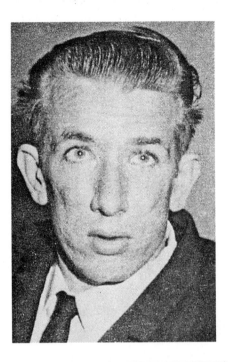

Photo 6.3

Crime also takes other forms, and often in a more organized fashion as is outlined in the Southwestern Pennsylvania La Cosa Nostra family, whose boss reigns over a family of terror. The "family" uses Capos and Soldiers to enforce its orders and keep its underworld activities intact, namely, drugs, prostitution, extortion, bribery, forgery, political influence and assorted RICO and other racketeering offenses. Harry and Mario Riccobene, as well as Thomas Delgiorno, are three other faces of crime.

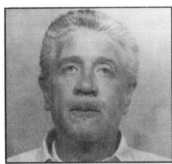
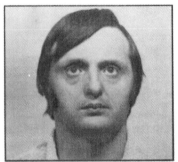

Harry Riccobene   **Mario Riccobene**   **Thomas Delgiorno**

Photo 6.4

The Riccobene brothers, Philadelphia mob figures, were convicted of first- and third-degree murder on November 18, 1984.

But crime takes many other forms as well. Consider the City of Chicago's 15th Police District at 5327 W. Chicago Avenue, Chicago, Illinois, whose telephone logs and ledgers over a 24-hour period involved 308 calls.

ASSIGNMENT #1
POLICE LEDGER

Time Allotted: 0.5 hours
Point Value: 5.0 points

REVIEW THE POLICE TELEPHONE LOG *FIGURE 6.1*. USING THE DATA IT PROVIDES COMPLETE THE PHONE LOG QUESTIONNAIRE *FORM 6.1*.

Typical phone day at W. Side district

THIS LIST of 308 calls contains those made over a typical 24-hour period to Chicago's 15th District, 5327 W. Chicago Av., starting at six minutes to midnight, July 12, through five minutes to midnight, July 13.

00:02 am— Domestic disturbance
00:03 am— Report of auto theft
00:12 am— Domestic disturbance
00:14 am— Suspicious man in car
00:25 am— Suspicious noise
00:26 am— Disturbance loud noise
00:30 am— Domestic disturbance
00:33 am— Wagon [prisoner transferred to hospital]
00:34 am— Domestic disturbance
00:34 am— Missing girl
00:38 am— Woman screaming
00:39 am— Suspicious auto
00:39 am— Suspicious man in alley
00:40 am— Domestic disturbance
00:55 am— Domestic disturbance
00:57 am— Attempted theft
01:30 am— Auto theft
01:34 am— Disturbance music in tavern
01:38 am— Suspicious man in alley
01:38 am— Fare dispute
01:39 am— Disturbance loud noise
01:48 am— Burglary alarm
01:48 am— Burglary alarm
01:50 am— Wagon [prisoner]
01:53 am— Disturbance loud noise
01:54 am— Disturbance two men
02:09 am— Wagon [prisoner]
02:13 am— Men with guns
02:19 am— Fireworks disturbance
02:24 am— Teenage disturbance
02:32 am— Wagon [prisoner]
02:41 am— Battery victim
02:43 am— Drunk report
02:46 am— Barking dog complaint
02:50 am— Open door complaint
02:52 am— Burglary alarm
03:00 am— Wagon [prisoner]

03:00 am— Disturbance in restaurant
03:07 am— Burglary alarm
03:07 am— Breaking into auto
03:08 am— Domestic disturbance
03:15 am— Robbery in progress
03:16 am— Teenage disturbance
03:37 am— Domestic disturbance
03:56 am— Wagon [prisoner]
03:58 am— Domestic disturbance
03:58 am— Woman screaming for help
04:01 am— Suspicious noises
04:04 am— Two men in disturbance
04:29 am— Burglary attempt
04:30 am— Burglary attempt
04:47 am— Report of men dumping car
05:52 am— Report of break-in
06:17 am— Burglary alarm
06:49 am— Report of man holding prisoner
07:05 am— Wagon [prisoner]
07:22 am— Domestic disturbance
07:23 am— Burglary alarm
07:33 am— Street cleaning [Police clearing area of illegally parked cars]
07:41 am— Wagon [prisoner]
07:42 am— Burglary alarm
07:55 am— Illegal parking
08:05 am— Criminal damage to property
08:10 am— Drug overdose victim
08:28 am— Suspicious auto
08:41 am— Theft from auto
08:42 am— Theft from auto
08:43 am— Residential alarm
08:48 am— Street cleaning
08:56 am— Illegal parking
08:57 am— Theft from auto
09:08 am— Suspicious auto
09:14 am— Burned-out auto
09:16 am— Burglary alarm
09:32 am— Illegal parking
09:34 am— Street cleaning
09:41 am— Criminal damage to auto
09:44 am— Burglary alarm
09:50 am— Theft victim
09:55 am— Information for police
09:56 am— Suspicious man
09:59 am— Battery victim

10:07 am— Criminal damage to property
10:11 am— Suspicious man
10:17 am— Street cleaning
10:23 am— Domestic disturbance
10:39 am— Illegal parking
10:58 am— Domestic disburbance
11:08 am— Battery victim
11:15 am— Information on arson
11:16 am— Theft victim
11:18 am— Injured person
11:19 am— Damage to property
11:19 am— Domestic disturbance
11:20 am— Suspicious teenagers
11:21 am— Landlord-tenant dispute
11:31 am— Robbery victim
12:06 pm— Theft victim
12:10 pm— Burglary alarm
12:13 pm— Damage to property
12:16 pm— Disturbance, employee with a gun
12:22 pm— Complaint about dog
12:22 pm— Domestic dispute
12:23 pm— Complaint about dog
12:30 pm— Child left alone
12:43 pm— Damage to car
12:46 pm— Domestic dispute
12:50 pm— Illegal vending
12:59 pm— Fire report
13:02 pm— Domestic disturbance
13:02 pm— Complaint about dog
13:09 pm— Theft victim
13:10 pm— Vicious dog report
13:11 pm— Fire report
13:15 pm— Burglary alarm
13:16 pm— Burglary attempt
13:39 pm— Theft from building
13:40 pm— Disturbance loud music
13:40 pm— Man fallen down
13:41 pm— Woman down in tavern
13:42 pm— missing girl
13:42 pm— Suspicious car
13:43 pm— Battery victim
14:02 pm— Damage to property
14:05 pm— Disturbance
14:06 pm— Fireworks disturbance
14:13 pm— Domestic disturbance
14:16 pm— Disturbance
14:28 pm— Information for police
14:30 pm— Teenage disturbance
14:33 pm— Disturbance loud music
14:41 pm— Suspicious car
14:43 pm— Man down in street
14:44 pm— Burglary alarm
14:47 pm— Fire hydrant open
14:50 pm— Burglary alarm
14:55 pm— Domestic disturbance

14:56 pm— Disturbance with neighbors
14:56 pm— Injured person
14:58 pm— Domestic disturbance
14:58 pm— Theft
15:03 pm— Open fire hydrant
15:05 pm— Disturbance loud music
15:06 pm— Illegal parking
15:09 pm— Robbery
15:13 pm— Teenage disturbance
15:33 pm— Burglary alarm
15:33 pm— Burglary alarm
15:44 pm— Theft of saw
15:50 pm— Threats
15:52 pm— Drug overdose victim
15:55 pm— Fire call
16:00 pm— Injured woman
16:07 pm— Purse snatch
16:07 pm— Battery victim
16:08 pm— Auto accident
16:12 pm— Domestic disturbance [proceed with caution]
16:12 pm— Suspicious auto
16:18 pm— Burglary in progress
16:19 pm— Fire
16:28 pm— Teenagers in tree
16:35 pm— Suspicious auto
16:35 pm— Stealing basketball nets
16:39 pm— Theft of bike
16:43 pm— Wagon [prisoner]
16:44 pm— Domestic dispute
16:49 pm— Damage to property
16:58 pm— Threatening phone calls
17:02 pm— Dog bit man
17:02 pm— Teenage disturbance
17:13 pm— Damage to property
17:16 pm— Burglary alarm
17:16 pm— Theft from auto
17:24 pm— Illegal parking
17:27 pm— Disturbance with two 'garbage hoppers' [bums]
17:39 pm— Illegal parking
17:48 pm— Open fire hydrant
17:49 pm— Vicious dog report
17:49 pm— Obscene phone call report
17:51 pm— Auto theft
17:55 pm— Illegal parking
18:00 pm— Hold-up alarm
18:09 pm— Information for police
18:09 pm— Domestic disturbance
18:14 pm— Wagon [prisoner]
18:17 pm— Injured person
18:20 pm— Teenagers in factory
18:21 pm— Information for police
18:28 pm— Fire report
18:28 pm— Disturbance loud music
18:31 pm— Domestic disturbance
18:34 pm— Teenagers playing ball
18:40 pm— Theft from auto
18:42 pm— Check for injured child

18:44 pm— Report two men with shotguns
18:45 pm— Theft of bicycle
18:52 pm— Auto theft
18:55 pm— Wagon [prisoner]
19:00 pm— Motorcycle gang disturbance
19:07 pm— Traffic control
19:08 pm— Theft victim
19:08 pm— Domestic disturbance
19:09 pm— Robbery alarm
19:18 pm— Suspicious man
19:18 pm— Confused man
19:22 pm— Illegal parking
19:22 pm— Dispute over money
19:24 pm— Wagon [prisoner]
19:27 pm— Information bike theft
19:29 pm— Suspicious auto
19:29 pm— Suspicious auto
19:29 pm— Teenage disturbance
19:33 pm— Domestic dispute
19:36 pm— Disturbance
19:38 pm— Children left alone
19:42 pm— Disturbance on street
19:46 pm— Disturbance on street
19:52 pm— Drunk causing disturbance
19:54 pm— Disturbance in apartment
19:56 pm— Suspicious auto
19:57 pm— Three men with guns
19:58 pm— Illegal parking
20:05 pm— Disturbance with neighbors
20:05 pm— Traffic control
20:06 pm— Illegal parking
20:06 pm— Illegal parking
20:08 pm— Man hanging out of second-floor window
20:11 pm— Disturbance at gas station
20:12 pm— Teenagers on roof
20:13 pm— Illegal parking
20:15 pm— Illegal parking
20:20 pm— Illegal parking
20:24 pm— Illegal parking
20:29 pm— Wagon [prisoner]
20:33 pm— Domestic disturbance
20:36 pm— Report of man drinking and throwing garbage
20:37 pm— Domestic disturbance
20:37 pm— Threatening phone calls
20:39 pm— Fight
20:41 pm— Information on stolen bike
20:45 pm— Youth firing gun
20:48 pm— Injured person
20:48 pm— Person breaking furniture
20:50 pm— Domestic dispute
20:51 pm— Man with gun
20:53 pm— Vicious dog report
20:53 pm— Dispute over child
20:54 pm— Fight on street
20:55 pm— Missing person
20:57 pm— Disturbance loud music
20:58 pm— Damage to property

21:09 pm— Man threatening woman
21:09 pm— Illegal parking
21:10 pm— Domestic dispute
21:10 pm— Gang fight
21:16 pm— Disturbance
21:17 pm— Domestic disturbance
21:17 pm— Domestic disturbance
21:18 pm— Domestic dispute
21:18 pm— Teenager disturbance
21:22 pm— Illegal parking
21:23 pm— Gang fight
21:23 pm— Disturbance
21:30 pm— Battery report
21:34 pm— Teenagers fighting
21:36 pm— Domestic dispute
21:39 pm— Illegal parking
21:40 pm— Domestic dispute
21:47 pm— Suspicious auto
21:47 pm— Teenagers fighting
21:49 pm— Domestic disturbance
22:02 pm— Domestic disturbance
22:04 pm— Domestic disturbance
22:08 pm— Disturbance man repairing cars
22:14 pm— Domestic disturbance
22:16 pm— Domestic disturbance
22:16 pm— Disturbance loud music
22:23 pm— Suspicious person
22:24 pm— Teenagers harassing cars
22:29 pm— Domestic disturbance
22:31 pm— Suspicious person
22:35 pm— Teenagers disturbing
22:38 pm— Man with knife
22:41 pm— Man creating disturbance
22:41 pm— Disturbance
22:42 pm— Domestic dispute
22:42 pm— Noisy teenagers back again
22:49 pm— Illegal parking
22:50 pm— Domestic disturbance
23:04 pm— Burglary alarm
23:07 pm— Fight—riot
23:08 pm— Man with gun
23:10 pm— Delivery of baby
23:10 pm— Burglary alarm
23:14 pm— Teenager disturbance
23:17 pm— Stolen bike
23:21 pm— Disturbance in alley
23:23 pm— Suspicious man
23:25 pm— Suspicious man in alley
23:28 pm— Disturbance loud music
23:28 pm— Noisy teens in alley
23:34 pm— Teenage disturbance
23:34 pm— Assault victim
23:35 pm— Burglary alarm
23:36 pm— Theft from auto
23:55 pm— Suspicious man in alley
23:55 pm— Auto alarm

Figure 6.1

PHONE LOG QUESTIONNAIRE

1. Name five specific crimes recorded:

    1._____

    2._____

    3._____

4._____

5._____

2. What types of activities, things or entities are considered suspicious?_____

_____

_____

3. What types of conduct could hardly be considered criminal yet still become a police function? Name four.

1._____

2._____

3._____

4._____

4. What types of activities called and responded to really surprise you? Why does it surprise you?_____

_____

_____

_____

5. Do you think that the image and stereotype of police work, especially that propounded by the media, correlates to this typical day in the life of a police station?   □ Yes   □ No

Explain:_____

_____

_____

Form 6.1

If the telephone log does anything, it should indicate that crime truly has many faces. There is also a blurring of the civil and criminal realms with the police and justice system involving itself in the affairs of families, the keeping of neighborhood boundaries and peace, and assorted activities that historically were the function of family and church rather than law enforcement entities.

The breadth and diversity of criminal conduct is staggering. New phenomena such as computer crime and counterfeit products are examples. See the figures below for two examples of garment and merchandise counterfeit activities.

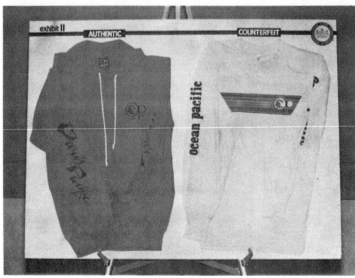

Figure 6.2

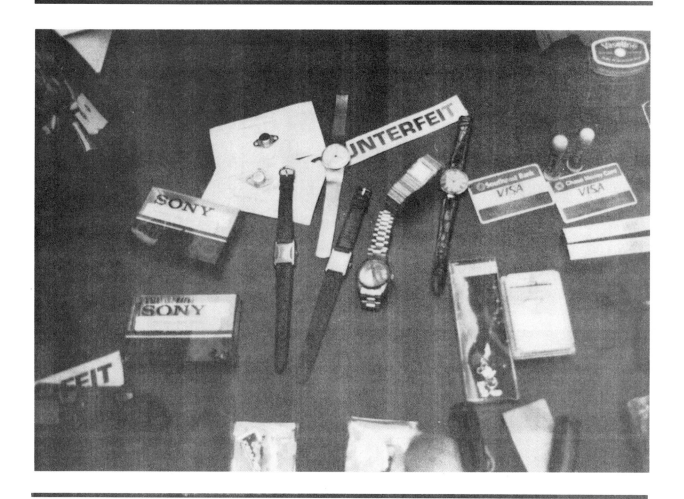

Figure 6.3

Regardless of the form of crime involved, it is a given that the criminal victimization of the American culture is on the rise.

ASSIGNMENT #2
VIOLENT CRIME QUESTIONS

Time Allotted: 0.5 hours
Point Value: 5.0 points

REVIEW THE CHART BELOW ENTITLED, *TABLE 3. PERCENTAGE OF U.S. POPULATION VICTIMIZED BY VIOLENT CRIME: RAPE, ROBBERY OR ASSAULT (COMBINED); RAPE, 1978-1982* AND COMPLETE THE QUESTIONNAIRE AT *FORM 6.2*.

Table 3. Percentage of U. S. population victimized by violent crime: rape, robbery or assault (combined); rape, 1978-82

Characteristic	Rape, robbery or assault (combined)					Rape				
	1978	1979	1980	1981	1982	1978	1979	1980	1981	1982
Total	**2.94%**	**3.23%**	**3.00%**	**3.21%**	**3.15%**	**.09%**	**.11%**	**.09%**	**.09%**	**.07%**
Sex										
Male	3.91	4.23	3.99	4.17	4.07	.01	.03	.02	.01	.00[a]
Female	2.04	2.31	2.11	2.34	2.31	.17	.18	.16	.17	.14
Race										
White	2.89	3.14	2.97	3.04	3.05	.08	.10	.09	.09	.07
Black	3.51	4.06	3.39	4.55	4.04	.17	.19	.11[a]	.14	.10
Other	2.17	3.11	2.62	3.80	2.78	.16[a]	.04[a]	.03[a]	.17[a]	.03[a]
Age										
12-15	5.08	5.31	4.62	5.57	4.83	.17	.17	.11	.13	.13
16-19	5.53	6.59	6.01	5.67	6.51	.19	.32	.31	.22	.19
20-24	5.76	6.32	6.13	6.41	6.22	.24	.25	.21	.24	.14
25-34	3.44	4.00	3.68	3.96	4.03	.10	.12	.12	.13	.12
35-49	1.91	2.01	1.94	2.07	2.09	.04	.05	.03	.04	.03[a]
50-64	1.04	1.10	1.02	1.29	1.03	.02[a]	.01[a]	.00[a]	.01[a]	.01[a]
65 and older	.69	.60	.60	.65	.60	.01[a]	.00[a]	.00[a]	.01[a]	.01[a]
Race, sex, and age summary										
White males, ages:										
12-15	6.40	6.63	5.95	6.50	5.85	.06[a]	.04[a]	.02[a]	.00[a]	.00[a]
16-19	7.35	8.60	8.48	7.37	8.45	.04[a]	.07[a]	.06[a]	.02[a]	.00[a]
20-24	8.02	8.19	8.50	8.29	8.13	.03[a]	.14[a]	.05[a]	.01[a]	.01[a]
25-34	4.42	5.41	4.52	4.87	4.88	.00[a]	.03[a]	.02[a]	.01[a]	.01[a]
35-49	2.29	2.30	2.28	2.44	2.45	.00[a]	.00[a]	.01[a]	.01[a]	.00[a]
50-64	1.12	1.21	1.17	1.46	1.24	.00[a]	.01[a]	.00[a]	.00[a]	.00[a]
65 and older	.79	.57	.88	.66	.65	.00[a]	.00[a]	.00[a]	.00[a]	.00[a]
White females, ages:										
12-15	3.50	4.09	3.06	3.90	3.59	.26	.33	.18[a]	.20[a]	.20[a]
16-19	4.22	5.03	4.06	3.62	4.58	.33	.52	.56	.37	.43
20-24	3.69	4.18	4.12	4.20	4.52	.37	.38	.35	.41	.26
25-34	2.45	2.47	2.70	2.98	3.12	.18	.16	.21	.27	.22
35-49	1.47	1.59	1.52	1.47	1.53	.11	.09	.07[a]	.06[a]	.06[a]
50-64	.72	.74	.84	.93	.71	.03[a]	.00[a]	.00[a]	.02[a]	.01[a]
65 and older	.54	.49	.37	.46	.43	.01[a]	.00[a]	.00[a]	.02[a]	.01[a]
Black males, ages:										
12-15	8.92	8.02	7.43	9.66	7.05	.12[a]	.13[a]	.00[a]	.12[a]	.15[a]
16-19	6.22	6.15	5.48	9.08	8.26	.00[a]	.00[a]	.00[a]	.26[a]	.00[a]
20-24	6.35	8.20	6.51	8.69	7.30	.00[a]	.00[a]	.00[a]	.00[a]	.00[a]
25-34	4.72	5.53	5.03	5.08	5.99	.00[a]	.09[a]	.00[a]	.00[a]	.00[a]
35-49	3.17	3.11	2.81	2.84	3.60	.00[a]	.00[a]	.00[a]	.00[a]	.00[a]
50-64	3.32	3.10	2.30	2.42	2.37	.00[a]	.00[a]	.00[a]	.00[a]	.00[a]
65 and older	1.49	1.15[a]	1.22[a]	2.46	1.54[a]	.00[a]	.00[a]	.00[a]	.00[a]	.00[a]
Black females, ages:										
12-15	2.94	2.44	3.11	5.16	4.46	.38[a]	.15[a]	.31[a]	.54[a]	.52[a]
16-19	2.59	5.16	4.49	4.64	5.03	.47[a]	.95[a]	.68[a]	.42[a]	.14[a]
20-24	4.23	5.84	4.54	6.52	4.38	.69[a]	.25[a]	.52[a]	.70[a]	.29[a]
25-34	2.89	4.03	3.35	3.91	3.49	.37[a]	.51[a]	.20[a]	.06[a]	.34[a]
35-49	1.70	2.24	1.98	2.94	2.45	.00[a]	.25[a]	.00[a]	.08[a]	.00[a]
50-64	1.39	1.88	.59[a]	2.47	1.38	.24[a]	.11[a]	.00[a]	.06[a]	.00[a]
65 and older	.97	1.49	.49[a]	1.07[a]	1.21	.12[a]	.07[a]	.00[a]	.00[a]	.09[a]
Marital status										
Male										
Never married	6.63	7.24	6.97	7.02	7.11	.03[a]	.06	.04[a]	.03[a]	.01[a]
Married	2.25	2.31	2.20	2.43	2.25	.00[a]	.01[a]	.00[a]	.00[a]	.00[a]
Widowed	2.01	1.70	1.17	1.69	1.40	.00[a]	.00[a]	.00[a]	.00[a]	.00[a]
Separated and divorced	6.40	7.80	6.34	6.42	5.87	.00[a]	.07[a]	.05[a]	.02[a]	.02[a]
Female										
Never married	3.30	4.08	3.46	3.92	3.92	.33	.38	.34	.35	.29
Married	1.18	1.13	1.15	1.24	1.19	.06	.04	.05	.07	.04
Widowed	.82	.86	.71	.92	.86	.04[a]	.03[a]	.02[a]	.01[a]	.03[a]
Separated and divorced	5.25	6.08	5.52	5.76	5.54	.52	.59	.39	.42	.36
Family income										
White, victims with:										
Less than $3,000	5.34	6.25	7.05	6.60	6.26	.17	.42	.29	.30	.20[a]
$3,000-$7,499	3.34	3.83	3.80	3.61	4.12	.14	.17	.12	.13	.17
$7,500-$9,999	3.42	4.05	3.58	3.53	3.67	.08	.13	.13	.17	.03[a]
$10,000-$14,999	3.04	3.05	3.28	3.41	3.53	.07	.08	.13	.14	.11
$15,000-$24,999	2.67	2.88	2.71	2.82	2.87	.06	.06	.07	.05	.05
$25,000 and over	2.34	2.81	2.35	2.59	2.50	.06	.08	.04	.05	.03
Black, victims with:										
Less than $3,000	3.98	5.48	4.59	6.25	5.57	.41	.41[a]	.29[a]	.41[a]	.21[a]
$3,000-$7,499	3.91	4.38	3.71	5.30	5.18	.09[a]	.14[a]	.25	.15[a]	.11[a]
$7,500-$9,999	3.72	3.70	3.99	4.42	4.06	.07[a]	.37[a]	.11[a]	.17[a]	.08[a]
$10,000-$14,999	3.37	4.17	3.41	5.45	4.12	.11[a]	.24[a]	.00[a]	.18[a]	.12[a]
$15,000-$24,999	2.75	2.43	3.05	3.74	3.04	.24[a]	.13[a]	.00[a]	.03[a]	.15[a]
$25,000 and over	2.31	4.31	2.00	2.54	2.74	.00[a]	.00[a]	.00[a]	.13[a]	.00[a]

Note: Detail may not add to total shown because of rounding.

[a] Estimate, based on about 10 or fewer sample cases, is statistically unreliable.

Figure 6.4

VIOLENT CRIME QUESTIONNAIRE

1. Who is more likely to be victimized by crime (check off)?

   a. _____ Individuals with more income
      _____ Individuals with less income

   b. _____ Persons who were/are married
      _____ Persons who were never married

2. Is there any racial context that you can discern in the calculation of crime rates?   ☐ Yes   ☐ No

   Explain:_____

   _____

   _____

3. Is it fair to say that the elderly suffer less from the crimes of rape and robbery than the younger?   ☐ Yes   ☐ No

   Explain:_____

   _____

   _____

4. Has there been a steady progression in criminal conduct in these areas since 1978?   ☐ Yes   ☐ No

   Explain:_____

   _____

   _____

Form 6.2

II.
TRACKING THE CRIMINAL CASE THROUGH THE LEGAL SYSTEM

The exercises that follow should give the student appreciation for the multi-faceted aspects of any criminal case. Some exercises require the filling in of your designed hypothetical information while others have more explicit instructions. From identification of criminal laws and statutes to an examination of avant-garde and novel criminal defenses, the student should leave this practicum with some understanding of the legal and human dynamics of criminal law practice.

A. Student Objectives

   (1) To assess and analyze various forms of criminal legislation interpreting language and the elemental qualifications and requirements in a criminal case;

   (2) To review various pieces of legislation determining the scope of definitions and regulatory authority;

   (3) To think creatively and constructively about specific crimes in the construction of a question-naire involving a case of arson;

   (4) To perform typical investigative functions and activities common to criminal cases including fingerprint identifications, diagram sketches, suspect descriptions and documentation for an arrest;

   (5) To review some procedural aspects of the criminal case including the preparation of a criminal complaint, an analysis of how criminal cases are disposed and a review of differing jurisdictions and their bureaucratic structures for the adjudication of crime; and

   (6) To learn about some unique defenses posed in criminal cases and their impact on criminal culpability.

B. Student Obligations

   (1) To complete all exhibits, charts, questionnaires, complaint forms and other documentation as is provided within this workbook or as provided by the instructor;

   (2) To compare, contrast and match criminal descriptions with specific crimes or statutes;

   (3) To prepare a fingerprint chart;

   (4) To prepare a suspect description;

   (5) To prepare a diagram or sketch;

   (6) To prepare a hypothetical case based upon a diagram;

   (7) To prepare a chart outlining criminal case dispositions in your local jurisdiction; and

   (8) To review local newspapers for unique or novel defenses.

C. Instructor Obligations

   (1) To provide students with local forms for the completion of assignments if so required. Instructors must provide a sample complaint if applicable in the preparation of the criminal complaint; and

   (2) To give guidance, general oversight and monitoring of all activities.

D. Time Allotted: 10.0 hours

E. Value of Assignment: 100.0 points

1.   Interpreting Criminal Laws and Legislation

The assignments below should leave the student with an appreciation for statutory language and construction in the area of criminal law. Minimally, precision of the language and the ease of understanding are important due process issues.

ASSIGNMENT #3
COMPARING AND CONTRASTING A HOMICIDE

Time Allotted: 0.5 hours
Point Value: 5.0 points

REVIEW THE STATUTES BELOW AND COMPLETE THE QUESTIONNAIRE AT *FORM 6.3*.

Manslaughter.
 a.   Criminal homicide constitutes aggravated manslaughter when the actor recklessly causes death under circumstances manifesting extreme indifference to human life;
 b.   Criminal homicide constitutes manslaughter when:
   (1)   It is committed recklessly; or
   (2)   A homicide which would otherwise be murder is committed in the heat of passion resulting from a reasonable provocation.
 c.   Aggravated manslaughter is a crime of the first degree. Manslaughter is a crime of the second degree.

Death by Auto.
 a.   Criminal homicide constitutes death by auto when it is caused by driving a vehicle recklessly.
 b.   Death by auto is a crime of the third degree and the court may not suspend the imposition of sentence on any defendant convicted under this section who was operating the vehicle under the influence of an intoxicating liquor, narcotic, hallucinogenic or habit-producing drug and any sentence imposed under this section shall include either a fixed minimum term of 270 days imprisonment during which the defendant shall be ineligible for parole or a requirement that the defendant perform a community related service for a minimum of 270 days.
 c.   For good cause shown the court may, in accepting a plea of guilty under this section, order that such plea not be evidential in any civil proceeding.

Aiding Suicide.

A person who purposely aids another to commit suicide is guilty of a crime of the second degree if his conduct causes such suicide or an attempted suicide, and otherwise of a crime of the fourth degree.

STATUTE COMPARISON QUESTIONNAIRE

1.   How do you distinguish a case of manslaughter from a case of death by auto? Be specific._____

_____

_____

_____

_____

_____

2. Can a case of manslaughter ever be considered a case of suicide?   ☐ Yes   ☐ No

    Why or Why Not?_____

    _____

    _____

    _____

3. Point out three other major distinctions, comparisons or differentiations in these three forms of homicide._____

    _____

    _____

    _____

    _____

    _____

Form 6.3

ASSIGNMENT #4
SEXUAL OFFENSES: TERMS AND DEFINITIONS

Time Allotted: 0.5 hours
Point Value: 5.0 points

Sexual offense law is certainly full of disagreement in terms of its construction and language. Think for a second about your own personal view about sexual offenses. Is your perception different from another's? Do you have difficulty in enforcing any portion of this statute considered below, at least in terms of its definitions? What are your social and personal positions regarding such controversial issues as the following:

— A person who is married cannot be raped by a spouse.
— Sexual intercourse as ordinarily defined receives highest felony treatment while deviate sexual intercourse often falls in lower categories.
— What about a person who is unconscious? Can they be raped?
— How do we define what a mentally defective person is in terms of the power to grant or give consent?

The complexities of the statute are not easy to fathom. Plainly, some things within this law may not sit well with you.

LOOK AT THE DEFINITIONS BELOW AND COMPLETE *FORM 6.4.*

130.00 SEX OFFENSES: DEFINITIONS OF TERMS

The following definitions are applicable to this article:

1. "Sexual intercourse" has its ordinary meaning and occurs upon any penetration however slight.
2. "Deviate sexual intercourse" means sexual conduct between persons not married to each other consisting of contact between the penis and the anus, the mouth and penis, or the mouth and the vulva.
3. "Sexual contact" means any touching of the sexual or other intimate parts of a person not married to the actor for the purpose of gratifying sexual desire of either party.
4. "Female" means any female person who is not married to the actor. For the purposes of this article "not married" means:
   a. the lack of an existing relationship of husband and wife between the female and the actor which is recognized by law, or
   b. the existence of the relationship of husband and wife between the actor and the female which is recognized by law at the time the actor commits an offense proscribed by this article by means of forcible compulsion against the female, and the female and actor are living apart at such time pursuant to a valid and effective:
      i. order issued by a court of competent jurisdiction which by its terms or in its effect requires such living apart, or
      ii. decree or judgment of separation, or
      iii. written agreement of separation subscribed by them and acknowledged in the form required to entitle a deed to be recorded which contains provisions specifically indicating that the actor may be guilty of the commission of a crime for engaging in conduct which constitutes an offense proscribed by this article against and without the consent of the female.
5. "Mentally defective" means that a person suffers from a mental disease or defect which renders him incapable of appraising the nature of his conduct.
6. "Mentally incapacitated" means that a person is rendered temporarily incapable of appraising or control-

ling his conduct owing to the influence of a narcotic or intoxicating substance administered to him without his consent, or to any other act committed upon him without his consent.

7. "Physically helpless" means that a person is unconscious or for any other reason is physically unable to communicate unwillingness to an act.

8. "Forcible compulsion" means physical force which is capable of overcoming earnest resistance; or a threat, express or implied that places a person in fear of immediate death or serious physical injury to himself or another person, or in fear that he or another person will immediately be kidnapped. "Earnest resistance" means resistance of a type reasonably to be expected from a person who genuinely refuses to participate in sexual intercourse, deviant sexual intercourse or sexual contact, under all the attendant circumstances. Earnest resistance does not mean utmost resistance.

9. "Foreign object" means any instrument or article which, when inserted in the vagina or rectum, is capable of causing physical injury.

After examining with a critical eye the statutes shown above, give three solid impressions, opinions or feelings you have regarding their construction.

1. _____

_____

_____

2. _____

_____

_____

3. _____

_____

_____

Form 6.4

ASSIGNMENT #5
ENFORCING A LAW: SMOKING IN PUBLIC

Time Allotted: 0.5 hours
Point Value: 5.0 points

Do you really think our law enforcement and judicial community should be required to prevent, deter and apprehend individuals who are smoking in public? In the State of New Jersey, under a law passed effective July 1985, persons who smoke or carry lighted tobacco in or upon any bus or public conveyance or in any public place where smoking is prohibited may be guilty of a disorderly persons offense.

READ THE REPRODUCED PORTIONS OF §2C:33-13, *SMOKING IN PUBLIC* AND COMPLETE *FORM 6.5*.

2C:33-13. Smoking in Public

a.   Any person who smokes or carries lighted tobacco in or upon any bus or other public conveyance, other than in the places provided, is a petty disorderly person.

b.   Any person who smokes or carries lighted tobacco in any public place, including but not limited to places of public accommodation, where such smoking is prohibited by municipal ordinance under authority of R.S. 40:48-1 and 40:48-2 or by the owner or person responsible for the operation of the public place, and when adequate notice of such prohibition has been conspicuously posted, is guilty of a petty disorderly persons offense. Notwithstanding the provisions of 2C:43-3, the maximum fine which can be imposed for violation of this section is $200.00.

c.   The provisions of this section shall supersede any other statute and any rule or regulation adopted pursuant to law.

After reading the above statute, ask yourself whether there will be difficulties in enforcing this provision. Discuss in detail what those difficulties might be.

Form 6.5

ASSIGNMENT #6
FIREARMS REGULATION

Time Allotted: 0.5 hours
Point Value: 5.0 points

State regulation on firearms is quite substantial, an example of which from Louisiana is the subject matter of this exercise.

READ THE STATUTE BELOW AND ANSWER THE QUESTIONS AT *FORM 6.6.*

**Louisiana
State Law**

Rev. Stat.—LA Stat. Ann.

TITLE 14.   CRIMINAL LAW

Chapter 1.   Criminal Code

91.   Unlawful sales to minors. Unlawful sales to minors is the selling, or otherwise delivering for value by anyone over the age of seventeen of any * * * firearm or other instrumentality customarily used as a dangerous weapon, to any person under the age of eighteen. Lack of knowledge of the minor's age shall not be a defense.

94.   Illegal use of weapons or dangerous instrumentalities

A.   Illegal use of weapons or dangerous instrumentalities is the intentional or criminally negligent discharging of any firearm, or the throwing, placing, or other use of any article, liquid, or substance, where it is foreseeable that it may result in death or great bodily harm to a human being.

B.   Whoever commits the crime of illegal use of weapons or dangerous instrumentalities shall be fined not more than one thousand dollars, or imprisoned with or without hard labor for not more than two years, or both.

C.   On a second conviction, the offender shall be imprisoned with or without hard labor for not more than five years.

D.   On a third and subsequent convictions, the offender shall be imprisoned with or without hard labor for not more than five years.

E.   The enhanced penalty upon second, third, and subsequent convictions provided for in this Section shall not be applicable in cases where more than five years have elapsed since the expiration of the maximum sentence, or sentences, of the previous conviction or convictions, and the time of the commission of the last offense for which he has been convicted; the sentence to be imposed in such event shall be the same as may be imposed upon a first conviction.

95.   Illegal carrying of weapons

A.   Illegal carrying of weapon is:

(1)   The intentional concealment of any firearm, or other instrumentality customarily used or intended for probable use as a dangerous weapon, on one's person; or

(2)   The ownership, possession, custody or use of any firearm, or other instrumentality customarily used as a dangerous weapon, at any time by an enemy alien; or

(3)   The ownership, possession, custody, or use of any tools, or dynamite, or nitroglycerine, or explosives, or other instrumentality customarily used by thieves or burglars at any time by any person with the intent to commit a crime; or
* * *

B.   Whoever commits the crime of illegal carrying of weapons shall be fined not more than five hundred dollars, or imprisoned for not more than six months, or both.

C.   On a second conviction, the offender shall be imprisoned with or without hard labor for not more than five years.

D.   On third and subsequent convictions, the offender shall be imprisoned with or without hard labor for not more than ten years without benefit of parole, probation, or suspension of sentence.

E.   The enhanced penalty upon second, third, and subsequent convictions shall not be applicable in cases where more than five years have elapsed since the expiration of the maximum sentence, or sentences, of the previous conviction or convictions, and the time of the commission of the last offense for which he has been convicted; the sentence to be imposed in such event shall be the same as may be imposed upon a first conviction.

F.   The provisions of this Section * * * shall not apply to sheriffs and their deputies, state and city police, constables and town marshals, or persons vested with police power when in the actual discharge of official duties.

95.1 Possession of firearm or carrying concealed weapon by a person convicted of certain felonies

A.   It is unlawful for any person who has been convicted of first or second degree murder, manslaughter, aggravated battery, aggravated or simple rape, aggravated kidnapping, aggravated arson, aggravated or simple burglary, armed or simple robbery, burglary of a pharmacy, burglary of an inhabited dwelling, or any violation of the Uniform

Controlled Dangerous Substances Law which is a felony or any crime defined as an attempt to commit one of the above enumerated offenses under the laws of this state, or who has been convicted under the laws of any other state or of the United States or of any foreign government or country of a crime which if committed in this state, would be one of the above enumerated crimes, to possess a firearm or carry a concealed weapon.

B.   Whoever is found guilty of violating the provisions of this Section shall be imprisoned at hard labor for not less than three nor more than ten years without the benefit of probation, parole, or suspension of sentence and be fined not less than one thousand dollars nor more than five thousand dollars.

C.   Except as otherwise specifically provided, this Section shall not apply to the following cases:

(1)   The provisions of this Section prohibiting the possession of firearms and carrying concealed weapons by persons who have been convicted of certain felonies shall not apply to any person who has not been convicted of any felony for a period of ten years from the date of completion of sentence, probation, parole, or suspension of sentence.

(2)   Upon completion of sentence, probation, parole, or suspension of sentence the convicted felon shall have the right to apply to the sheriff of the parish in which he resides, or in the case of Orleans Parish the superintendent of police, for a permit to possess firearms. The felon shall be entitled to possess the firearm upon the issuing of the permit.

(3)   The sheriff or superintendent of police, as the case may be, shall immediately notify the Department of Public Safety, in writing, of the issuance of each permit granted under this section.

95.2.   Additional penalties for possession of a firearm or explosive device in the commission of certain crimes. Notwithstanding any other provisions of law to the contrary, any person who uses a firearm or explosive device at the time he commits or attempts to commit the crime of second degree murder, manslaughter, aggravated battery, simple kidnapping, aggravated escape, aggravated burglary, or aggravated arson or attempted aggravated rape, attempted first degree murder or attempted aggravated kidnapping shall upon conviction serve a term of two years imprisonment for the first conviction and upon conviction for each second and subsequent offense listed in this Section, he shall serve a term of five years imprisonment. The penalty provided herein shall be in addition to any other penalty imposed under the provisions of this Title and such person shall serve the additional term of imprisonment without benefit of parole, probation, suspension of sentence or credit for good time and any adjudication of guilt or imposition of sentence shall not be suspended.

The prison terms provided under the provisions of this Section, shall run consecutively to any other penalty imposed upon conviction of any of the crimes listed in this Section.

TITLE 40.   PUBLIC HEALTH AND SAFETY

Chapter 9.   Weapons

PART I: MACHINE GUNS

1751.   Definitions. For purposes of this Part, "**machine gun**" includes all firearms of any caliber, commonly known as machine rifles, machine guns, and sub-machine guns, capable of automatically discharging more than eight cartridges successively without reloading, in which the ammunition is fed to the gun from or by means of clips, disks, belts, or some other separable mechanical device. "**Manufacturer**" includes all persons manufacturing machine guns; "**Merchants**" includes all persons dealing with machine guns as merchandise.

1752.   Handling of machine guns unlawful; exceptions. No person shall sell, keep or offer for sale, loan or give away, purchase, possess, carry, or transport any machine gun within this state, except that:

(1)   All duly appointed peace officers may purchase, possess, carry, and transport machine guns.

(2)   This Part does not apply to the Army, Navy, or Marine Corps of the United States, the National Guard, and organizations authorized by law to purchase or receive machine guns from the United States or from this state. The members of such Corps, National Guard, and organizations may possess, carry, and transport machine guns while on duty.

(3)   Persons possessing war relics may purchase and possess machine guns which are relics of any war in which the United States was involved, may exhibit and carry the machine guns in the parades of any military organization, and may sell, loan, or give the machine guns to other persons possessing war relics.

(4)   Guards or messengers employed by common carriers, banks, and trust companies, and pay-roll guards or messengers may possess and carry machine guns while actually employed in and about the shipment, transportation, or delivery, or in the guarding of any money, treasure, bullion, bonds, or other thing of value. Their employers may purchase or receive machine guns and keep them in their possession when the guns are not being used by their guards or messengers.

(5)   Manufacturers and merchants may sell, keep or offer for sale, loan or give away, purchase, possess, and transport machine guns in the same manner as other merchandise except as otherwise provided in this Part. Common carriers may possess and transport unloaded machine guns as other merchandise.

1753.   Transfer of possessions permitted in certain cases; method. No manufacturer or merchant shall permit any machine gun to pass from his possession to the possession of any person other than:

(1)   A manufacturer or merchant.

(2)   A common carrier for shipment to a manufacturer or merchant.

(3)   A duly authorized agent of the government of the United States or of this state, acting in his official capacity.

(4)   A person authorized to purchase a machine gun under the provisions of paragraphs (1) and (4) of R.S. 40:1752.

Manufacturers or merchants shall not deliver a machine gun to any of the persons authorized to purchase it under the provisions of paragraphs (1) and (4) of R.S. 40:1752 unless the person presents a written permit to purchase and possess a machine gun, signed by the sheriff of the parish in which the manufacturer or merchant has his place of business or delivers the machine gun. The manufacturer or merchant shall retain the written permit and keep it on file in his place of business. Each sheriff shall keep a record of all permits issued by him.

1754. Registers to be kept; inspection thereof. Every manufacturer or merchant shall keep a register of all machine guns manufactured or handled by him. This register shall show:

(1) The date of the sale, loan, gift, delivery, or receipt of any machine gun;

(2) The name, address, and occupation of the person to whom the machine gun was sold, loaned, given, or delivered, or from whom it was received; and

(3) The purpose for which the person, to whom the machine gun was sold, loaned, given, or delivered, purchased or obtained it.

Upon demand, every manufacturer or merchant shall permit any sheriff or deputy sheriff or any police officer to inspect his entire stock of machine guns, and parts and supplies therefor, and shall produce the register required in this Section and all written permits to purchase or possess a machine gun, which he has retained and filed in his place of business.

1755. Penalty.

A. Any manufacturer who:

(1) Passes possession of or delivers a machine gun to any person in violation of R.S. 40:1753; or

(2) Fails to keep an accurate register, as required in R.S. 40:1754; or

(3) Fails to produce or account for a sheriff's permit for each machine gun sold by him for which a permit is necessary under the provisions of R.S. 40:1753,

shall be imprisoned at hard labor for not less than one year nor more than five years.

B. Any person who violates R.S. 40:1752 shall be imprisoned at hard labor for not less than one year nor more than ten years.

C. Whoever, having been convicted of murder, armed or simple robbery, aggravated or simple burglary, or aggravated battery, or an attempt to commit any one of those crimes, thereafter violates any of the provisions of this Part shall be imprisoned at hard labor for not less than three years nor more than ten years.

PART II: REGISTRATION

1781. Definitions. For the purpose of this Part, the following terms have the meanings ascribed to them in this Section:

(1) "**Dealer**" means any person not a manufacturer or importer engaged in this state in the business of selling any firearm. The term includes wholesalers, pawnbrokers, and other persons dealing in used firearms.

(2) "**Department**" means the Department of Public Safety.

(3) "**Firearm**" means a shotgun having a barrel of less than eighteen inches in length; a rifle having a barrel of less than sixteen inches in length; any weapon made from either a rifle or a shotgun if said weapon has been modified to have an overall length of less than twenty-six inches; any other firearm, pistol, revolver or shotgun from which the serial number or mark of identification has been obliterated, from which a shot is discharged by an explosive, if that weapon is capable of being concealed on the person; or a machine gun or gas grenade; and includes a muffler or silencer for any firearm, whether or not the firearm is included within this definition. Pistols and revolvers and those rifles and shotguns which have not previously been defined in this Paragraph as firearms from which serial numbers or marks or identification have not been obliterated are specifically exempt from this definition.

(4) "**Importer**" means any person who imports or brings into the state any firearm.

(5) "**Machine gun**" means any weapon, including a submachine gun, which shoots or is designed to shoot automatically more than one shot without manual reloading, by a single function of the trigger.

(6) "**Manufacturer**" means any person who is engaged in this state in the manufacture, assembling, alteration, or repair of any firearm.

(7) "**Muffler**" or "**silencer**" includes any device for silencing or diminishing the report of any portable weapon such as a rifle, carbine, pistol, revolver, machine gun, submachine gun, shotgun, fowling piece, or other device from which a shot, bullet, or projectile may be discharged by an explosive and is not limited to mufflers and silencers for firearms as defined in this Section.

(8) "**Transfer**" includes the sale, assignment, pledge, lease, loan, gift or other disposition of any firearm.

1782. Exemptions from Part. This Part does not apply to the following persons and things:

(1) Sheriffs or equivalent municipal officers in municipalities of over ten thousand, when they are acting in their official capacity.

(2) The arms, accoutrements, and equipment of the military and naval forces of the United States or of other officers of the United States authorized by law to possess weapons of any kind.

(3) The arms, accoutrements, and equipment of the militia.

(4) Any firearm which is unserviceable and which is transferred as a curiosity or ornament.

1783. Registration with department of public safety. Every person possessing any firearm shall register with the department the number or other mark identifying the firearm, together with his name, address, and place of business or employment, the place where the firearm is usually kept, and, if the person is other than a natural person, the name and home address of the executive officer thereof having control of the firearm and the name and home address of the person having actual possession thereof.

1784.   Application to possess or transfer. No person shall continue to possess or shall transfer any firearm without the prior approval of the department. Interested persons shall file written application in duplicate on application forms issued in blank for those purposes by the department. In the case of transfers of any firearm, applications shall be filed by both the proposed vendor and the proposed vendee.

The applications shall set forth, in the original and duplicate, the manufacturer's number or other mark identifying the firearm. Both the original and duplicate shall be forwarded to the department. If approved, the original shall be returned to the applicant. * * *

1785.   Possession or dealing in unregistered or illegally transferred weapons. No person shall receive, possess, carry, conceal, buy, sell, or transport any firearm which has not been registered or transferred in accordance with this Part.

1787.   Importation, manufacture, or dealing in without registration. Upon first engaging in business, every importer, manufacturer, and dealer in firearms shall register with the department his name or style, principal place of business and other places of business in this state. No person required to register under the provisions of this Section shall import, manufacture, or deal in any firearm without having registered as required by this Section.

1788.   Identification with number or other mark; obliteration or alteration or number or mark.

A.   Each manufacturer, importer, and dealer in any firearm shall identify it with a number or other identification mark approved by the department and shall mark or stamp or otherwise place the number or mark thereon in a manner approved by the department.

B.   No one shall obliterate, remove, change, or alter this number or mark. Whenever, in a trial for a violation of this Section, the defendant is shown to have or to have had possession of any firearm upon which the number or mark was obliterated, removed, changed, or altered, that possession is sufficient evidence to authorize conviction unless the defendant explains it to the satisfaction of the court.

1789.   Records of importers, manufacturers, or dealers. Importers, manufacturers, and dealers shall keep such books and records and render such returns in relation to the transactions in firearms specified in this Part as the department requires.

1790.   Rules and regulations; importation of firearms. The department may prescribe such rules and regulations as are necessary for carrying out the provisions of this Part.

Under regulations prescribed by the department, any firearm may be imported or brought into this state or possessed or transferred when the purpose thereof is shown to be lawful.

PART III: PURCHASE OF RIFLES AND SHOTGUNS

1801.   Declaration of policy. It is declared that it is in the public interest to authorize residents of this state to purchase or otherwise obtain rifles and shotguns or ammunition in states contiguous to this state in compliance with such other laws of this state or its political subdivisions as may be applicable and in compliance with Section 102 of the Gun Control Act of 1968, Public Law 90–618, 18 U.S.C. §921 et seq. and it is the declared intention of this state that the sale of shotgun and rifles and the sale of ammunition in this state to residents of adjacent states is hereby authorized pursuant to regulations issued under the Gun Control Act of 1968.

1802.   Definitions. As used in this Part:

(1)   **"A state contiguous to this state"** shall mean any state having a common border with this state.

(2)   All other terms shall be given the meaning prescribed in 18 U.S.C. Sec. 921 (The Gun Control Act of 1968, Public Law 90–618), and the regulations duly promulgated thereunder as presently enacted or promulgated and as hereafter modified.

1803.   Purchase of rifle or shotgun or ammunition. It shall be lawful for any person residing in this state, including any corporation or other business entity maintaining a place of business in this state, to purchase or otherwise obtain a rifle or shotgun or ammunition in any state which is contiguous to this state and to receive or transport such rifle or shotgun or ammunition into this state and to permit any person residing in a contiguous state to purchase shotguns, rifles or ammunition in this state and to receive or transport such rifles, shotguns or ammunition in this state.

1804.   Application. This Part shall not apply or be construed to affect in any way the purchase, receipt or transportation of rifles or shotguns or ammunition by federally licensed firearms manufacturers, importers, dealers or collectors except to permit such purchase, receipt or transportation.

PART IV: ARMOR-PIERCING BULLETS

1810.   Definitions. As used in this Part, **"armor-piercing bullet"** shall mean any bullet, except a shotgun shell or ammunition primarily designed for use in rifles, that:

(1)   Has a steel inner core or core of equivalent density and hardness, truncated cone, and is designed for use in a pistol or revolver as a body armor or metal piercing bullet; or

(2)   Has been primarily manufactured or designed, by virtue of its shape, cross-sectional density, or any coating applied thereto, to breach or penetrate body armor when fired from a handgun.

1811.   Prohibitions

A.   No person shall import, manufacture, sell, purchase, possess, or transfer armor-piercing bullets.

B.   Whoever violates the provisions of this Section shall be fined not more than one thousand dollars or imprisoned with or without hard labor for not more than one year, or both.

1812.   Exemptions. The provisions of this Part shall not apply to:

(1)   Law enforcement officers and employees acting in the lawful performance of their duties.

(2)   Law enforcement or other authorized agencies conducting a firearms training course, operating a forensic ballistics laboratory, or specializing in the development of ammunition or explosive ordnance.

(3)   Department of Corrections officials and employees authorized to carry firearms while engaged in the performance of their official duties.

(4)   Members of the armed services or reserve forces of the United States or Louisiana National Guard while engaged in the performance of their official duties.

(5)   Federal officials authorized to carry firearms while engaged in the performance of their official duties.

(6)   The lawful manufacture, importation, sale, purchase, possession, or transfer of armor-piercing bullets exclusively to or for persons authorized by law to possess such bullets.

(7)   A bona fide collector licensed by the Department of Public Safety.

TITLE 47.   REVENUE AND TAXATION

Occupational License Tax

382.   Wholesale dealers in pistols, rifles, or cartridges. Every wholesale dealer in pistols, pistol cartridges, blank pistols, blank cartridges, and all rifles except .22 and .25 calibers, and rifle cartridges, except .22 and .25 calibers, shall pay an annual license on the said business, graduated as follows:

First Class—When the gross sales are ten thousand dollars or more, the license shall be fifty dollars ($50.00).

Second Class—When the gross sales are five thousand dollars or more, and less than ten thousand dollars, the license shall be thirty-five dollars ($35.00).

Third Class—When the gross sales are less than five thousand dollars, the license shall be twenty-five dollars ($25.00).

No dealer shall be deemed a wholesale dealer unless he sells to dealers for resale.

383.   Retail dealers in pistols, rifles or cartridges.

A.   Every retail dealer in pistols or pistol cartridges, blank pistols or blank pistol cartridges, or any rifles, except rifles of .22 and .25 calibers, or any rifle cartridges, except rifle cartridges of .22 and .25 calibers, shall pay an annual license tax on the said business. The amount of said license shall be as shown in the following table:

If the Gross Sales Are:

As Much As	But Less Than	The Annual License Shall Be:
$ 0	$ 2,500	$ 25
2,500	5,000	50
5,000	7,500	100
7,500	10,000	150
10,000	. . .	200

B.   No person shall sell, at wholesale or retail, pistols or pistol cartridges, blank pistols or blank pistol cartridges, or any rifles, except rifles of .22 and .25 calibers or any rifle cartridges, except rifle cartridges of .22 and .25 calibers, without first obtaining the license required in this Section or in R.S. 47:382, or without first obtaining the license which may be imposed by any municipal or parochial authority for the sale of pistols or pistol cartridges, blank pistols or blank pistol cartridges, rifles or rifle cartridges.

Whoever violates the provisions of this Sub-section shall be fined not less than fifty dollars nor more than two hundred dollars, or imprisoned for not more than sixty days, or both.

Figure 6.5

1.   Certain persons convicted of certain crimes such as manslaughter, aggravated battery, murder, aggravated and simple rape, and kidnaping do not have a right to possess a firearm or carry any weapons.   ☐ True   ☐ False

Why or Why Not?_____

_____

_____

2. Guards and messengers employed by common carriers, banks, or trust companies may possess and carry a machine gun while actually employed in and about the shipment, transportation, or delivery, or in the guarding of any money, treasure, bullion, bonds, or other thing of value.   □ True   □ False

Why or Why Not?_____

_____

_____

3. Armor piercing bullets can be permissibly sold to Department of Correction Officials and employees authorized to carry firearms while engaged in the performance of their official duties.   □ True   □ False

4. Which of the following information is not required to be kept in a register by a manufacturer or merchant selling machine guns?

a. Date of the sale.   □ Yes   □ No

b. Name, address and occupation of person buying machine gun.   □ Yes   □ No

c. Political party and religious affiliation of purchaser.   □ Yes   □ No

Form 6.6

ASSIGNMENT #7
MATCHING TEST: CONDUCT WITH CRIMINAL OFFENSES

Time Allotted: 0.5 hours
Point Value: 5.0 points

COMPLETE *FORM 6.7.*

In the short assignment below, match the descriptive words which outline what is required for a finding of guilt under a criminal charge. Look closely and make certain that your choice is correct. In many forms of criminal behavior, there can be cross-over.

OFFENSE

GAMBLING _____

WEAPONS _____

NARCOTICS, HEROIN, MARIJUANA _____

FIREARMS _____

PROSTITUTION _____

DISORDERLY CONDUCT _____

LOITERING _____

VAGRANCY _____

DESCRIPTION OF CONDUCT

a. Possession of proscribed substances; selling of proscribed substances; use of proscribed substances; giving away proscribed substances.

b. Proscribed behavior in both public and private places; economic transaction for sexual conduct.

c. Duty imposed to prevent proscribed behavior; can include paraphernalia; can include games of chance; can include conduct in both public and private places.

d. Duty imposed to prevent proscribed behavior; individual behaviors listed; failure to leave location; language-/fighting words; obstructing traffic.

e. Duty imposed to prevent proscribed behavior; individual behaviors listed; failure to leave location; distinguished from homelessness.

f. Duty imposed to prevent proscribed behavior; individual behaviors listed; failure to leave location; obstructing public passage.

g. Duty imposed to prevent proscribed behavior; confiscation permitted; use or possession exemptions; regulation of sales; prohibition of buying, using or possessing.

h. Duty imposed to prevent proscribed behavior; confiscation permitted; concealment prohibited; prohibit use or possession; sale regulated; sale prohibited; use or possession exemptions.

Form 6.7

ASSIGNMENT #8
AN IMAGINARY CASE OF ARSON

Time Allotted: 0.5 hours

Point Value: 5.0 points

Arson is a crime that can have multiple motives, from political and domestic reasons, to its chief cause, economic collusion and insurance fraud.

The arson for profit scheme requires legal specialists, particularly investigators for the district attorney's office, who are paralegals or legal assistants, to raise a series of telling questions. Thinking hypothetically prepares the practitioner for the real cases to come. A large, comprehensive questionnaire from the U.S. Department of Justice's Law Enforcement Assistance Administration entitled, *Enforcement Manual: Approaches for Combatting Arson for Profit Schemes, A Practical Guide,* raises every conceivable issue. Again, the student is required to think in a hypothetical sense. Answer these questions using creativity and imagination. No one expects uniform or standardized answers. Completion of the assignment should lead to understanding of the complex evidentiary issues in a case of arson.

CREATE YOUR OWN HYPOTHETICAL ARSON CASE AND COMPLETE *FORM 6.8.*

Sources of Interview Information

The following is a list of some of the possible witnesses to acts committed in connection with an arson-for-profit scheme and the types of questions they should be asked:

I.   Interview of Witnesses at Scene of Fire
    A.   Possible Witnesses:
- Tenants of building
- Tenants of surrounding buildings
- Businessmen in building
- Businessmen in surrounding buildings
- Customers of businesses in building
- Customers of businesses in surrounding buildings
- Passersby including: bus route drivers, taxi drivers, deliverymen (milk, bread), garbage collectors, police patrols, people waiting for buses and taxis

    B.   Questions to Be Asked:
- Did you observe the fire?
- At what time did you first observe the fire?
- In what part of building did you observe the fire?
- What called your attention to the building?
- Did you see anyone entering or leaving the building prior to the fire?
- Did you recognize them?
- Can you describe them?
- Did you observe any vehicles in the area of the fire?
- Can you describe them?
- Can you describe the smoke and the color of the flame?
- How quickly did the fire spread?
- Was the building burning in more than one place?
- Did you detect any unusual odors?
- Did you observe anything else?
- What else did you observe?

II.   Interview of Fire Officers and/or Firefighters at Scene

   A.   Questions to Be Asked:
      • What time was alarm received?
      • What time did you arrive at scene of fire?
      • Was your route to the scene blocked?
      • What was the extent of burning when you arrived?
      • Were doors and windows locked?
      • Was the entrance and/or passageways blocked?
      • What kind of fire was it?
      • What was the spread speed of the fire?
      • In what area(s) did the fire start?
      • What was the proximity of the fire to the roof?
      • Was there evidence of the use of an accelerant?
      • Was there any evidence of arson recovered?
      • Did the building have a fire alarm system?
      • Was it operating?
      • Was there any evidence of tampering with the alarm system?
      • Did the building have a sprinkler system?
      • Did it operate?
      • Was there any evidence of tampering with the sprinkler system?
      • Was there anyone present in the building when you arrived?
      • Who was that person in the building?
      • Did he say anything to you?
      • Were there any people present at the scene when you arrived?
      • Who were they?
      • Did you observe any vehicles at the scene or leaving when you arrived?
      • Can you describe them?
      • Were there contents in the building?
      • Was there evidence of contents removed?
      • Was the owner present?
      • Did he make a statement?
      • What did he say?
      • What is the prior fire history of the building?
      • What is the prior fire history of the area?

III.   Interview of Insurance Personnel

   The profit in many arson-for-profit cases is the payment from an insurance policy or policies. There are three classes of people who may be interviewed in order to determine if the profit centers around an insurance claim. They are the insurance agent/broker, the insurance adjuster, and the insurance investigator.

   A.   Questions to Ask the Agent or Broker
      • Who is the insured?
      • Is there more than one insured?
      • Is the insured the beneficiary?
      • What type of policy was issued?
      • What is the amount of the policy?
      • When was it issued?
      • When does it expire?
      • What is the premium cost?
      • Are payments up-to-date?
      • Have there been any increases in amount of coverage?
      • What amount?
      • When did increase take effect?
      • What was the reason for the increase?
      • Are there any special provisions in the policy? (E.g., interruption of business or rental income.)
      • What are they, and when did they take effect?
      • Has the insured ever received a cancellation notice on this property? If so, when? Why?
      • Does the insured have any other policies?
      • Were there previous losses at location of fire?
      • Were there losses at other locations owned by the insured?

   B.   Questions to Ask the Insurance Claims Adjuster:
      • Did you take a sworn statement from the insured?

- Did the insured submit documents regarding proof of loss, value of contents, bills of lading, value of building, etc.?
- Did you inspect the fire scene?
- Did you inspect the fire scene with a public insurance adjuster?
- Did you and the public adjuster agree on the cost figure of the loss?
- Have you dealt with this public adjuster before?
- Has he represented this owner before?
- Has the insured had any other losses with this company? If so, get details.

C. Questions to Ask the Insurance Investigator:
- Were you able to determine the cause of the fire?
- Did you collect any evidence?
- Who analyzed the evidence?
- What were the results of the analysis?
- Was the cause of the fire inconsistent with state of building as known through underwriting examination?
- Have you investigated past fires involving the location?
- Have you investigated past fires involving the insured?
- What were the results of the investigations?
- Have you had prior investigations involving the public adjuster?
- Have you had prior investigations involving buildings handled by the same insurance agent/broker?
- What were the results of these investigations?
- Does this fire fit into a pattern of fires of recent origin in this area?
- What are the similarities?
- What are the differences?
- Have you taken any statements in connection with this burning?
- Whose statements did you take?
- What do they reveal?

There may be restrictions on the amount of information insurance personnel can turn over without a subpoena, but the investigator should be able to determine enough to indicate whether the issuance of a subpoena or search warrant would prove fruitful.

IV. Other Witnesses Concerning Finances of Insured

There are a number of other people who may have information relating to the finances of the owner which may indicate how he stood to profit from the burning. These witnesses would include business associates, creditors, and competitors. (See also the guide by Harvey Schmidt in Part II of this manual.) Following are the types of questions these witnesses may be able to answer:

- How long have you known the owner/insured?
- What is the nature of your relationship with him?
- Do you have any information on the financial position of his business?
- Is he competitive with similar businesses?
- Have there been recent technological advances which would threaten his position?
- Has there been a recent increase in competition which would affect his position?
- Have changes in the economy affected his position?
- Has he experienced recent difficulty in paying creditors?
- Has his amount of debt increased recently?
- Has he lost key employees recently?
- Has the location where he does business changed for the worse recently?
- Has he increased his mortgage or taken out a second or third mortgage?
- Has he had difficulty making mortgage payments?
- Do you have any other information about his financial position?

Form 6.8

ASSIGNMENT #9
FINGERPRINT IDENTIFICATION

Time Allotted: 0.5 hours
Point Value: 5.0 points

As most people know, fingerprint evidence is considered to be the most credible and verifiable source of evidence. The collection of fingerprints is a crucial tool in most major felonies. All fingerprints can be categorized into various types, including arches, loops, deltas and whorls. A chart outlining basic human print characteristics is provided for you to identify your fundamental print patterns.

A PLAIN ARCH is that type of pattern in which the ridges enter upon one side, make a rise or curve in the center, and flow or tend to flow out upon the opposite side, without forming an angle or upthrust, and lacking two of the basic characteristics of the loop.

A TENTED ARCH is that type of pattern which posseses either an angle, an upthrust, or two of the three basic characteristics of the loop.

A LOOP is that type of pattern in which one or more ridges enter upon either side, recurve, touch or pass an imaginary line between delta and core and pass out or tend to pass out upon the side from which such ridge or ridges entered.

A SUFFICIENT RECURVE consists of the space between the shoulders of a loop, free of any appendages which abut upon it at a right angle.

TYPE LINES are the two innermost ridges which start or go parallel, diverge, and surround or tend to surround that pattern area.

THE DELTA is that point on a ridge at or nearest to the point of divergence of two typelines, and located at or directly in front of the point of divergence.

DELTA RULES:

1. when there are two or more possible deltas which conform to the definition, the one nearest the core should be chosen.

2. the delta may not be located in the middle of a ridge running between the typelines toward the core, but at the nearer end only.

3. the delta may not be located at a bifurcation which does not open toward the core.

4. where there is a choice between a bifurcation and another type or delta, the bifurcation is selected.

A PLAIN WHORL consists of one or more ridges which make a complete circuit, with two deltas, between which, when an imaginary line is drawn, at least one recurving ridge is cut or touched.

A CENTRAL POCKET LOOP consists of at least one recurving ridge, or an obstruction at right angles to the line of flow, with two deltas, between which, when an imaginary line is drawn, no recurving ridge within the pattern area is cut or touched.

THE LINE OF FLOW of a central pocket loop is determined by drawing an imaginary line between the inner delta and the center of the innermost recurving ridge.

A DOUBLE LOOP consists of two separate loop formations, with two separate and distinct sets of shoulders and two deltas.

AN ACCIDENTAL consists of a combination of two different types of patterns with the exception of the plain arch, with two or more deltas, or a pattern which possesses some of the requirements for two or more different types of a pattern which conform to none of the definitions.

Figure 6.6

Use an ink pad, paste, water color paint or other similar technique to gain an impression of your fingerprints. A typical example of a fingerprint identification card is reproduced below for your use in this assignment.

KEEP IN A SAFE PLACE
(CONFIDENTIAL)

CHILDS LAST NAME		FIRST NAME		MIDDLE		PHONE NO.

ADDRESS		SOCIAL SECURITY NO.	DATE OF BIRTH	PLACE OF BIRTH

RACE	AGE	EYES	WEIGHT	HEIGHT	SEX	COMPLEXION

SCARS	ALIAS	SCHOOL ATTENDED

PARENTS OR GUARDIAN'S NAME	ADDRESS	PHONE

1. RIGHT THUMB	2. RIGHT FORE FINGER	3. RIGHT MIDDLE FINGER	4. RIGHT RING FINGER	5. RIGHT LITTLE FINGER

6. LEFT THUMB	7. LEFT FORE FINGER	8. LEFT MIDDLE FINGER	9. LEFT RING FINGER	10. LEFT LITTLE FINGER

LEFT FOUR FINGERS TAKEN SIMULTANEOUSLY	LEFT THUMB	RIGHT THUMB	RIGHT FOUR FINGERS TAKEN SIMULTANEOUSLY

PRINTS TAKEN BY

OFFICER	RANK	AGENCY	DATE FINGERPRINTED

FORM # CFP-1   G.A. THOMPSON   BOX 64681   DALLAS, TEXAS 75206

Form 6.9

The technique of fingerprinting is fundamentally a rolling technique — that is, you roll your fingers from left to right across the paper following the instructions on the card. Your instructor can give you more guidelines on this particular process. Once you have imprinted the impression of your fingerprints on the card, this exercise calls for the identification of your print types.

1. Is the predominant pattern in your fingerprints an arch, whorl or loop?

    _____

2. Do you have deltas or islands?_____

    _____

3. Do you have combinations of different types?_____

    _____

    _____

ASSIGNMENT #10
DIAGRAMS FROM A NARRATIVE

Time Allotted: 0.5 hours
Point Value: 5.0 points

Reconstructing a diagram from the testimony of a witness or other interested parties calls for communicative precision. The student will see how challenging this particular exercise can be, and once you thoroughly analyze the facts and draw your own representation of what you feel those facts are, you can compare your end result with the official police report that is included in this section or will be provided to you by your instructor. If confused as to methodology, an excellent police diagram is reproduced at *Figure 6.7* for illustrative purposes.

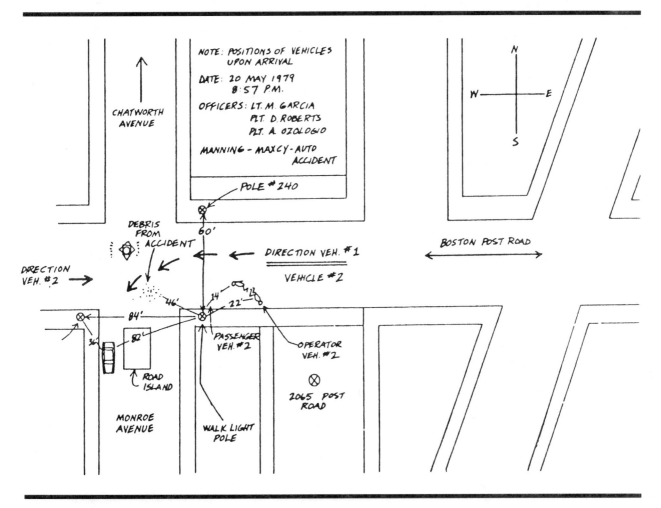

Figure 6.7

REVIEW AND ANALYZE THE POLICE REPORT DATA BELOW AND PICTORIALLY REPRESENT THAT DATA IN A DIAGRAM.

POLICE REPORT DATA:

Unit #1 was traveling north on Morton Avenue when it struck Unit #2 in the rear which was stopped behind a line of cars also stopped for the light at Morton & Michigan Aves.

Unit #2, in a chain reaction, by force of Unit #1, then struck Unit #3 and Unit #3 then struck Unit #4, all stopped for the light at Morton & Michigan Aves.

Damage to Unit #1 was severe to front end and was towed to Mills Auto Body by Voigts Arco.

Damage to Unit #2 was to front and rear ends, moderate. Operator complained of pain but refused treatment on the scene.

Damage to Unit #3 was to the tail gate and tail light and front grill. Passenger complained of neck pain and stated she was going to hospital on her own.

Damage to Unit #4 was to the tail gate which buckled.

DRAW DIAGRAM BELOW:

ASSIGNMENT #11
DIAGRAM OF A SCENE OR LOCATION

Time Allotted: 0.5 hours
Point Value: 5.0 points

Baseline and triangulation methods are the easiest form of graphic portrayal of a crime scene. No artistic talent is required, but there must be some serious adherence paid to scale measurements and a code or legend which explains the setting. Examples of both methods are reproduced below.

EXAMPLE OF BASELINE OR COORDINATE METHOD OF SKETCHING

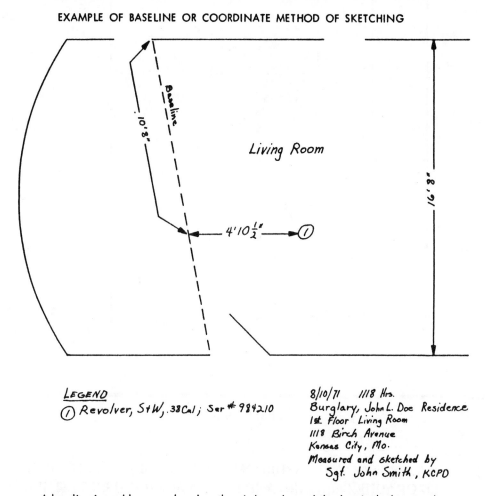

Living Room

Baseline

10' 8"

4' 10 1/2"

16' 8"

LEGEND
① Revolver, S&W, .38Cal; Ser # 984210

8/10/71   1118 Hrs.
Burglary, John L. Doe Residence
1st Floor Living Room
1118 Birch Avenue
Kansas City, Mo.
Measured and sketched by
    Sgt. John Smith, KCPD

A baseline is used here, anchored on the window edge and the door jamb, because the near (west) wall is not straight. If the west wall were straight it could be used as the baseline.

Figure 6.8

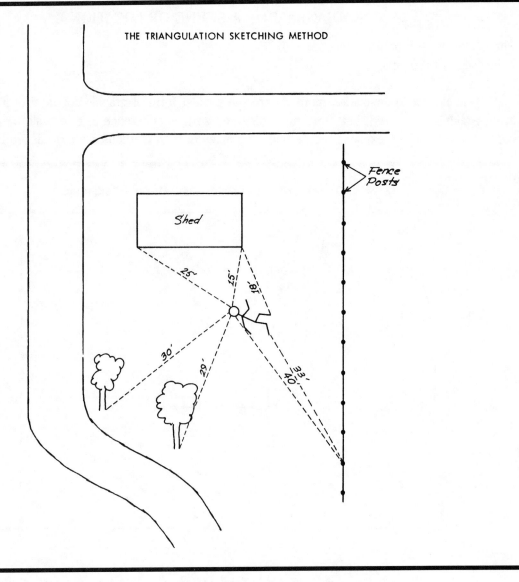

Figure 6.9

PICK ANY LOCATION, SAY, YOUR BEDROOM, YOUR HOUSE, THE BLOCK IN WHICH YOUR HOUSE IS LOCATED OR YOUR BACKYARD AND DRAW A SKETCH USING EITHER METHOD OR ANOTHER METHOD WITH WHICH YOU ARE COMFORTABLE.

PLACE SKETCH HERE:

ASSIGNMENT #12
SUSPECT DESCRIPTIONS

Time Allotted: 0.5 hours
Point Value: 5.0 points

Police employ varied techniques and methods, both scientific and mechanical, which track down, trace and identify suspects. Victims and other witnesses are your best source of information in the preparation of a suspect description.

USING THE DESCRIPTION FORM AT *FORM 6.10*, DESCRIBE AN INDIVIDUAL OF YOUR CHOOSING, WHETHER A FRIEND, PARENT, BROTHER, SISTER OR OTHER PARTY.

DETAILS DESCRIPTION

1. SEX (Male, Female)

2. RACE (White, Black, Red, Yellow)

3. AGE _____

4. HEIGHT (Compare with persons with whom you work)

   _____ Feet _____ Inches

5. WEIGHT (Compare with persons with whom you work)

   _____ Pounds

6. PROBABLE NATIONALITY (Latin, Chinese, Scandinavian, Etc.)

   _____

7. BUILD (Slender, Medium, Heavy, Stocky, Athletic, Very Heavy, Very Thin)

8. POSTURE (Stooped, Erect, Slumped)

9. COMPLEXION (Rough, Smooth, Tanned, Dark, Fair, Freckled, Pale, Pimply, Red, Olive)

10. HEAD (Large, Medium, Small, Round, Square, Oblong, Broad, Inclined forward, backward, sideways)

11. HAIR (Color _____, Color at Temples _____; Baldness, frontal, top, receding at hairline, totally bald, thick, thin, course, wavy, straight, kinky, curled, bushy; parted on right, left, no part)

12. EYES (Brown, Blue, Green, Grey, Hazel, Yellow, Clear, Bloodshot; large, small deep-set, protruding, straight, slanted, cross-eyed, narrow, squinting, wide, glass eye; close set, wide apart, piercing, dull, brilliant, fixed, mobile; eyelashes long, short. If glasses worn: Type, color of rims, etc.)

13. FOREHEAD (Broad, Narrow, High, Low, Receding, Vertical, Bulging)

14. EYEBROWS (Thin, Bushy, Penciled, Natural, Arched, Horizontal, Slanting up or down, meeting)

    Same color as hair?_____ if not, color _____

15. NOSE (Long, Medium, Short; Thin, Thick, Straight, Concave, Convex, Pointed, Flat, Turned up, Turned down, Pointed to right, left; Nostrils large, small, high, low, flared)

16. MUSTACHE OR BEARD (Short, Medium, Long, Pointed or Dull ends, Ends turned up or down; Thick, thin, straight type of beard or sideburns) Compare with color of hair.

17. CHEEKS (Full, Fleshy, Sunken)

18. CHEEKBONES (High, Low, Prominent, Not Prominent)

19. MOUTH (Turned up or down at corner, Held open, or closed, Distorted by speech or laughter)

20. LIPS (With reference to either upper or lower: Thick, Thin, Puffy, Overhanging, Compressed, Protruding, Retracted over teeth; Red, Pale, Blue, Cracked, Scarred)

21. TEETH (Yellow, White, Dull, Stained, Loose, Decayed, Broken, Filled, Braced, Capped, Receding or Projecting, False, Prominent bridgework)

22. CHIN (Small, Large, Square, Curved, Pointed, Flat, Double, Dimpled, Protruding, Vertical, Normal, Receding)

23. JAW (Long, Short, Wide, Narrow, Thin, Fleshy, Heavy)

24. EARS (Small, Medium, Large, Close to or projecting from head, Oval, Round, Rectangular, Triangular, Pierced, Cauliflowered, hairy; Contour of the lobe, lower portion: Descending, Square, Medium, Gulfed)

25. NECK (Small, Medium, Long, Straight, Curved, Thin, Flat, Prominent, Medium or absent Adam's apple, Crooked, Heavy, Goiterous)

26. SHOULDERS (Small, Heavy, Narrow, Broad, Square, Round, Stooped, Not equal)

27. HANDS (Long, Short, Broad, Narrow, Thin, Fleshy, Rough, Bony, Soft, Smooth, Hairy, Square, Tapered)

28. FINGERS (Short, Long, Slim, Thick, Tapered, Square, Stained, Mutilated)

29. FINGERNAILS (Length, Description, Foreign matter under nails such as paint, grease, etc.)

30. VOICE (Pleasant, Well-modulated, Low, High, Lisp, Other impediment of speech, Gruff, Polite, Southern or foreign accent)

REMEMBER EXACT LANGUAGE USED:_____

_____

_____

_____

_____

_____

_____

_____

31. WALK (Long or short stride, energetic, slow, fast, springy step)

32. APPEARANCE (Loud, conservative, neat, sloppy)

_____

_____

33. CLOTHING   COLOR   PATTERN   TYPE   MATERIAL   CONDITION   HOW WORN

Hat or Cap_____

Overcoat_____

Coat_____

Slacks_____

Suit_____

Dress_____

Shirt_____

Tie_____

Shoes_____

Socks_____

Belt_____

Mask_____

34. JEWELRY

Lapel pins, Rings, Watches, Watch bobs, Chains, Earrings, Tie pins, Identification bracelets, Tie clasp, Cuff links (Describe:)

_____

_____

35. PECULIARITIES (Most Important of All)

(A) Scars, Marks, Tattoos, Moles, Birthmarks (Describe:)

_____

_____

36. TYPE OF GUN USED - Below

(A) Color - Blued, nickel, gray, other (Describe:)

_____

_____

(B) Revolver, automatic, single shot, rifle, shotgun, submachine gun

(C) Length of barrel _____

(D) Condition - blue worn off, rusty, well-kept

(E) In which hand was the gun held (right, left - both)

(F) Did suspect appear to be familiar with the weapon? (Yes - No)

NAME _____

ADDRESS _____

DATE _____

Form 6.10

ASSIGNMENT #13
CRIME REPORT: FROM DIAGRAM TO NARRATIVE
A HYPOTHETICAL SITUATION

Time Allotted: 0.5 hours
Point Value: 5.0 points

This exercise lets students use their imagination, something a little different and not done too often in the study of law.

USE THE DIAGRAM BELOW TO CREATE A CRIMINAL, NARRATIVE REPORT FROM A SET OF FACTS THAT YOU HYPOTHETICALLY DRAFT AND ARE RESPONSIBLE FOR. THE ONLY REQUIREMENT IS THAT YOU REMAIN WITHIN THE CONTEXT OF THE PICTURE. YOUR REPORT SHOULD BE NO MORE THAN ONE DOUBLE-SPACED, TYPED PAGE.

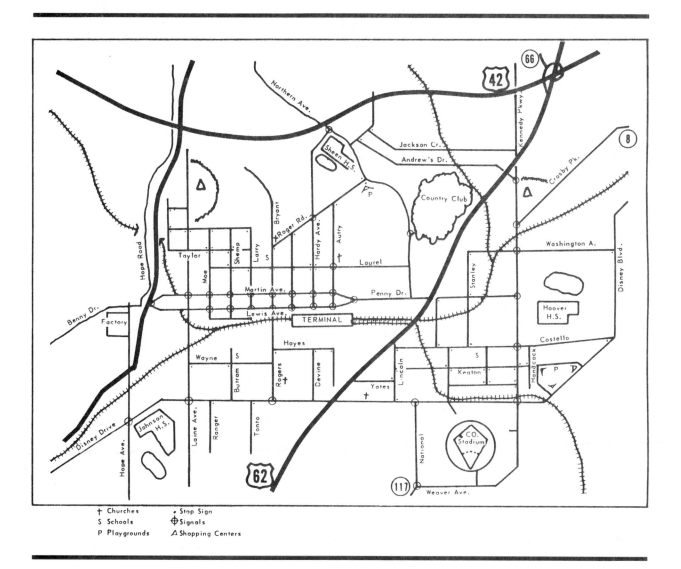

Figure 6.10

ASSIGNMENT #14
THE ARREST

Time Allotted: 0.5 hours
Point Value: 5.0 points

The initial stages of these exercises concerned themselves with the identification of laws and statutes and their proper applicability and, secondly, the investigative steps the justice system takes to identify suspects. If the evidence is substantial enough and probable cause exists, an arrest process will follow. Of course, police act as the gatekeepers to the justice system and must exercise discretion based on reason and rationality. Adherence to constitutional rights, warrant requirements, *Miranda* warnings and other permissions need to be considered before effecting an arrest. The standard arrest form is the subject matter of this exercise.

USE THE FACTS LISTED BELOW TO COMPLETE THE ARREST FORM AT *FORM 6.11*. FOR THOSE SPACES OR SECTIONS NOT ADDRESSED, FILL IN INFORMATION OF YOUR OWN CHOOSING.

FACT PATTERN:

Suspect's Height: 6'9"
Suspect's Name: George O. Nelson
Place of Birth: Ewing, California
Date of Birth: August 2, 1945
Suspect's Weight: 210
Suspect's Address: 19 Simpson Rd., Ewing, CA
Crime: Assault
Suspect's Race: Caucasian
Social Security No.: 111-18-8888
Vehicle: Not Applicable
Suspect's Employment: None
Suspect's Hair: Blond
Suspect's Eyes: Blue
Arrest No.: 467-1986
Weapon: Not Applicable
Time of Arrest/Rights Read: 5:23 p.m.
Arrived at Station: 5:35 p.m.
Processed: 5:40 p.m.
Interviewed: 6:00 p.m.
Arraignment: Upcoming
Arresting/Transporting Officer: Patrolman Samuel Ellis
Alcohol/Narcotics: Not Applicable
Details of Arrest: Monday, 10-20-86, 5:18 p.m., at residence at 13 Ambler Drive, Springfield, PA
Victim: Mona Nelson, 13 Ambler Drive, Springfield, PA; phone 765-4367
Details of Incident: (By student)

ARREST REPORT

| 14. REP. AREA | 1. SUSPECT'S NAME (LAST, FIRST, MIDDLE) | 1 A. M.O. NO. | 2. COMPLAINT NO. |

| 15. LOCATION OF ARREST | 3. SUSPECT'S RES. ADDRESS | CITY | 4. ARREST NO./GRADE |

16. DESCRIBE TYPE OF PREMISES

| 5. SEX   RACE   D.O.B.   HT.   WT.   HAIR   EYES | 6. I.D. NO. |

17. DAY. DATE/TIME ARRESTED

| 7. N.C.I.C. CHECK   TIME   8. SOCIAL SECURITY NO. |

18. BREATHALYZER / OPERATOR / TIME READING
19. PARENT/GUARDIAN / TIME NOTIFIED   ☐ YES ☐ NO
9. PLACE OF BIRTH   10. WEAPON (DESCRIBE)   SERIAL NO.

20. RESIST? ☐ YES ☐ NO   21. NARCOTIC? ☐ YES ☐ NO   22. ARMED? ☐ YES ☐ NO
11. OCCUPATION   12. RES. PHONE   13. BUS. PHONE

23. WHERE SUSPECT EMPLOYED OR SCHOOL   24. DAY, DATE/TIME OCCURRED   25. DATE/TIME REPORTED

26. SUSPECT OPERATOR'S LIC. NO.   STATE   27. FORMAL CHARGE(S)   28. U.C.R.

29. HOLD PLACED ON VEHICLE ☐ YES ☐ NO   TOWED TO   30. CHARGES CHANGED TO   DATE/TIME

31. VEHICLE INVOLVED   YEAR - MAKE - MODEL   COLOR(S)   REG. NO. STATE YEAR   31A. VEHICLE REGISTERED OWNER   ADDRESS

CODE: C - COMPLAINANT V - VICTIM W - WITNESS P - PARENT/GUARDIAN CO - SUSPECT

32. NAME	CODE	RESIDENCE ADDRESS	CITY	RES. PHONE	BUS PHONE
(1)					
(2)					
(3)					
(4)					
(5)					

33. ARREST PROCEDURE

(A) ARRESTED _____ HRS. (B) RIGHTS _____ HRS. (C) TRANSPORTED _____ HRS. (D) ARRIVED _____ HRS.

(E) PROCESSED & RIGHTS _____ HRS. (F) INTERVIEWED _____ HRS. (G) ARRAIGNED _____ HRS. (H) RELEASED COMMITTED _____ HRS.

ITEM NO.	34. NARRATIVE. (1) CONTINUATION OF ABOVE ITEMS (INDICATE "ITEM NUMBER" AT LEFT. (2) DESCRIBE DETAILS OF INCIDENT NOT LISTED ABOVE. (3) IDENTIFY ADDITIONAL WITNESSES, VICTIMS ETC. FROM BLOCK NO. 32.

35. TRANSPORTING OFFICER   NO.   36. ARRESTING OFFICER   NO.   37. BOOKING OFFICER   NO.

38. TRANSPORTING OFFICER   NO.   39. ARRESTING OFFICER   NO.   40. SEARCHED BY   NO.

41. SUSPECT'S MONEY   42. SUPERVISOR APPROVING   43. DAILY BULLETIN ☐ YES ☐ NO   PAGE   OF

Form 6.11

ASSIGNMENT #15
THE CRIMINAL COMPLAINT

Time Allotted: 0.5 hours
Point Value: 5.0 points

FACT PATTERN:

Issuing Authority: Judge Robert Stevens
Complainant: Trooper Warren Michaels
Political Subdivision: Jamestown, Pennsylvania
Date of Complaint: August 1, 1989
Defendant's Name: Sally R. Jones
Incident No.: 1612
UCR No.: 1190
OTN: 39-59-89
Complaint No.: CA-81-1989
Year: 1989
Affiant: Trooper Warren Michaels, Midway Police Department, Jamestown, Pennsylvania
Defendant's Address: 1814 Unitary Drive, Ellicottville, Pennsylvania
Nicknames: None
Acts Committed: Select any legislation, law or statute considered in previous assignments.
Act or Legislation No.: To be created by student

USING THE FACTS LISTED ABOVE, PREPARE AND COMPLETE THE STANDARDIZED MODEL CRIMINAL COMPLAINT AT *FORM 6.12.*

CRIMINAL COMPLAINT   (POLICE)

DISTRICT JUSTICE
MAGISTERIAL DISTRICT NO.

COMPLAINT NUMBER	YEAR	TYPE	NUMBER
Complaint Numbers if Other Participants			

INCIDENT NUMBER	UCR NO.	OTN

DEFENDANT: **VS.**

I, _____
(Name of Affiant)

of _____
(Identify department or agency represented and political subdivision)

NAME
AND
ADDRESS

R.S.A.
A K A

do hereby state:

(1) ☐ I accuse the above named defendant, who lives at the address set forth above or,

☐ I accuse an individual whose name is unknown to me but who is described as _____

☐ his nickname or popular designation is unknown to me and, therefore, I have designated him herein as John Doe;
with violating the penal laws of the Commonwealth of Pennsylvania at_____
(Place-Political Subdivision)

_____ in _____County on or about _____

(Check appropriate box)

Participants were *(if there were participants, place their names here, repeating the name of above defendant):*

(2) The acts committed by the accused were: Ⓐ

all of which were against the peace and dignity of the Commonwealth of Pennsylvania and contrary to the Act of Assembly,
or in violation of_____and_____ of the Act of_____
(Section)   *(Sub-section)*

or the_____Ordinance of _____.
(Political Sub-division)

(3) I ask that a warrant of arrest or a summons be issued and that the accused be required to answer the charges I have made.

(4) I verify that the facts set forth in this complaint are true and correct to the best of my knowledge or information and belief. This verification is made subject to the penalties of Section 4904 of the Crimes Code (18 Pa. C. S. § 4904) relating to unsworn falsification to authorities.

_____ , 19 _____   _____
(Signature of Complainant)

AND NOW, on this date_____ , 19____, I certify the complaint has been properly completed and verified, and that there is probable cause for the issuance of process.

_____   _____ (SEAL)
(Magisterial District)   *(Issuing Authority)*

AOPC 411-86   **ORIGINAL**   SEE REVERSE SIDE FOR WAIVER AND FOOTNOTES

Form 6.12

ASSIGNMENT #16
INITIAL DISPOSITION OF A CASE

Time Allotted: 0.5 hours
Point Value: 5.0 points

Wide differences exist in the disposition of criminal cases across the 50 American jurisdictions, with even more striking local traditions and practice. Rely fully on your instructor for his or her advice as relates to local issues. This assignment asks you to calculate and gauge what happens initially to a criminal case. Two diagrams are outlined below — the first of which entitled, *Golden: Felony arrest dispositions*; and the second, *Manhattan: Felony arrest dispositions*.

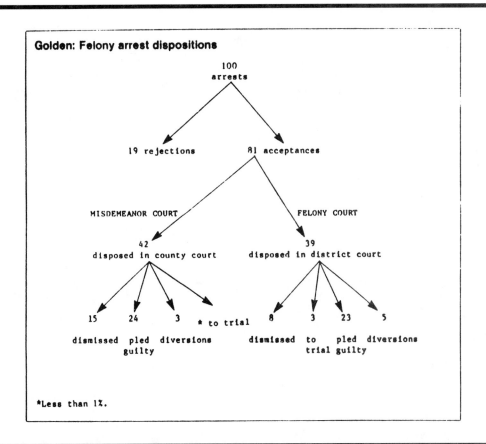

Figure 6.11

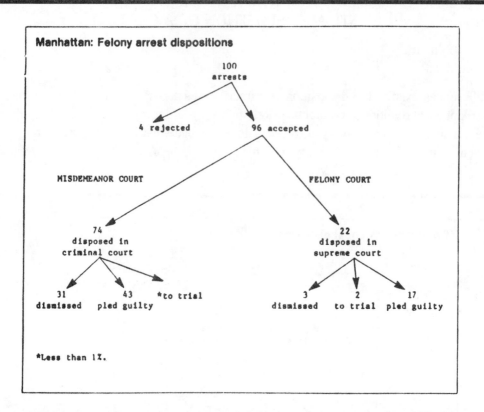

Figure 6.12

These diagrams provide a statistical basis for this exercise. Both figures highlight the same information but from differing jurisdictions, namely, Golden, Colorado, and Manhattan, New York. As you can easily see, what happens at the arrest level is tracked to the appropriate court and jurisdiction until trial, dismissal or eventual pleading.

CONSIDER THESE FIGURES AND ANSWER THE FOLLOWING QUESTIONS.

1. Which jurisdiction rejects more cases than the other?_____

    _____

2. Do you have any ideas or reasons why this might be true?_____

    _____

    _____

3. Is it true that in both jurisdictions, a majority of cases are resolved in misdemeanor courts rather than courts of felony jurisdiction?   ☐ Yes   ☐ No

    Do you know of any reasons why that might be true?_____

    _____

    _____

4. Manhattan dismisses more cases, on a statistical and percentage basis, than Golden, Colorado.

☐ True ☐ False

Explain:_____

_____

_____

5. The minority of cases in both jurisdictions go to trial.

☐ True ☐ False

Explain:_____

_____

_____

6. What percentage of felony cases in both jurisdictions that eventually go to a court of original jurisdiction, that is, are not rejected or dismissed on earlier motion, go to trial? Please explain your method.

_____

_____

ASSIGNMENT #17
PROCESSING THE CRIMINAL CASE: JURISDICTIONAL DIFFERENCES

Time Allotted: 0.5 hours
Point Value: 5.0 points

The U.S. Department of Justice in its major study entitled, *Prosecution of Felony Arrests* (1980), statistically and graphically outlined the different case flow systems adopted in numerous American jurisdictions, two examples of which with accompanying narrative are reproduced below.

Tallahassee, Florida (2nd Judicial Circuit)

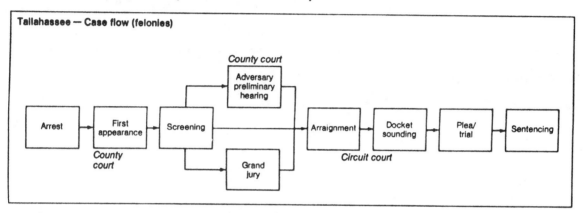

Tallahassee — Case flow (felonies)

Demographic characteristics and crime rate

This six-county jurisdiction had a 1980 population of about 202,000. Approximately 83,725 residents (74% white, 24% black) lived in Tallahassee at that time, a 15% increase over the 1970 figure.

Tallahassee's crime rate was 11,970 per 100,000 population in 1980, the violent crime component being 1,149. The corresponding rates for 280 cities of comparable size averaged 7,137 and 602, respectively.

Criminal justice setting

The state's attorney for the 2nd Judicial District has jurisdiction over misdemeanors arising in the district, which includes the counties of Leon, Jefferson, Gadsden, Liberty, Franklin, and Wakulla. Jurisdiction also extends to child-support cases, URESA hearings (involuntary hospitalization for alcohol, drug, or mental-health-related conditions), juvenile matters, and probation violations.

In 1980, 28 law enforcement agencies presented an estimated 11,000 felony and misdemeanor arrests to the office. About 70% of the office's case load is from Leon County, the Tallahassee police department and Leon County department being the major law enforcement agencies.

The eight-judge county court (lower court) has jurisdiction over misdemeanors, felony first appearances, and felony adversary preliminary hearings.

Serving as the upper court, the circuit court has jurisdiction over felonies, among other matters. Three criminal division judges hear all felony cases in the 2nd Circuit, one on a full-time basis and two handling civil cases as well.

State's Attorney's Office: Size, organization, and procedures

The office employs approximately 25 attorneys. In Leon County, 10 assistants handle felonies; 4, misdemeanors; 2, traffic violations; 1, juvenile matters; and 1, worthless check cases. Assistants in the outlying counties prosecute all cases arising in their respective counties. The office also employs six investigators.

All cases are screened by the first assistant. After arraignment on the information (circuit court), a given case is prosecuted by one attorney until disposition.

Flow of felony cases—arrest through sentencing

After arrest, the officer completes a state's attorney information worksheet (SAIW), a primary document

used by the office. A law enforcement screening officer assigns the charges. The SAIW is taken to county court, where a complaint and probable cause are filed.

First appearance in county court occurs within 24 hours of arrest unless the defendant has already posted bond. At first appearance, the judge reads the complaint to the defendant, advises him of his rights, appoints an attorney if necessary, sets bail, and routinely finds probable cause.

After first appearance, the first assistant screens the case. He notes the probable-cause affidavit, the SAIW, complaint, offense report, and he may have the defendant's rap sheet. If the case is a capital offense, potentially controversial, or weak, the first assistant may present it to a grand jury.

Following screening, an information is filed in circuit court, where the defendant's first appearance is arraignment on the information, approximately 2 weeks after first appearance in county court. If an information is not filed within 21 days, the defendant is entitled to an adversary preliminary hearing (county court) and may call witnesses and obtain discovery. Such hearings are rare.

Approximately 90 to 95% of felony arrests are brought to circuit court for arraignment, which is the first appearance for defendants who were released on bond prior to the probable cause hearing in county court. At arraignment, the information is read and a trial date set. For those defendants making their first court appearance, their rights are read and a public defender is appointed, as appropriate.

The trial date is usually set 6 to 8 weeks after arraignment. Florida's speedy trial rule requires that felonies be disposed of within 180 days from the date of arrest. Prior to trial, "docket sounding" occurs. The prosecutor and public defender alert the judge to what is likely to happen in the case. At this point, the judge can push the attorneys to dispose of the case by not granting continuances or encouraging them to negotiate a plea.

The office encourages prosecutors to obtain pleas to the lead charge, but the primary focus of plea negotiations is on the terms of the sentence or agreement by the State to remain silent at sentencing. If a plea agreement is reached, sentencing usually occurs about 6 weeks after the plea is taken.

Figure 6.13

Washington, D.C.

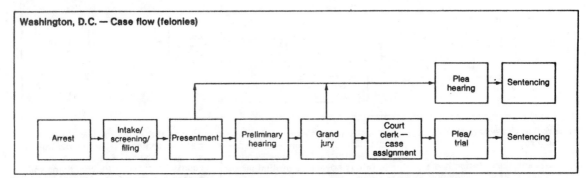

Washington, D.C. — Case flow (felonies)

Arrest → Intake/screening/filing → Presentment → Preliminary hearing → Grand jury → Court clerk — case assignment → Plea/trial → Sentencing; and Plea hearing → Sentencing

Demographic characteristics and crime rate

In 1980, Washington's population was 637,651 (70% black), 16% under the 1970 total.

The 1980 crime rate was 10,026 per 100,000 population, 2,011 being the violent crime component. Corresponding rates in 1980 for 17 cities of comparable size were 9,106 and 1,162, respectively.

Criminal justice setting

The superior court division of the United States Attorney's Office (USAO) for the District of Columbia has jurisdiction over non-Federal misdemeanors and felonies committed in Washington, D.C. Traffic and petty offenses, ordinance violations, and juvenile cases are handled by the District's corporation counsel.

Most of the non-Federal misdemeanors and felonies brought to the USAO (22,000 annually) are presented by the D.C. metropolitan police department, although other law enforcement agencies also bring cases to the U.S. Attorney.

Part of a unified court system, the superior court of the District of Columbia (equivalent to a State court of general jurisdiction) exercises jurisdiction over non-Federal misdemeanors and felonies. (The Federal district court adjudicates Federal and dual-jurisdiction crimes.) Twelve judges staff the superior court's felony trial division; eight staff the misdemeanor trial division. The judges maintain individual calendars.

Three of the felony judges handle cases involving first degree murder, rape, or cases with more than four co-defendants (Felony I cases). Other felonies are assigned to one of the eight Felony II judges, except cases being handled by the vertical prosecution team (pilot project), which has its own felony judge.

Felony presentment and preliminary hearings are conducted by two commissioners. Another commissioner handles misdemeanor arraignments.

USAO, Superior Court Division: Size, organization, procedures

The superior court division of the USAO employs 121 attorneys, assigned among six sections: grand jury (incorporates intake and screening), felony trial, misdemeanor trial, and such small sections as the vertical prosecution pilot project, witness assistance, and career criminal units. With the exception of cases assigned to the vertical prosecution unit and, to some extent, the career criminal unit, cases are prosecuted horizontally through indictment. After indictment cases are assigned to individual attorneys.

About 21 attorneys staff the grand jury section; 40 (divided into 7 teams) the misdemeanor trial section; and 36 (12 teams) the felony trial section. Each of the misdemeanor and felony trial teams always prosecutes cases before its own judge.

Flow of felony cases—arrest through sentencing

Arrestees taken into custody have their cases screened within a day of arrest. (See accompanying chart of felony case flow.) Police take their arrest reports to the intake unit at superior court, where any criminal history information pertaining to the accused is retrieved from various data bases. The screening unit supervisor decides whether the case should be pursued as a felony. If so, a staff attorney from the grand jury section, who is working intake that week, reviews the arrest report and evidence to determine the merits of the case; charge and bond recommendations are made, and the case is filed.

For defendants in custody, felony presentment occurs on the same day as filing; otherwise, presentment is usually scheduled 3 days after arrest. Charges may be read (usually waived by the defense), bond established, and dates set for the preliminary hearing (normally in 10–20 days) and grand jury (within 30 days after preliminary hearing).

Most cases for which probable cause is not found at the preliminary hearing are appealed to the grand jury as grand jury originals. Cases not indicted are almost always

dismissed. Indicted cases are randomly assigned to a felony trial judge by the clerk of the superior court. After indictment, the chief of the trial section assigns prosecution of the case to a member of the trial team assigned to that judge.

If a plea bargain is to be offered by the prosecutor, a form letter outlining the offer is prepared at screening and given to the defense attorney at presentment. The offer expires on the date of the preliminary hearing. However, very few cases plead out prior to indictment.

Routinely, another plea offer is made after indictment, but it is usually less generous than the one

extended at screening. All plea offers must be approved by a supervisor. Although counts and charges are normally included in the plea negotiation process, the substance of the offer concerns the right to speak at the sentence hearing. The office does not bargain on incarceration or nonincarceration recommendations; that decision is considered the sole domain of the judge. The routine recommendation is for "a substantial period" of incarceration (but not actual amounts of time). The most substantial concession an attorney can make to the defense is to waive the right to speak at the sentence hearing. Judges do not participate in the plea bargaining process.

Figure 6.14

If you have difficulty understanding any aspects of these exercises, please consult your instructor.

PART 1

POINT OUT THREE MAJOR DIFFERENCES IN HOW FELONY CASES ARE PROCESSED THROUGH THE TALLAHASSEE AND WASHINGTON, D.C. SYSTEMS. BE SPECIFIC AND EXACTING IN YOUR DESCRIPTION.

1. _____

_____

_____

2. _____

_____

_____

3. _____

_____

_____

PART 2

USING THE TALLAHASSEE AND WASHINGTON, D.C. MODELS, PLEASE PRODUCE A BLOCK REFERENCED AND CAPTIONED CASE FLOW FELONY SYSTEM FOR YOUR LOCAL JURISDICTION.

ASSIGNMENT #18
DEFENSE ISSUES: INSANITY

Time Allotted: 0.5 hours
Point Value: 5.0 points

The insanity defense raises both ire and consternation amongst the general citizenry and professionals in the legal system. These workbook assignments cannot begin to ask the student to fathom the dynamics of the insanity defense, but instead will give the student an understanding of what types of diagnosis and diseases can qualify as a form of legal excuse or defense in a given criminal case. Needless to say, the popular perception is that the defense is easily made and as easily proven. Nothing could be further from the truth. Defendants can escape liability only if they can prove that their mental disease or defect was the producer, the prime cause of the criminality. The defenses popularly reviewed throughout history include the Daniel McNaghten Test (also known as the right or wrong rule), irresistible impulse, the Durham Rule (the product rule), and the ALI Rule (the substantial capacity test).

The disorders listed below are, at best, medical descriptions. Your obligation under this assignment is to define at least 20 of these clinical diagnoses and disorders. Standard, comprehensive dictionaries will certainly assist, but of greater use would be medical data bases, medical journals and medical reference manuals. Your instructor can give you some idea of a local or public library that would contain such sources. When you complete these twenty definitions, please consider whether or not these forms of conduct or behavior should qualify as a means of criminal defense.

Acute Brain Disorders

Chronic Brain Disorders

Psychotic Disorders
　　Involutional Psychotic Reaction
　　Affective Reactions
　　　　Manic depressive reaction, manic type
　　　　Manic depressive reaction, depressed type
　　　　Manic depressive reaction, other
　　　　Psychotic depressive reaction
　　Schizophrenic Reactions
　　　　Schizophrenic reaction, simple type
　　　　Schizophrenic reaction, hebephrenic type
　　　　Schizophrenic reaction, catatonic type
　　　　Schizophrenic reaction, paranoid type
　　　　Schizophrenic reaction, acute undifferentiated type
　　　　Schizophrenic reaction, chronic undifferentiated type
　　　　Schizophrenic reaction, schizo-affective type
　　　　Schizophrenic reaction, childhood type
　　　　Schizophrenic reaction, residual type
　　Paranoid Reactions
　　　　Paranoia
　　　　Paranoid state

Psychophysiologic Autonomic and Visceral Disorders
    Psychophysiologic Skin Reaction
    Psychophysiologic Musculoskeletal Reactions

Psychoneurotic Disorders
    Psychoneurotic Reactions
        Anxiety Reactions
        Dissociative Reaction
        Conversion Reaction
        Phobic Reaction
        Obsessive Compulsive Reaction
        Depressive Reaction

Personality Disorders
    Personality Pattern Disturbance
        Inadequate Personality
        Schizoid Personality
        Cyclothymic Personality
        Paranoid Personality
    Personality Trait Disturbance
        Emotionally Unstable Personality
        Passive-aggressive personality
        Compulsive personality
    Sociopathic Personality Disturbance
        Antisocial reaction
        Dyssocial reaction
        Sexual deviation
        Alcoholism (addiction)
        Drug addiction
    Special Symptom Reaction
        Learning disturbance
        Speech disturbance
        Enuresis
        Somnambulism

Transient Situational Personality Disorders
    Transient Situational Personality Disturbance
        Gross stress reaction
        Adult situational reaction
        Adjustment reaction of infancy
        Adjustment reaction of childhood
        Adjustment reaction of adolescence
        Adjustment reaction of late life

Mental Deficiencies
    Mental Deficiency (Familial or Hereditary)
        Mild
        Moderate
        Severe
    Mental Deficiency, Idiopathic
        Mild
        Moderate
        Severe

USE YOUR OWN STATIONERY TO COMPLETE THIS ASSIGNMENT.

ASSIGNMENT #19
NOVEL DEFENSES

Time Allotted: 0.5 hours
Point Value: 5.0 points

Criminal defense attorneys specialize in the advocacy of the novel defense claims. In more recent times, we have heard of the Twinkie defense, the heavy metal defense, and the television-zombie condition which prompts criminal behavior. Over the years, defenses related to astrology, alignment of the planets and barometric pressure have also been attempted. Defenses which raise a great deal of discussion and heated debate are the Spousal Defenses, that is, women who have been continuously battered and abused by their husbands set out to and do kill them. This is sometimes referred to as the "Burning Bed Phenomenon." Also, a recent explanation of criminality, the Pre-Menstrual Syndrome, known as the PMS defense, has attained notoriety.

PART 1

READ THE FOLLOWING ARTICLES AND GIVE YOUR IMPRESSIONS OF THE LEGITIMACY, ETHICS AND EFFICACY OF RAISING SUCH A DEFENSE IN A CRIMINAL HOMICIDE CASE IN THE SPACE BELOW.

_____

_____

_____

_____

_____

_____

_____

_____

_____

_____

_____

_____

_____

Battered-woman defense back in court

BY BEN L. KAUFMAN
The Cincinnati Enquirer

Adversaries Thomas Miller and Claude Crowe renewed a courtroom battle this week that they'd set aside eight years ago:

Is the "battered-woman syndrome" a justification for homicide?

Attorney Miller wants to invoke that defense — used by many battered wives — on behalf of Diane Arlene Hafford, 34, of Pleasant Hill Drive in Springfield Township.

She is charged with murdering boyfriend Cecil A. Welch last September with one shot from a .22-caliber revolver.

Miller says Welch abused Hafford, as did her former husband and father.

Assistant Prosecuting Attorney Claude Crowe says the Ohio Supreme Court has declared expert testimony on the battered-wife syndrome inadmissible because it's more prejudicial than helpful.

Hafford sat gently rocking in a chair at the defense table Monday as Miller and Welch fought it out with legal citations, appeals to common sense and barbs.

Their audience was Hamilton County Common Pleas Judge Ann Marie Tracey, who must try Hafford's murder case later this year.

After hearing them out, Tracey promised an answer Friday.

Eight years ago, it was a different defendant and a different judge and the legal environment was less restrictive.

In 1981, Miller overcame Crowe's objections and Ruth Williams escaped a murder conviction for shooting her husband.

Sympathetic jurors heard details of her miserable life as a victim of abuse and found her guilty of the lesser charge of involuntary manslaughter.

Within weeks, however, the world turned upside down for defense attorneys.

In an unrelated case, the Ohio Supreme Court said defendants pleading self-defense could not bring in experts on the battered-wife syndrome.

The syndrome was not sufficiently developed as a matter of commonly accepted scientific knowledge, the Supreme Court said, and the evidence was likelier to prejudice a jury than to help it. But Miller argued Monday that's no longer the case.

The battered-wife syndrome is so closely related to the recognized Post Traumatic Stress Disorder, he said, that expert testimony is admissible.

Crowe insisted it was not.

Moreover, Crowe argued, it's in the defense's interests for Tracey to reject the expert testimony. He offered these reasons:

■ If Hafford is convicted, Miller can appeal. If Hafford's conviction is reversed because Tracey would not admit expert testimony on the battered-wife syndrome, then the law truly is changed and every battered woman in Ohio benefits.

■ If Tracey admits the evidence and Hafford is acquitted or convicted of a lesser charge, Hafford wins, but it does not undo the Supreme Court ban on expert testimony on the battered-woman syndrome.

Judge refuses to ban 'battered' defense

BY BEN L. KAUFMAN
The Cincinnati Enquirer

Hamilton County Common Pleas Judge Ann Marie Tracey refused Friday to ban the "battered-woman syndrome" defense during Diane Hafford's murder trial.

Her ruling rejected arguments by Assistant Prosecuting Attorney Claude Crowe that the Ohio Supreme Court barred this defense eight years ago.

However, Tracey said defense attorneys may not refer to the syndrome until she admits it as evidence.

Hafford, 34, is charged with murdering boyfriend Cecil Welch, 31, last September with one shot from a .22-caliber pistol at her Springfield Township home.

To establish self-defense, attorney Thomas Miller must show Hafford had an "honest belief that she was in imminent danger of death or great bodily harm and that the use of force was her only means of escape from such danger."

History of abuse

Miller says Hafford was abused by her father, her former husband and Welch, and that is a significant factor in what she believed to be her situation.

Tracey said he would have a chance to prove his point.

"Clearly, evidence tending to show whether the defendant in her circumstances had an honest belief that she was in imminent danger would be relevant to a material issue in this case."

Crowe misunderstood the Supreme Court decision, Tracey said. Rather than ban the evidence, she explained, the court said enough was known about the syndrome in 1981 for someone to qualify as an expert.

That shouldn't be a problem in 1989. "There have been significant leaps in the general acceptance of the battered-woman syndrome in the scientific community," she said, adding that many states also are admitting the syndrome itself as a defense.

Tracey's order said the syndrome includes the psychological after-effects "of victimization by physical, sexual and psychological abuse from an intimate partner."

Possible distortion

Those effects can involve the victim's emotions, thinking, physical responses and behavior after each instance of abuse, she said.

Battered women find ways of coping "that may not appear reasonable, such as continuing to live with the abuser," Tracey continued. "Ultimately, they may fight back, but may perceive threatening behavior in a distorted manner."

Figure 6.15

PART 2

PMS is being used as a legal defense

Associated Press

PRE-MENSTRUAL syndrome, a severe form of the emotional and physical distress that afflicts some women before their monthly periods, is being accepted as a legal defense in criminal cases in some countries, according to a medical journal report.

"The ramifications of this are tremendous," Dr. Katharina Dalton, who is treating dozens of women for the syndrome, wrote in the April 10 issue of the *Journal of the American Medical Association.*

The report cited the cases of three young women, imprisoned in Britain for theft and murder, who broke the law only during their pre-menstrual ·

days. As a result, PMS was accepted as a mitigating factor in female crime in the United Kingdom.

In France, PMS can be grounds for a plea of temporary insanity.

Ms. Dalton has given the women doses of natural progesterone, a hormone, as part of a controversial new treatment.

Although physicians are unsure what causes physical and emotional distress before menstruation, doctors are focusing research on physiological origins.

PMS, a term usually reserved for severe cases of the syndrome, should be recognized as a real "clinical entity affecting a large segment of the female population," wrote gynecologists in one report.

A small minority find their lives

seriously disrupted. Doctors say such people have been known to abuse their children or commit violent crimes. Some are said to be suicidal.

Common drugstore remedies provide only partial relief for some women.

Ms. Dalton has prescribed progesterone for about 30 years to ease the symptoms of PMS. She now is treating 50 female criminals with the hormone and has treated hundreds of women who suffer from PMS impairment not linked to crime.

Since virtually no long-term experiments have been done on the therapy, some doctors are skeptical about her treatment. One reported giving progesterone by injecton and finding that it aggravated rather than alleviated symptoms.

Figure 6.16

IN THE CASE OF PMS, WHAT IS YOUR GENERAL PERCEPTION? DO YOU THINK THIS IS LEGITIMATE DEFENSE? WHY OR WHY NOT?

_____

_____

_____

_____

_____

_____

_____

_____

_____

_____

ASSIGNMENT #20
TECHNOLOGY IN A CRIMINAL CASE

Time Allotted: 0.5 hours
Point Value: 5.0 points

Forensic evidence is becoming extensively relied on in the prosecution of criminal cases. Requirements for this exercise call for you to research your own newspapers to come up with two articles which rely on the use of forensic evidence in a criminal case.

Cut out two articles from a newspaper which zero in on forensic science in a criminal case. Paste the articles in the space provided below.

ARTICLE #1:

ARTICLE #2: